JOURNAL FOR THE STUDY OF THE OLD TESTAMENT
SUPPLEMENT SERIES
70

Editors
David J A Clines
Philip R Davies

BIBLE AND LITERATURE SERIES
17

General Editor
David M. Gunn

Assistant General Editor
Danna Nolan Fewell

Consultant Editors
Elizabeth Struthers Malbon
James G. Williams

Almond Press
Sheffield

First published by Sifriat Poalim (Tel Aviv) in Hebrew in 1979.
Second edition 1984.

Translated by Dorothea Shefer-Vanson in conjunction with the
author.

Narrative Art
in the Bible

Shimon Bar-Efrat

The Almond Press · 1989

Bible and Literature Series, 17

General Editor: David M. Gunn
(Columbia Theological Seminary, Decatur, Georgia)
Assistant General Editor: Danna Nolan Fewell
(Perkins School of Theology, Dallas, Texas)
Consultant Editors: Elizabeth Struthers Malbon
(Virginia Polytechnic Institute & State University, Blacksburg, Virginia)
James G. Williams
(Syracuse University, Syracuse, New York)

Copyright © 1989 Sheffield Academic Press

Published by Almond Press
Editorial direction: David M. Gunn
Columbia Theological Seminary
P.O. Box 520, Decatur
GA 30031, U.S.A.
Almond Press is an imprint of
Sheffield Academic Press Ltd
The University of Sheffield
343 Fulwood Road
Sheffield S10 3BP
England

Typeset by Sheffield Academic Press
and
printed in Great Britain
by Billing & Sons Ltd
Worcester

British Library Cataloguing in Publication Data

Bar-Efrat, Shimon
    Narrative art in the bible. —(Bible and
    literature series, ISSN 0260-4493: V. 17
    Journal for the study of the Old Testament
    supplement series, ISSN 0309-0787: V. 70)
    1. Bible. Literary aspects
    I. Title   II. Series
    809'. 93522

ISBN 1-85075-138-2

CONTENTS

PREFACE

The purpose of this book is to provide a guide to the biblical narrative as a literary work of art. It aims at presenting a way of reading which is based on the employment of tools and principles current in the study of literature, and it combines summary and methodical survey with the observation of new aspects.

The literary features dealt with in the book are lavishly illustrated with examples designed to clarify as well as to throw new light on narratives or parts of narratives. The examples have been selected from all sections of narrative literature in the Bible, but in particular from Genesis and the books of Samuel.

No examples are given from the Joseph Narrative and the book of Ruth, in spite of their literary excellence. These narratives have been omitted for the benefit of those readers who are not satisfied with passive reading but wish to study the biblical narrative actively. These readers can use the Joseph Narrative and the book of Ruth in order to apply the methods and principles set forth in this book.

Footnotes have been kept to a minimum. The publications pertaining to biblical narrative which have contributed to this book are included in the bibliography at the end. At this point I would like to note the inspiration I have derived from the work of Professor Meir Weiss, from whose writings and lectures I have profited greatly.

The writing of this book was possible thanks to Lea, who provided optimal conditions, and to Idit and Ohad, who showed much consideration. In the present edition some minor changes were introduced and a few passages added.

It is my hope that the approach presented here, focusing on the artistic shape of biblical narrative, will contribute to a more profound and exact understanding of these narratives as well as to a fuller appreciation of their beauty.

Shimon Bar-Efrat, Jerusalem 1987

Note: Quotations from the Bible are based for the most part on the Revised Standard Version. In those cases where it was necessary for the sake of the argument to render stylistic features of the Hebrew text in a precise form we often had to make our own translations, even though these sometimes resulted in awkward English.

INTRODUCTION

More than one third of the Hebrew Bible consists of narratives. It is generally recognized that these are of the highest artistic quality, ranking among the foremost literary treasures of the world. In conventional biblical scholarship, however, the literary study of biblical narratives has been only of marginal concern. Most Bible scholars have directed their attention to approaches such as source- and textual-criticism, and later also to the criticism of traditions and redaction, while the investigation of the narratives' artistic qualities has been pushed aside. It is true that some work has been done in this respect, especially in recent years, but this has not caused the literary study of the Bible to become a major current in scholarly endeavour.

Even the work done by the well-known German scholar, Gunkel, who evinced a deep interest in the literary facets of the Bible, did not serve to change this trend appreciably. In discussing the narratives in Genesis, Gunkel claimed that anyone who did not pay attention to their artistic form was not only deprived of considerable pleasure but also failed to clarify their meaning. The precise source of their unusual beauty was fundamentally a scientific issue which also bore upon their content and the religious view they reflected. In the third part of his introduction to Genesis, Gunkel dealt with such aspects as the simplicity of style, internal structure, the number of people and their characterization, the relationship between plot, dialogue and description, aspects of the plot and the absence of explicit evaluation.

Despite Gunkel's vast influence on Bible scholarship, however, this aspect of his work was not really continued, and these matters remained in the background of research. The foreground was occupied by other subjects dealt with by Gunkel, such as the history of forms and genres, which constituted an aperture whereby it was possible to penetrate to the earlier stages of the narratives and the history of the traditions before they were recorded in writing.

Thus, alongside the study of the history of the written narratives, there developed an attempt to examine their pre-history, when they were still transmitted orally. The avowedly historical approach is evident not only in the overriding interest in the changes which the narratives have undergone over the course of time and in attempts to reconstruct their original form, but also in the tendency to regard the narratives as a means of uncovering the historico-cultural reality, such as the 'setting/function in life' (Sitz im Leben) or the changing views, institutions and religious customs.

The various historical approaches have undoubtedly contributed greatly to our knowledge of the world and literature of the Bible. The literary approach and methods are no less important than the historical ones, however, since the *being* of biblical narrative is equally as interesting as its *becoming*. Anyone who wishes to study its being must use the avenue of literary analysis, for it is impossible to appreciate the nature of biblical narrative fully, understand the network of its component elements or penetrate into its inner world without having recourse to the methods and tools of literary scholarship.

In accordance with a prevailing trend in the study of literature today, attention in this book will be directed mainly to the formal and structural aspects of biblical narratives, including details of their linguistic fashioning. In other words, we will not approach the narratives through their facts, plot-contents or motifs, even though these will be touched upon from time to time, but will rather focus upon the study of techniques, modes of design, types of narration and other matters connected with the shape of the narratives. We should by no means underestimate these facets of the narratives, that is, the way the narrative material is organized and presented. The subject-matter, themes and values of the narrative cannot exist separately from the techniques, which define its character no less than the content. It is through the techniques that the meaning of the facts of the narrative is determined. Techniques and forms can emphasize or minimize narrative materials, bring a topic into the foreground or push it into the background. They hint at causal and other connections between events and constitute the principal means whereby the narrative impresses itself upon the reader, directing the attitudes and reactions to what is related. It makes no difference if the author used the techniques consciously or not, the crucial point is what formal methods are actually present in the work, what they contribute and how they function.

Thus, by paying attention to methods, structures and forms, the foundations on which the meanings and influence of the narrative are based will become clear to us, so that the ensuing interpretation will rest upon firm ground. The examination of form and design will also reveal additional, subtler and more precise meanings.

Though every narrative is a unique creation, it consists of universal components and techniques which are shared by other narratives. Through being combined and utilized in particular ways, they build the structure of the individual narrative. The components and techniques are closely inter-connected, operating in concert and influencing one another. In order to attain a systematic and organized understanding of the various forms, however, it is necessary to unravel the fabric of the complete narrative and examine the techniques separately and consecutively.

This book will deal first with the narrator and modes of narration, then with the shaping of the characters, the structure of the plot, time and space, and the details of style. After examining the various aspects individually, an analysis of an entire narrative, encompassing all these aspects, will be undertaken.

Chapter 1

THE NARRATOR

The relation between narrator and narrative is not like that between painter and painting or composer and a musical composition. It is distinguished by the fact that the narrator is, quite simply, inside the narrative; he or she is an integral part of the work, one of its structural components, even one of the most important ones. Sometimes narrators are obvious and palpable features of the narrative (for instance, in first-person narratives), while sometimes they are not apparent or defined, and we consequently tend to forget their existence. Even in the second instance, however, it is clear that within the narrative there is someone who brings the events before us and addresses us.

The existence of the narrator within the narrative distinguishes narrative from its sister art, drama. Both in drama and in narrative the characters are presented to us, we witness what befalls them and hear their conversations, but in drama the author is felt only indirectly, through the characters, whereas in narrative the narrator exists alongside the characters, and the narrator's voice is heard as well as theirs. While drama brings the characters and their world directly in front of us, creating an immediate encounter between the characters and the audience, the nature of narrative is such that the epic world embodied within it will not reach our awareness without the narrator's mediation. We do not have direct access to the characters of a narrative, and their speech is even embedded in the narrator's through such phrases as, 'And he said', 'And she answered'. We see and hear only through the narrator's eyes and ears. The narrator is an apriori category, as it were, constituting the sole means by which we can understand the reality which exists within a narrative. The nature of this reality, and the essence of the narrative world, with its characters and events, and, above all, their significance, is entirely dependent on the narrator, through whom we apprehend. Consequently, the character of the narrators and the way in which they mediate is of supreme importance.

The narrator within the narrative should not be identified with the writer as a real person. Knowledge of the writer's life and familiarity with biographical details do not contribute to a better understanding of the narrator in the narrative, since the value systems, attitudes and characteristics of the two are not necessarily identical. The figure of the 'implied author' (i.e. the author who emerges through the story, as opposed to the actual writer) and his or her way of looking at and presenting things is part of the character of the work and is revealed to us only through reading and studying it.

It is also customary to make a distinction between the (implied) author and the narrator. It is the latter who tells us what is happening and which character is speaking at any given time. The former becomes known to us through what the narrator says, through the speech of the characters (which is formulated by the author) and through the organization of the narrative materials, plot, time, space, etc.

The best way of approaching narrators and their narrative modes is by examining the viewpoint from which they observe the events and through which the relationship between them and the narrative world is expressed. There are many possibilities in this respect, the most important for biblical narrative being:

1. Narrators who know everything about the characters and are present everywhere, as opposed to narrators whose knowledge is limited. The former see through solid walls into secret corners, even penetrating the hidden recesses of people's minds. The latter observe things from the outside, seeing what people do and hearing what they say, leaving it to us to draw conclusions about their inner lives.

2. Narrators who intrude into the story, adding comments and explanations, and whose existence is evident, as opposed to narrators who tend to be silent and self-effacing. The former type may refer to themselves or their methods in creating the narrative, they may address the reader directly or offer interpretations and evaluations of what is happening, while the latter will merely communicate the story itself.

3. Narrators who relate what is happening from a remote perspective, offering a wide, panoramic view, as opposed to

narrators who are close to the events, depicting them with the minimum of mediation, presenting scenes and letting the characters speak for themselves.

4. Narrators who watch things from above, seeming to hover above the characters, as opposed to narrators who look at events from the viewpoint of one of the participants.

5. Neutral or objective narrators as opposed to narrators who adopt a definite attitude about what they are relating. The formers' mode of narration will be business-like, factual and devoid of personal involvement, while the latters' will evince approval or disapproval, acceptance or rejection, praise or censure, and perhaps even identification or abhorrence.

These distinctions represent the extremes, and in actual fact the viewpoint of a narrative may be found anywhere between them. It is also obvious that these features can occur in any narrative in a variety of different combinations. It is not obligatory for a certain point of view to be maintained consistently throughout a narrative. One viewpoint may well predominate, but there is no reason why it should not be replaced by another from time to time.

The point (or points) of view of a narrative are important for several reasons.

First of all, the point of view is one of the factors according unity to a work of literature, which naturally involves diffuseness and variety as regards characters, events, places and times. It has been said that the narrator's point of view is the 'fourth unity' (after Aristotle's three: unity of time, place and plot), because it blends the multiplicity of viewpoints of the characters within one general vista.

Secondly, the point of view which has been selected dictates what will be narrated and how, what will be related from afar and what from close to. The narrator is like a photographer who decides what will and will not be included in a picture, from what distance and angle, with what degree of sharpness and in what light. Just as the nature of a film is dependent on the position of the camera and the way it is operated, the nature of the narrative depends on the point of view from which the events are presented.

Thirdly, the appropriate point of view can make a crucial contribution to enhancing the interest or suspense of the narrative. The narrative should be moulded in such a fashion that it will be interesting, even gripping if possible, in order to enthrall the reader and make him or her share in what is happening. A narrative which is not read, or which does not capture the reader's attention, cannot fulfil its task. The reader's involvement in what is going on is dependent to a great extent on the way the narrative is presented, and this includes both the dominant point of view and the shifts in the various viewpoints.

Fourthly, the point of view is one of the means by which the narrative influences the reader, leading to the absorption of its implicit values and attitudes. Naturally, the reader's attitude to what is being related is dependent to a considerable extent on values and ideas which are held beforehand, but the author can also influence these judgments. Generally, if the author adopts a positive stance, the reader will follow suit, and the same applies if the author's attitude is one of disapprobation. For, on the whole, the reader identifies less with the characters of the narrative than with the author, seeing the characters through the author's eyes and adopting that stance towards them. The author's attitudes and views are not necessarily expressed separately from the facts of the narrative (as is the case in a certain kind of fable, where the moral is always appended at the end), but are usually intertwined with them, being manifested in the way the narrative unfolds. The narrative affects the reader through the combination of 'what' and 'how', namely, what is related and how this is done. Among the most important of the 'how' factors are the various points of view by which the author perceives and moulds the characters and their actions, determining the way in which the reader apprehends and is influenced by them. The effectiveness of the narrative is, therefore, dependent to a considerable extent on the technique of the viewpoint.

This technique is of particular importance in biblical narrative, which attempts to influence its audience and to impart its outlook on life, people, good and evil, God and divine activity in the world. Whereas the Prophetic and Wisdom literature express their views directly, openly urging that they be accepted, the narrative operates in an oblique and unobtrusive way, and in this respect narrative modes in general, and the technique of the viewpoint in particular, fulfil a decisive role.

1. *The Narrator's Omniscience*

The narrator in most biblical narratives appears to be omniscient, able to see actions undertaken in secret and to hear conversations conducted in seclusion, familiar with the internal workings of the characters and displaying their innermost thoughts to us.

Omniscience involves omnipresence. God knows everything because He is everywhere all the time. An author is like God in many respects, creating a world and fashioning people, examining the inner workings of characters and knowing the outcome of things at the outset, but the author cannot be everywhere at the same time. This is not because of being mere flesh and blood but because of the limitations of the medium, language. Language limits the author to describing events consecutively, thus creating the impression that the narrator is now here and then there, looking first into one man's heart and then into another's, constantly transferring the point of view from one place to another.

In real life we are unable to shift our point of view wherever we wish at any moment. We are restricted to one place, and can only transfer ourselves by making an effort, generally seeing everything from one point of view, our own. We are slow to move and cannot leap easily over large distances, nor can we vault across time. These things can, however, be done by the narrator in a work of literature. The narrator does not always exploit these possibilities, and is sometimes voluntarily restricted to describing events in one place and from only one point of view. When such possibilities are exploited, then we have an omniscient narrator.

In many biblical narratives the narrator is in one place, as, for example, in the narratives of the Garden of Eden (Genesis 3), the purchase of the cave of Machpelah (Genesis 23) and the queen of Sheba's visit to king Solomon (1 Kings 10). In many more narratives, however, the narrator shifts from one place to another in a flash: one moment being in the land of Canaan with Abraham, and the next in Mesopotamia with Abraham's servant, visiting Bethuel's house (Genesis 24); one moment in Aphek with the armies of Israel and the Philistines, and the next in Shiloh with the aged Eli (1 Samuel 4); one moment in Jerusalem with Absalom, and the next in Mahanayim with David (2 Samuel 17). The narrator bounds freely to and fro, not tarrying on the way.

The biblical narrator also enters the innermost chambers, is present at highly intimate situations, and hears private conversations. Consequently, we know that David does not have sexual intercourse with Abishag the Shunammite, the beautiful girl brought to share his bed in order to warm him (1 Kgs 1.4). The narrator remains in Amnon's chamber after everyone has been ordered to leave it, is present during the rape, sees how Amnon overcomes Tamar's opposition and hears the exchange of words between them before and after the deed (2 Samuel 13). The narrator is even privy to the contents of the secret letter which David sends to Joab giving detailed instructions as to how to get rid of Uriah the Hittite (2 Sam. 11.15). The narrator is sometimes even an ear- and eye-witness to conversations conducted in heaven by God and His minions (Job 1.6-12; 2.1-6). Nothing remains hidden to the omniscient narrator.

It has been claimed that the biblical narrator tends to imply the feelings of characters through their speech and actions rather than reporting them directly, and that readers have to draw their own conclusions about inner emotions from external behaviour. It is true that in most cases this is the approach adopted by the narrator but, as the following examples will show, the narrator repeatedly penetrates into the minds of the characters, revealing their thoughts and emotions, aspirations and motives clearly. These inside views are sometimes given separately and independently, that is, without any record of actions or speech from which they could be inferred. On occasions, the information about the inner life of characters is given alongside reports of external behaviour which reflects their internal situation. When an inside view accompanies an account of external behaviour, the information about the character's inner life should be regarded not as an explanation or conclusion on the narrator's part, based on the external behaviour, but as a category of facts no different in its standing and validity from any other feature of the narrative, enjoying the same imprimatur of the narrator's authority. In this respect, there is a fundamental difference between a work of literature and a historical-scientific treatise, which sometimes also contains pronouncements about the inner workings of people who lived in the past, describing their hopes, beliefs, aspirations or considerations, even though there is no direct evidence for them. In a historical treatise the reader accepts, by convention, that these are merely interpretations or assumptions made by the author on the basis of the known, external actions, while this is not the case with a work of literature.

In the examples below, the narrator gives an account of the characters' inner feelings either independently or in association with information about allied external behaviour.

The evidence *par excellence* of the narrator's unlimited knowledge is undoubtedly what is reported about God, whose feelings, thoughts, intentions, opinions and judgments the narrator purports to know:

> And the Lord was sorry that he had made man on the earth, and it grieved him to his heart (Gen. 6.6).
>
> But Noah found favour in the eyes of the Lord (Gen. 6.8).
>
> And God saw the people of Israel, and God knew (Exod. 2.25).
>
> Then the anger of the Lord was kindled against Moses (Exod. 4.14).
>
> But the thing that David had done displeased the Lord (2 Sam. 11.27).
>
> For the Lord had ordained to defeat the good counsel of Ahithophel, so that the Lord might bring evil upon Absalom (2 Sam. 17.14).

The narrator does not often provide us with information about God's inner feelings. In consequence, we can assume that when such information is given, the matter is of special importance. This is the case, for example, in God's judgment on David's actions concerning Bathsheba and Uriah. Judgment by God is not like that by one of the characters in the plot, and is far more effective and convincing even than judgment by the narrator; for God is the absolute and supreme authority, and this naturally reflects upon the value and importance of His judgments (although it should not be forgotten that we know what God's attitude is only on the narrator's authority). In the narratives preceding the one about Bathsheba and Uriah David was usually presented in a positive way, influencing the reader's attitude towards him. An explicit judgment will function as a counterweight here, overcoming the positive predisposition towards David which has been built up in the reader. In addition, the reader may judge David's actions in accordance with a special code of norms, assuming that the king is not subject to the limitations imposed on ordinary citizens, that he is entitled to take any woman he desires, and that as supreme military commander he has the right to decide about the life and death of his soldiers in the field. It is well known that in the ancient east kings were empowered to act precisely in this way. By attributing the judgment to God, a system of absolute norms, to which the king is also subject and according to which he should be judged, is set above this 'royal' canon. The absoluteness of the ethical norms—necessary here, because the object of the judgment is not an ordinary individual—would not have been reflected had the judgment been presented as the narrator's own.

Just as narrators know God's opinions, feelings and intentions, they are also familiar with the inner workings of the human characters in the spheres of cognition, emotion and volition.

Cognition

> Now Jacob did not know that Rachel had stolen them (Gen. 31.32).

> When Judah saw her, he thought her to be a harlot (Gen. 38.15).

> Then Eli understood that the Lord was calling the boy (1 Sam. 3.8).

> And the advice was good in the eyes of Absalom and all the elders of Israel (2 Sam. 17.4).

In all these cases, as well as in many others, the inside views play an important role. In the final example, for instance, referring to the opinion of Absalom and the elders regarding Ahithophel's advice, it is made clear to us that before Hushai gave his counsel, all those present had been convinced of the wisdom of Ahithophel's plan. By clarifying this, the narrator maximalizes the tension and makes the rejection of Ahithophel's advice at the last moment extremely surprising.

Emotion

The narrator discerns and reports different kinds of emotions, such as love and hate, joy and sorrow, anger, fear, shame, etc.

> So Jacob served seven years for Rachel, and they seemed to him but a few days because of the love he had for her (Gen. 29.20).

> Then Amnon hated her with very great hatred; so that the hatred with which he hated her was greater than the love with which he had loved her (2 Sam. 13.15).

> So Jonah was exceedingly glad because of the plant (Jon. 4.6).

> And the men were indignant and very angry (Gen. 34.7).

And Moses' anger burned hot (Exod. 32.19).

And Adonijah feared Solomon (1 Kgs 1.50).

And the man and his wife were both naked, and were not ashamed (Gen. 2.25).

For his heart trembled for the ark of God (1 Sam. 4.13).

For he was comforted about Amnon, seeing he was dead (2 Sam. 13.39).

Volition
The narrator sometimes explicitly informs us of an individual's will or the lack of it to undertake a certain action. In these cases the willingness or unwillingness is accorded emphasis.

Then Saul said to his armour-bearer: 'Draw your sword and thrust me through. . . ' But his armour-bearer would not (1 Sam. 31.4).

. . . and he would not drink it (2 Sam. 23.16, 17).

. . . and all that Solomon desired to build (1 Kgs 9.1).

Haman aspired to destroy all the Jews (Esth. 3.6).

In actual fact, the narrator penetrates into the minds of the characters even when simply telling us what they are seeing or hearing. An outside observer can see that a person is looking, but is unable to tell what the person is seeing; in contrast to the verb 'look', the verb 'see' relates to internal occurrences, as is the case with the verb 'hear'. There is no need to point out that both these verbs occur frequently in biblical narrative, and that the narrator often tells us what the characters are seeing or hearing. Seeing is mentioned more often than hearing, and this is not surprising since the individual usually learns about the situation through the sense of sight. The other senses feature much less. It is noteworthy, however, that in the story of Isaac's blessing (Genesis 27) reference is made to all the five senses, either by the narrator or by the characters, since they all play an important part in the development of the plot. Isaac, who is an old man whose *sight* is failing, asks Esau to prepare him the *tasty* food he likes; when Jacob brings him the food (which Rebekah has cooked) Isaac *feels* him, and although the voice *sounds* like Jacob's the hands are Esau's; finally Isaac *smells* his son's clothes and declares that the smell of his son is like that of a field, and then he blesses him.

The indication of perceptions, desires and intentions, emotions, knowledge and understanding fulfil a definite role within their contexts, whether it be to delineate characters, to advance the plot or to clarify it. Information about the internal states of characters is not distributed evenly throughout biblical narratives, some having a far higher proportion of information of this kind than others which have none or very little, and this determines the character of the narrative to a considerable extent.

Thus, it is clear that the narrator's penetration into the characters' minds is by no means a rare and unusual phenomenon. It is impossible, however, to ignore the fact that these disclosures provide a brief and succinct report of an existing state of mind, and do not describe its evolution. The mental life of the characters does not become a subject in its own right, and the narrator hardly ever provides direct information about the *processes* going on in their minds. We may search biblical narratives in vain for direct descriptions of internal deliberations, mental conflicts or psychological uncertainties and vacillations. The narrator is content with providing brief glimpses of the inner lives of characters, informing us from time to time of the current situation in their minds.

In many cases, moreover, the narrator does not let the reader share this unlimited knowledge, failing to reveal even a fraction of the characters' inner world. In the story of the sacrifice of Isaac, for example (Genesis 22), the narrator does not tell us what Abraham's emotions were when he received the command to go and sacrifice his son, what he felt and what he thought about during the three days' journey and what was going on in his mind as he ascended the mountain together with his son. The narrator does not inform us of Isaac's thoughts and feelings either. Isaac's question, 'Behold, the fire and the wood; but where is the lamb for a burnt offering?' hints at what is going on in his mind, but we do not know what he felt and understood after his father's evasive reply: 'God will provide himself the lamb for a burnt offering, my son'.

In the narrative of David and Bathsheba (2 Samuel 11) the narrator does not furnish any information whatsoever about the feelings of the characters, despite the fact that powerful and deep emotions play a crucial role in this episode. Did David love Bathsheba? How did she feel towards him? What did she think when she was summoned to appear before the king, and what was her reaction when she discovered that she was pregnant by him? What were Uriah's feelings towards David, and what were David's towards Uriah? The narrator does not provide answers to these and many other questions in biblical narratives.

In some cases the characters' intentions, which are known to the narrator, are not revealed to us until they are translated into the language of action. Thus, the narrator does not disclose David's intentions when he summons Uriah the Hittite to Jerusalem from the battle-field at Rabbah of the Ammonites (after Bathsheba has conceived), but they become clear to us, later in the narrative, from David's repeated attempts to persuade Uriah to go down to his house.

Similarly, we are not informed of Absalom's reasons for standing by the way of the gate and flattering everyone who comes there on his way to be judged before the king (2 Sam. 15.1ff.). These reasons become apparent to the reader later on, when Absalom rebels against his father.

In the examples cited here the characters in the narrative wish to keep their intentions secret. Accordingly the narrator also refrains from revealing them, at the same time contributing to the heightening of tension.

In all these instances, as well as in many others, the narrator does not give a direct report of the characters' innermost thoughts and feelings. There is simply a description of their external behaviour, their actions and their conversations. To all intents and purposes, the narrator is simply capturing the situation as it is revealed to the outside observer.

2. *The Narrator's Manifestations*

A. *The Overt Narrator*

In the study of literature a distinction is usually made between editorial omniscience, when the narrator inserts comments about the characters and events into the narrative, and neutral omniscience, when the narrative is allowed to speak for itself. In the former, the narrator's existence is very obvious, while in the latter it is scarcely felt. This distinction is convenient but its relative nature should not be forgotten, since there is a continuum of intermediate situations between these two opposing ones.

The presence of narrators within narratives is felt most when they refer to themselves, in either the first or the third person, when they mention the activities undertaken in creating the narrative, such as writing it down or consulting sources, or when they address their readers directly. In all these cases a double structure is created within the narrative: in addition to the stratum of events, which is the main one, there is the stratum of the narrator, who stands forward as the intermediary between the world of the narrative and us.

Biblical narrators do not usually mention themselves. The 'first person' narratives in the books of Ezra and Nehemiah, in which the narrator and the protagonist are identical, can be cited as exceptions. Objective aspects of the events are intertwined with subjective ones in these narratives. At the beginning of the book of Nehemiah, for example, the narrator makes it clear to us what has led him to go from his home in Susa, the Persian capital, to Jerusalem; and in several verses in the book, after recounting events, he adds the words: 'Remember for my good, O my God (all that I have done for this people)' (5.19; 13.14, 22, 31).

Biblical narrators make no reference to their activity in writing the narrative, with the exception of the authors of the books of Kings and Chronicles, who cite works where additional material can be found and which apparently served as their sources, such as the book of the Acts of Solomon (1 Kgs 11.41), the book of the Chronicles of the Kings of Israel (1 Kgs 14.19), the book of the Chronicles of the Kings of Judah (1 Kgs 14.29), the book of the Kings of Israel and Judah (2 Chron. 27.7), the Chronicles of Samuel the seer, the Chronicles of Nathan the prophet and the Chronicles of Gad the visionary (1 Chron. 29.29). The comments made by the authors of the books of Kings and Chronicles mentioning these sources occur, however, at the end as an appendix to the actual stories and not as an integral part of them.

Despite the fact that in most biblical narratives the narrators do not mention themselves or their sources or address their audience directly, the stratum of the narrator exists in many of them alongside that of the events, as the following examples show.

> And Jacob set up a pillar upon her grave; it is the pillar of Rachel's tomb, which is there to this day (Gen. 35.20).

> So Joshua burned Ai, and made it for ever a heap of ruins, as it is to this day (Josh. 8.28).

> And they went up and encamped at Kiriath Jearim in Judah, on this account that place is called Mahaneh Dan to this day; behold, it is west of Kiriath Jearim (Judg. 18.12).

Now Absalom in his lifetime had taken and set up for himself the pillar which is in the King's Valley, for he said, 'I have no son to keep my name in remembrance'; he called the pillar after his own name, and it is called Absalom's monument to this day (2 Sam. 18.18).

Their descendants who were left after them in the land, whom the people of Israel were unable to destroy utterly—these Solomon made a forced levy of slaves, and so they are to this day (1 Kgs 9.21).

The phrase 'to this day' refers to the narrator's time and not to that when the events described took place. By mentioning their own period, narrators divert attention from the stratum of the narrated events to that of their own time.

The expression 'to this day' is usually regarded as an aetiological term, namely, one indicating that the object of the narrative is to explain the origin of a name or phenomenon which exists in the narrator's time. In some of the instances, however, the phrase 'to this day' can also be regarded as an attempt to provide evidence substantiating the story, linking the world projected in the narrative with that of the narrator and the audience, and thus giving the story credibility. By referring to the present the narrator impairs the immediacy of the narrative and the audience's ability to become immersed in the world thus created; on the other hand, however, the narrator furnishes proof of the story which the people in the audience can verify for themselves.

Narrators refer to their own time indirectly by using the phrase 'in those days'. This expression denotes the time of the story from the narrator's perspective, indicating that there is distance between the period in which the events took place and that of the narrator. By noting this fact, both the time of the story, which is referred to directly by the phrase 'in those days', and the time of the narrator, which is hinted at indirectly, are brought to the reader's attention.

In the vast majority of cases when the expression 'in those days' occurs in the Bible, it serves to express the contrast between the situation in the narrator's time and that during the period which is being described in the narrative. For example: 'The Nephilim were on the earth in those days' (Gen. 6.4), or, 'In those days there was no king in Israel; every man did what was right in his own eyes' (Judg. 17.6; 18.1; 19.1; 21.25). Reservations about the situation are often sensed as well as contrast, as in the last example.

There are also cases when the phrase 'in those days' serves to connect different narratives by noting that they occurred at the same period. For example: 'In those days the Philistines gathered their forces for war, to fight against Israel' (1 Sam. 28.1), or, 'In those days the Lord began to cut off parts of Israel. Hazael defeated them throughout the territory of Israel' (2 Kgs 10.32).

In every instance this expression creates distance between the narrator and the story and, as a result, between the reader and the story too. Distance is necessary in order to make it possible to consider the significance of the events. The reader is no longer borne along by the stream of incidents, and can observe them from above.

The narrator is also revealed through those passages which contain an explanation or comment about what is happening rather than an account of a specific event. For at a key point the narrator stops the narrative and adds explanations or clarifications. Whenever this is done, it shifts the readers out of the stratum of the plot and transfers them to the narrator's own sphere. Explanations of events are a powerful tool in the hands of the narrator, enabling clear and unequivocal messages to be conveyed to the readers.

'Thus God requited the crime of Abimelech, which he committed against his father in killing his seventy brothers; and God also made all the wickedness of the men of Shechem fall back upon their heads, and upon them came the curse of Jotham the son of Jerubbaal' (Judg. 9.56-57). These verses, which conclude the narrative of Abimelech, explain what befell him and the men of Shechem as requital for the evil which they had done and as the fulfilment of Jotham's curse. Thus it is made clear that natural political and military events have a deeper significance and embody divine justice.

'Now in those days the counsel which Ahithophel gave was as if one consulted the oracle of God; so was all the counsel of Ahithophel esteemed, both by David and by Absalom' (2 Sam. 16.23). This comment by the narrator indicates that an unseen hand was directing events behind the scenes. In the contest between Ahithophel and Hushai it is almost certain that Ahithophel will gain the upper hand. Not only had his previous advice recommending that Absalom go in to his father's concubines been adopted, but whatever he counselled had always been accepted; both David and Absalom regarded Ahithophel's recommendations as if they were the word of God. Consequently, at this critical moment the reader fears that Hushai will not succeed in confuting Ahithophel's advice and it is on this that the fate of the rebellion and of king David are dependent! When, further on, it transpires that, contrary to expectations, Ahithophel's advice has been dismissed this time, the reader immediately suspects that some extraordinary element is involved. The narrator confirms this supposition, making it clear exactly what the nature of that element and the meaning of the events is by intervening again (in the following chapter): 'For the Lord had ordained to defeat the good counsel of Ahithophel, so that the Lord might bring evil upon Absalom' (2 Sam. 17.14).

Both of the incursions by the narrator—the first at the start of the decisive scene when Ahithophel and Hushai give their respective advice (the scene which is the axis upon wich the entire story of Absalom's rebellion revolves) and the second at its conclusion—ensure that every reader will grasp the full significance of the narrative in the same way that the narrator does. If the narrator had not intervened and had let the events speak for themselves, it is doubtful whether this end would have been achieved.

But was the narrator obliged to intervene *twice* in order to obtain this result? Would not the second intervention alone have sufficed, making it quite clear that Ahithophel's advice was not accepted because God had thus ordained? What does the first intervention contribute?

Although the second comment explains that what happened was the result of God's command, it does not make it clear just how it was implemented. Sometimes God acts through direct and open interference in the causal chain of events, through miracles, in which case divine action replaces human action. Sometimes the divine purpose is effected unobtrusively as part of the natural course of events, as in the example of Abimelech, in which case all that is perceptible is the ordinary human action, though everything that happens is interpreted as being the result of God's concealed activity.

The rejection of Ahithophel's advice would appear to fall into neither category, since it is neither a supernatural occurrence (a miracle) nor is it an ordinary event. It is something between the two, namely, an unlikely incident. God so disposes events that something happens which, while not going contrary to the laws of nature, is improbable and totally unexpected. This view of the way God moves is insinuated by the narrator's first intervention, which makes it plain how unlikely it is that Ahithophel's advice will not be accepted.

God's actions are not separate from those of humanity in this instance but are intertwined with them. The narrator does not tell us precisely how this is to be understood. Did God make Hushai exceedingly shrewd or Absalom foolish in order to arrange matters as He desired? Or is this perhaps a case of double causality, namely, an event that occurs because of both human and divine causes? The concept of two causal systems existing simultaneously on two separate levels and giving rise to one and the same event can be found in the Bible, in the ancient east and in the world of classical Greece. In this particular case, the assumption of double causality is supported by David's reaction on hearing that Ahithophel has joined Absalom's side. On this occasion David addresses both God and Hushai: 'O Lord, I pray thee, turn the counsel of Ahithophel into foolishness' (15.31), '... then you will defeat for me the counsel of Ahithophel' (15.34).

A similar instance of explicit intervention by the narrator occurs in 1 Kgs 2.27: 'So Solomon expelled Abiathar from being priest to the Lord, thus fulfilling the word of the Lord which he had spoken concerning the house of Eli in Shiloh'. Here, too, it is clear that the narrator believes that a latent power is operating behind the overt events, and double causality is evident. Abiathar's expulsion is not the outcome of a human decision alone—although this decision is wholly understandable against the background of Abiathar's support for Adonijah, Solomon's rival—but also results from a divine resolution made long before. In the narrator's opinion the expulsion of Abiathar should not be regarded solely in the short-term framework of immediate events, but in a wider historical perspective extending far beyond the period described. The extensive historical view is even more apparent if we note that the explanation given here, namely, that Abiathar's expulsion fulfils the word of God, is merely one link in a long chain of similar explanations which recur throughout the book of Kings.[1]

> So the king did not hearken to the people; for it was a turn of affairs brought about by the Lord that he might fulfil his word, which the

1. G. von Rad, 'The Deuteronomic Theology of History in I and II Kings', *The Problem of the Hexateuch and other Essays* (Edinburgh and London, 1966), pp. 209-11.

Lord spoke by Ahijah the Shilonite to Jeroboam the son of Nebat (1 Kgs 12.15).

And as soon as he was king, he killed all the house of Jeroboam; he left to the house of Jeroboam not one that breathed, until he had destroyed it, according to the word of the Lord which he spoke by his servant Ahijah the Shilonite (1 Kgs 15.29).

Thus Zimri destroyed all the house of Baasha; according to the word of the Lord, which he spoke against Baasha by Jehu the prophet (1 Kgs 16.12).

In his days Hiel of Bethel built Jericho; he laid its foundation at the cost of Abiram his firstborn, and set up its gates at the cost of his youngest son Segub, according to the word of the Lord, which he spoke by Joshua the son of Nun (1 Kgs 16.34).

So he died according to the word of the Lord which Elijah had spoken (2 Kgs 1.17).

And as Josiah turned, he saw the tombs there on the mount; and he sent and took the bones out of the tombs, and burned them upon the altar, and defiled it, according to the word of the Lord which the man of God proclaimed, who had predicted these things (2 Kgs 23.16).

And the Lord sent against him bands of the Chaldeans, and bands of the Syrians, and bands of the Moabites, and bands of the Ammonites, and sent them against Judah to destroy it, according to the word of the Lord which he spoke by his servants the prophets (2 Kgs 24.2).

This chain of explanations creates a system of prophecies on the one hand, and their fulfilment on the other, indicating that history was regarded as the fulfilment of the word of God. The events are the result of both human behaviour and a divine plan.

Throughout the books of Kings we find verses passing judgment, which also shift the reader from the level of the narrated events to that of the narrator. For example: 'So Solomon did what was evil in the sight of the Lord, and did not wholly follow the Lord, as David his father had done' (1 Kgs 11.6); 'After this thing Jeroboam did not turn from his evil way' (1 Kgs 13.33); 'And Asa did what was right in the eyes of the Lord, as David his father had done' (1 Kgs 15.11); 'Before him there was no king like him, who turned to the Lord with all his heart and with all his soul and with all his might, according to all the law of Moses; nor did any like him arise after him' (2 Kgs 23.25).

Outside the books of Kings there are very few instances in which the narrator passes judgment (for the judgment embodied in direct characterization see below, p. 53). Only rarely do we encounter such verses as: 'Now the earth was corrupt in God's sight, and the earth was filled with violence' (Gen. 6.11) or, 'And David did justice and equity to all his people' (2 Sam. 8.15). The judgments are usually put into the characters' mouths, as, for example, in Judg. 20.6: 'And I took my concubine and cut her in pieces, and sent her throughout all the country of the inheritance of Israel; for they have committed abomination and wantonness in Israel'. In some cases the narrator attributes the judgment to God: 'But the thing that David had done was evil in the eyes of the Lord' (2 Sam. 11.27).

Some explanations given by the narrator, which are fairly frequent in biblical narrative, differ in both form and function from those discussed above. In form, because they begin with the word, 'for' (*kî*); in function, because they do not hint at deeper significances, indicating other, hidden levels, but simply clarify details and point to internal links on the level of the actual events. The form is appropriate for the function, since the word 'for' reflects the fact that the explanations are integrated within the narrative and adjacent to the events to which they refer. Here are a few examples:

> And the land could not support both of them dwelling together; for their possessions were so great that they could not dwell together (Gen. 13.6).

> Come, let us go to the seer; for he who is now called a prophet was formerly called a seer (1 Sam. 9.9).

> Now she was wearing a long robe with sleeves; for thus were the garments worn by the virgin daughters of the king (2 Sam. 13.18).

> And he had provided the king with food while he stayed at Mahanaim; for he was a very wealthy man (2 Sam. 19.32).

Occasionally, the narrator uses explanations of this kind not in order to elucidate the material background, customs, etc., as in the examples given above, but to explain the psychological motives which led to the activity described. Because the author also conveys values to us through the characters, it is important that we understand their actions and assess them correctly. By giving explicit accounts of the motives for their actions, the narrator moulds our attitude to the characters and prevents us from interpreting them wrongly. The narrator knows and understands the nature of the characters, and sometimes lets the reader share in this.

> When the men of the place asked him about his wife, he said, 'She is my sister'; for he feared to say, 'my wife' (Gen. 26.7).

> Manoah said to the angel of the Lord, 'Pray, let us detain you, and prepare a kid for you'. . . For Manoah did not know that he was the angel of the Lord (Judg. 13.15-16).

> But Absalom spoke to Amnon neither good nor bad; for Absalom hated Amnon, because he had forced his sister Tamar (2 Sam. 13.22).

> Now Hiram king of Tyre sent his servants to Solomon, when he heard that they had anointed him king in place of his father; for Hiram always loved David (1 Kgs 5.15).

> And no one spoke a word to him, for they saw that his suffering was very great (Job 2.13).

In conclusion, the effect of the explanations, judgments and interpretations of the kinds cited above is to create distance and reduce the reader's emotional involvement. A reader who is totally absorbed in the plot will be able neither to see the events dispassionately, nor to judge them and assess their significance. A certain emotional distance is a precondition for clear thinking, and without it it is impossible to grasp the ideas in the narrative. The explanations help in understanding the narrative, emphasizing certain points and influencing the formation of the reader's opinion in accordance with the author's ideas and values.

There is another side to the coin, however, since a large number of interventions by the narrator mar the illusion of reality in the narrative, diverting attention from the events of the narrative to the craft of narration and from the incidents themselves to the attitude towards them. The narrative will be more vivid, dramatic, gripping and realistic the less the narrator's existence is felt, the less aware we are of the fact that someone is mediating between us and the events, and the less we sense that someone is selecting and interpreting them for us.

If narrators wish to refrain from overdoing things in this respect they must keep interpretation and explanation to a minimum. A small number of interventions will not impair the illusion of reality, and this, indeed, is the method adopted by narrators in the Bible. Direct interventions are neither numerous nor extensive, and this contributes considerably to the vividness and immediacy of the biblical narratives, although it is not, of course, the only factor which gives them their dramatic character.

B. *The Covert Narrator*

As has been stated above, the distinction between an overt narrator, whose presence is clearly apparent, and a covert one, whose existence is minimized, should not be regarded as an absolute and unequivocal one. Whenever the flow of the narrative is interrupted in order to supply explanations and interpretations, the narrator's existence is felt quite clearly. But even in those parts of the narrative—and they constitute the majority—when the narrator reveals the actual events to us, there are some slight indications of a guiding and elucidating hand. And in these sections of the narrative too, it is possible to speak of different levels of the narrator's existence, sometimes more covert and sometimes less so.

It is true that there are many readers whose attention is geared towards events and characters. Their main interest is in the development of the plot, and they will not sense the narrator's covert existence. There are also, however, readers who read in a more sensitive and thoughtful way. They will pay attention to the more or less subtle techniques of the narrative and will be aware of the fact that even in the actual presentation of events the narrator's existence can be perceived.

Be that as it may, at this juncture we will discuss the narrator's method in those parts of the narrative which, omitting interpretation or explanation, focus on genuine narration, and we will clarify how the narrator's presence is felt and in what way personal views are expressed. The more obvious manifestations of the narrator's activity and attitudes will be considered first, followed by those which are less evident.

Biblical narrators' objectivity and lack of tendentiousness in representing characters and events has often been noted. This quality of objectivity has been attributed to them for two main reasons: a. They do not usually conceal the negative aspects of the protagonists (David's behaviour towards Bathsheba and Uriah is the classic example of this). b. They generally relate events in a factual and impassionate manner, refraining from pathos, expressions of sympathy or joy, praise or censure, and describing even the most shocking incidents in a restrained way, without going into gory details (the narrative of the sacrifice of Isaac is a characteristic example).

Despite these facts, it cannot be said that the biblical narrators are completely objective. In actual fact, there is no such thing as a totally objective narration, for even if they do not conceal the characters' negative aspects and use a controlled and factual style, as biblical narrators do, this does not mean that they remain impartial towards their protagonists. It is true that their stance is indicated by implication rather than explicitly or obtrusively, but this method is no less efficacious than the direct and obvious one. On the contrary, just because it is not conspicuous and functions covertly, it tends to be more effective in transmitting narrators' values to the readers.

Thus, the narrator's elucidatory activity is evident whenever we find evaluative terms characterizing the protagonists within the text of the narrative and as an integral part of it. For example:

> When the boys grew up, Esau was a skilful hunter, a man of the field, while Jacob was a *blameless* man, dwelling in tents (Gen. 25.27).

> As they were making their hearts merry, behold, the men of the city, *base* fellows, beset the house round about (Judg. 19.22).

> And he had a son whose name was Saul, *choice and fine*. There was not a man among the people of Israel *finer* than he (1 Sam. 9.2).

> Then a *wise* woman called from the city, 'Hear! Hear! Tell Joab, Come here, that I may speak to you' (2 Sam. 20.16).

The narrator's attitude is sometimes expressed through the connotations of the words used to convey the characters' actions. To all intents and purposes the narrator simply describes facts and events, but because of the charge of the words the stance towards those facts is conveyed together with the factual information. For example:

> Then Sarai *ill-treated* her, and she fled from her (Gen. 16.6).

> As soon as Gideon died, the people of Israel turned again and *played the harlot* after the Baals (Judg. 8.33).

> So the man seized his concubine, and put her out to them; and they knew her, and *abused* her (Judg. 19.25).

So Absalom *stole* the hearts of the men of Israel (2 Sam. 15.6).

But he forsook the counsel which *the old men* gave him, and took counsel with *the children* who had grown up with him and stood before him (1 Kgs 12.8).

The words which have been emphasized are not neutral but are imbued with a powerful positive or negative charge and thus, while giving what appears to be a factual account of events, the narrator's attitude is transmitted.

Narrators have at their disposal two principal ways of presenting events in the narrative (these form either end of a continuum, with intermediate points between them). The first method is to provide a summary account of what has happened, while the second is to show the events themselves. When narrators give a summary account they regard the events from a remote (optical) point of view, unfolding a wide, comprehensive panorama in front of us. When they display the actual incident they view it from close to, showing us a vivid and detailed scene. In the first instance we receive a report of what has taken place, in the second we see things happening with our own eyes, as it were. Each approach complements the other, for while the second one is dramatic and concentrated it is limited, failing to give a comprehensive view. In order to achieve this the first approach, which provides an extensive report, is required.

When the method of summary account is used narrators are more evident than when that of showing scenes is employed, since the more they summarize and compress many events into one broad picture, the more their activity as intermediaries between us and the events is felt. This activity inevitably entails a certain assessment and interpretation of what is happening, since narrators will include only those incidents which they consider to be essential.

Both these approaches occur in biblical narrative, as can be demonstrated by comparing the extensive summary of David's wars against the nations of the region (2 Sam. 8) with the intensive representation of David's flight from Jerusalem in the narrative of Absalom's revolt (2 Sam. 15–16). Whereas the review of the wars gives us a general picture virtually devoid of details, David's flight is depicted through a series of scenes showing us vividly and at close quarters his various meetings with Ittai, with Zadok and Abiathar, with Hushai, with Ziba and with Shimei the son of Gera.

This scenic, or dramatic, method is found in a large number of biblical narratives, such as the Garden of Eden (Genesis 3), the visit of the three men to Abraham (Genesis 18), David and Goliath (1 Samuel 17) and many others. There is a clear tendency to prefer this method in biblical narrative, and it is this which gives it its lively and dramatic character. Because scenic representation creates the illusion of looking at the event itself, it increases the reader's ability to be absorbed in the world displayed and to share in what happens, like a spectator at the theatre.

Although, as has been stated above, the reader should be able to be detached from time to time from the world of the narrative in order to ponder the significance of the events, emotional involvement is also necessary, for without it the reader will not adopt the values embodied in the narrative. It is true that if the emotional involvement is too great, amounting to total identification, the reader will not consider the meaning of the incidents nor judge the moral conduct of the characters, but if it is too small and the reader remains indifferent to the characters and their fate the narrative will not have any effect. The reader's involvement is carefully directed and controlled even in those passages where the narrator hides behind the events or the characters.

Narrators' perceptions of events sometimes accord with those of one of the characters. In this case, even though they use the third person for their narration, the narrators adopt the optical or psychological point of view of that character, while they themselves are concealed, as it were. Below are a few examples of this kind of narration.

In many cases where we find the word 'behold' (*hinnēh*) the narrator shows us a certain detail from the point of view of one of the characters. This is clearly evident when 'behold' occurs after a verb denoting seeing, as in the verses: 'And Isaac went out to meditate in the field in the evening; and he lifted up his eyes and looked, *and behold*, there were camels coming' (Gen. 24.63); 'When he was gone out, his servants came; and when they saw that, *behold*, the doors of the parlour were locked. . . ' (Judg. 3.24); 'And the watchman went up to the roof over the gate unto the wall, and lifted up his eyes, and looked, *and behold* a man running alone' (2 Sam. 18.24). In these cases the narrator explicitly informs us that what is being described is what one of the characters is seeing at that moment, even though it has been proved to us that the narrator actually knew this beforehand or knows more than that character discerns at that moment. Even when 'behold' occurs without being preceded by a word denoting perception, and what we appear to have before us is the narrator's report, in actual fact the events are often described from the point of view of one of the characters.

> When they came to Gibeah, *behold*, a band of prophets was coming towards him (1 Sam. 10.10).

> When David came to the summit, where God was worshipped, *behold*, coming towards him was Hushai the Archite with his coat rent and earth upon his head (2 Sam. 15.32).

> When David had passed a little beyond the summit, *behold*, Ziba the servant of Mephibosheth was coming towards him. . . (2 Sam. 16.1).

> And as Obadiah was on the way, *behold*, Elijah was coming towards him. . . (1 Kgs 18.7).

In these examples the word, 'behold' relates to the character who sees the object described, not to the narrator. The narrator discerns something, and as a result we perceive it too, together with the character and through the latter's eyes. In the example of Hushai (2 Sam. 15.32) the word order is the reverse of what is customary in the Bible. Whenever the term 'coming towards' (*liqrā'tô*) occurs in the Bible it is preceded by the subject (see the examples above), but this is not so in this instance. The unusual order of the words here may indicate that first David saw someone coming towards him but could not yet make out who it was, and only afterwards realized that it was Hushai the Archite.

The names or designations used to refer to the characters in the narrative also often reveal that the narrator has adopted the viewpoint of one of the characters. Thus, in Gen. 21.9-21 we are told about Ishmael, but he is not mentioned by name; instead various designations are used reflecting the attitude of the other characters towards him.[2]

> But Sarah saw *the son of Hagar the Egyptian*, whom she had borne to Abraham, playing with her son Isaac (v. 9).

> And the thing was very displeasing to Abraham on account of *his son* (v. 11).

---

2. N. Leibovitz, 'How to Read a Chapter of the Bible', *Nefesh weShir* (Jerusalem, 1953), pp. 100-101 (Hebrew).

And he took bread and a skin of water, and gave it to Hagar, putting it on her shoulder, along with *the child*, and sent her away (v. 14).

When the water in the skin was gone, she cast *the child* under one of the bushes (v. 15).

And God heard the voice of *the lad* (v. 17).

And God was with *the lad*, and he grew up (v. 20).

Thus, for Sarah Ishmael is merely the son of Hagar, the Egyptian woman, for Abraham he is his son, for Hagar he is the child, her child, while for God he is what he is, namely, the lad. The narrator refers to him by different terms in accordance with the various attitudes to Ishmael.

Two of the sons of Jacob, Simeon and Levi, *Dinah's brothers*, took their swords and came upon the city unawares (Gen. 34.25).

Simeon and Levi are referred to as Dinah's brothers by the narrator because they think about her, act for her, take her out of Shechem's house and for her sake kill Shechem, his father, and all the men of the city.

The narrator's designations of Bathsheba (2 Sam. 11–12) reflect David's attitude to her. In the first verses of the story (11.2, 3a) she is simply called 'a woman', and this is not surprising since Bathsheba's name is not yet known (neither to David nor to us). But in verse 5, after her name has been disclosed, she is still referred to as 'the woman', not Bathsheba, and in the remainder of chapter 11 her name is not mentioned either, indicating David's attitude to her as merely a woman, an object for the satisfaction of his desires. Only after Nathan's rebuke, David's remorse and the death of the child does David's attitude to her change, and she becomes an end in herself and no longer simply a means. This change is reflected in the fact that in 12.24 she is referred to by her name, Bathsheba: 'Then David comforted his wife, Bathsheba, and went in to her, and lay with her'. The first verb in the verse also makes it clear that David is more concerned about her and her feelings now, and that their sexual intercourse this time is different in its significance, being more for her sake than his. In this verse she is referred to not only as Bathsheba but also as 'his wife', the possessive pronoun indicating the relationship which has developed between them.

The relationship between Bathsheba and Uriah is hinted at in
11.26: 'When the wife of Uriah heard that Uriah her husband was
dead, she made lamentation for her husband'. The repetitions of the
name Uriah, the designation 'husband', the possessive pronouns, as
well as the phrase 'the wife of Uriah', emphasize the fact that they
were husband and wife, for the verse could also have been phrased
thus: 'When Bathsheba heard that Uriah was dead, she made
lamentation for him'. The relationship at which the narrator is
hinting in this verse need not necessarily be an emotional one; the
reference may be to the objective situation, stressing it here in order
to indicate David's sin. By causing Uriah's death David separated
people who had been bound together in marriage. The indirect
reference to David's sin is made even clearer if we pay attention to
the fact that the subject of this verse, 'the wife of Uriah', is carried
over into the next one, 'and she became his wife', indicating that
David took as his wife someone who was the wife of another (this is
said explicitly by Nathan: 'You have taken *the wife of Uriah the
Hittite* to be *your wife*' [12.10]). The same way of hinting at the sin,
carrying the pronoun over into the next verse, is also found in 11.3, 4:
'Is not this Bathsheba, the daughter of Eliam, *the wife of Uriah the
Hittite*? So David sent messengers and took her; and she came to
him, and he lay with her'. The indirect reference to the sin by means
of the designation 'Uriah's wife', is most manifest in 12.15: 'Then
Nathan went to his house. And the Lord struck the child that *Uriah's
wife* bore *to David*, and it became sick'.

In the light of what has been said above, it is hardly surprising that
in the narrative of the enthronement of Solomon, in 1 Kings 1, the
narrator invariably refers to Bathsheba by her first name: 'So
Bathsheba went to the king into his chamber; Bathsheba bowed. . . '
(vv. 15, 16, 31). Here there is no occasion to hint at a sin, nor any
sexual intercourse; on the other hand Bathsheba appears here in an
active role (though not as the initiator), as a personality in her own
right with interests of her own, in contrast to the way she was
represented in 2 Samuel.

Particular attention should be paid to the fact that when Nathan
attempts to persuade Bathsheba to intercede with the king on behalf of
her son, Solomon, the author refers to her as 'the mother of
Solomon': 'Then Nathan said to Bathsheba the mother of Solomon. . . '
(1 Kgs 1.11). When Adonijah asks Bathsheba to use her influence
with her son so that he should give him Abishag the Shunnamite for

his wife, the narrator again calls her 'the mother of Solomon': 'Then Adonijah the son of Haggith came to Bathsheba the mother of Solomon' (1 Kgs 2.13).

Thus, the way the narrator refers to a person reflects either the narrator's own attitude or that of another character (if the attitude changes, as does David's to Bathsheba, this may be expressed through changing designations). This constitutes a remarkable coalescence of two points of view, merging the character's subjective view with the narrator's 'objective' one.[3] At the same time a balance is achieved between excessive affinity and aloofness on the part of the narrator. This way of narration expresses the narrator's empathy for the character whose point of view is adopted. Empathy, however, is not the same as identification and may even include criticism. Be that as it may, this mode of narration enables the author to enter the character's mind while at the same time being an outside observer.

Another example is to be found in the way the narrator refers to David in the narrative of Absalom's revolt (2 Sam. 15-19). Sometimes the term 'the king' is used, sometimes the name 'David' and sometimes 'king David'. When the narrator describes David's meetings with Ittai the Gittite and Zadok the priest, David is designated 'the king' (except in 15.22, where he is called 'David'; a few exceptions are only to be expected, however, if we take into account the process by which the biblical texts were transmitted, involving inaccuracies in copying, etc.). When David's meeting with Hushai on the Mount of Olives is depicted, however, the narrator refers to him as 'David'. During his meeting with Ziba, Mephibosheth's servant, he is referred to as 'the king' again, while in the incident in which Shimei the son of Gera curses and stones him, he is called 'David'. During the conversation between David and Abishai concerning Shimei, the term used is 'the king'. In describing David's return to Jerusalem after the revolt has been suppressed (ch. 19) the term 'the king' is always employed (except in v. 23): this appellation features in his second meeting with Shimei the son of Gera, in his encounter with Mephibosheth and when he takes his leave of Barzilai the Gileadite.

3. Coalescence and merging, not mere juxtaposition. An example of the juxtaposition of two points of view can be found in Exod. 2.23: 'And it came to pass in those many days. . . ' 'many' from the point of view of the suffering people, 'those' from the point of view of the narrator, observing events from a later point in time.

These ways of referring to David reflect the attitude of the character mentioned in the context. For Ittai, Zadok and Ziba he is the king, for Hushai and Shimei he is David. For Hushai this reflects the close relationship between the two men—Hushai is David's devoted friend—while for Shimei this expresses his contempt and refusal to acknowledge the legitimacy of David's rule. The fact that at the second meeting between David and Shimei the narrator uses the term 'the king' indicates a change in Shimei's attitude, at least externally. (The change in attitude is manifest even more forcefully in what Shimei says himself. Whereas at the first meeting he calls David 'man of blood, worthless fellow!', at the second he addresses David as 'my lord the king', and refers to himself as 'your servant'.)

When David crosses the Jordan eastwards in his flight he is referred to as 'David', while when he crosses the river westwards on his return he is called 'the king' and this is not without significance either. This time, however, the narrator is intimating what David's situation and status is rather than how other characters see him. During his flight he is merely David, barefoot, tired, destitute, accompanied by only a handful of loyal subjects; on his return he is the king once more, and is recognized as such by both Judah and Israel.

Nevertheless, there are instances when the use of either 'David' or 'the king' or the phrase 'king David' does not appear to have any significance. In these cases all that can be said is that we are unable to explain the use of alternate references other than for the sake of variety.

What has been said above about the use of names and designations in order to reflect the characters' attitudes applies to places as well as to people. This is indicated by the following example, which is also taken from the narrative of Absalom's revolt. In 2 Sam. 15.37 we read: 'So Hushai, David's friend, came into the city, just as Absalom was entering Jerusalem'. Is it coincidence that initially, when the subject is Hushai, the place is called 'the city', while afterwards, when the subject is Absalom, it is referred to as 'Jerusalem?' This switch is not arbitrary, it would seem. Whenever the passage is about Absalom and his supporters the place is called Jerusalem: 'Now Absalom and all the people, the men of Israel, came to Jerusalem, and Ahithophel with him' (16.15); 'When Absalom's servants came to the woman at the house... And when they had sought and could not find them, they returned to Jerusalem' (17.20). In connection with David and his followers, however, the place is usually (though not invariably) called 'the city'. When Absalom's servants are trying to find Ahimaaz and Jonathan, unsuccessfully, we read, as mentioned just before, that they return to Jerusalem, whereas Ahimaaz and Jonathan themselves, who belong to David's faction, are said to be waiting at En-Rogel, '. . . for they must not be seen entering the city' (17.17). This term also occurs in 15.24: 'Abiathar came up . . . and they set down the ark of God, until the people had all passed out of the city'. The weightiest evidence, however, is the fact that David himself speaks of 'the city' in this narrative: 'Arise and let us flee; or else there will be no escape for us from Absalom; go in haste, lest he overtake us quickly, and bring down evil upon us, and smite the city with the edge of the sword' (15.14); 'Carry the ark of God back into the city' (15.25); 'Go back to the city in peace' (15.27); 'But if you return to the city' (15.34). In contrast to the objective reference to the place as 'Jerusalem', the use of the term 'the city' reveals David's special relationship with it. Here, too, the narrator enters David's mind, transmitting the facts from his point of view.

It should not, of course, be claimed that whenever the name of a city or the term 'the city' is used it has the same meaning as it has here. On the contrary, it can be assumed that the meaning will change in accordance with the context and the general character of the narrative. Even in the account of Absalom's rebellion David uses the term 'the city' only when he is talking to his associates—his servants, Zadok and Hushai—whereas when he is addressing Barzilai the Gileadite he adapts his speech to his listener and calls the place 'Jerusalem' (19.33). Thus it appears that the use of names and designations in referring to people and places is neither accidental nor devoid of significance.

Whenever the characters use direct speech in the narrative their point of view is, naturally, reflected. In these instances the narrator's existence is least apparent, being pushed aside and becoming practically imperceptible. When the characters' voices are heard the narrator's voice is silent; and then to all intents and purposes the narrator is absent. In actual fact, however, the narrator is never absent from the narrative, for when the characters speak in their own voices, their speech does not have the same independence as that of characters in a play, because in narrative literature, as has been

stated above, the narrator prefaces the characters' speech with a
phrase, such as: 'And he asked', 'And she replied', 'And X said to Y'
etc., making it clear that we hear the characters' conversations only
by virtue of the narrator's assistance. The protagonists' speech is
always imbedded in that of the narrator, who gives them the floor.
The narrator not only informs us who is speaking and to whom, but
also sometimes defines the nature of the speech.

For example, in 2 Sam. 18.5 the king says: 'Deal gently for my sake
with the young man Absalom'. The narrator prefaces this sentence
by stating: 'And the king ordered Joab and Abishai and Ittai', thus
giving it the force of an explicit order (which is not the case with
everything the king says; compare 2 Sam. 15.19, 25 etc.), and the
responsibility for obeying the order is placed upon each of the three
commanders explicitly mentioned by name. Because of this, it is
clear that when Joab kills Absalom he is not simply ignoring a
request made by the king but is knowingly disobeying an order. The
definition of the king's words as an order (and this definition occurs
twice in this chapter, in vv. 5 and 12) makes Joab's offence
particularly grave, while at the same time emphasizing the importance
of the matter for David.

In the same chapter (2 Sam. 18.28) we read: 'Then Ahimaaz cried
out to the king, "All is well"'. The narrator uses the verb 'cried out'
(*qārā'*) in order to show that Ahimaaz shouted from afar in order to
calm the king, who was waiting anxiously for news from the
battlefield (the Hebrew word *shalom* means 'all is well' here, and is
not a greeting, compare 2 Kgs 4.26). This is also intimated by the
order of events: 'Then Ahimaaz cried out to the king, "All is well".
And he bowed before the king with his face to the earth, and said,
"Blessed be the Lord your God, who has delivered up the men who
raised their hand against my lord the king"'. First Ahimaaz calls out
that all is well, then he bows down before the king, then he passes on
his news. The use of the verb 'cried out' also fits in with the
description of Ahimaaz's gradual approach: first the watchman on
the roof of the gate discerns someone a long way off but cannot
identify him, then he perceives that it is Ahimaaz, then it is possible
to hear what he is shouting, and finally the messenger stands before
the king, bows down and delivers his message.

David's reaction on hearing of Absalom's death comes immediately
afterwards: 'O my son Absalom, my son, my son Absalom', etc.
(2 Sam. 18.33), and again a few verses later: 'O my son Absalom,

O Absalom, my son, my son!' (2 Sam. 19.4). On the first occasion the narrator precedes David's speech with the phrase 'and as he went, he said', while the second time he states: 'and the king cried with a loud voice'. This indicates that initially David spoke with restraint, while later on he was unable to control himself and cried out loud.

In the vast majority of cases the narrator uses the neutral term 'and he said' ('and she said', 'and they said', etc.) in order to denote the speech of a character. The phrase 'and he said' is occasionally repeated, even though the same character continues speaking. When this is the case the narrator is hinting that there has been a break in the character's words.[4] A pause of this kind can occur in order to allow for a reply or a reaction. For example: 'But Abram *said*, "O Lord God, what wilt thou give me, for I continue childless, and the heir of my house is Eliezer of Damascus?" And Abram *said*, "Behold, thou hast given me no offspring; and a slave born in my house will be my heir"' (Gen. 15.2-3). After Abram asks 'what wilt thou give me', meaning what is the point of a rich reward if I have no offspring, he waits for a reply from God, and when there is none he says explicitly: Because you have not given me a son a stranger will be my heir.

'The king sent and summoned Shimei, and *said* to him, "Did I not make you swear by the Lord, and solemnly admonish you, saying, "Know for certain that on the day you go forth and go to any place whatever, you shall die?" And you said to me, "What you say is good; I obey". Why then have you not kept your oath to the Lord and the commandment with which I charged you?" The king *said* to Shimei, "You know in your own heart all the evil that you did to David my father; so the Lord will bring back your evil upon your own head"' (1 Kgs 2.42-44). The repetition of '(the king) said', indicates that after Solomon asked: 'Why then have you not kept your oath to the Lord and the commandment with which I charged you?' he waited a few moments for Shimei's response. Shimei's answer is not given, indicating that he did not reply, because he had nothing to say. After a brief pause, Solomon begins speaking again, hinting to Shimei that he will die not only because of the formal reason that he broke his oath not to leave the city, but also for the substantive reason that he cursed and mocked David when the king fled from Jerusalem during Absalom's revolt.

4. M. Shiloh, 'And he said . . . and he said', *Sefer Korngreen* (Tel Aviv, 1963) (Hebrew).

'When Uriah came to him, David *asked* how Joab was doing, and how the people fared, and how the war prospered. Then David *said* to Uriah, "Go down to your house, and wash your feet"' (2 Sam. 11.7-8). Although the narrator uses two different verbs to denote David's speech, there is no intervening speech by any other character, nor any action of any kind. Uriah's answer to David's questions is not given, but this time there is no doubt that Uriah did reply. The omission of the answer suggests that Uriah's reply was of no significance to David, or that David did not even listen to Uriah's replies. From this we can infer that the questions were asked simply as camouflage. Uriah was to think that he had been summoned from Rabbah of the Ammonites to Jerusalem in order to report on Joab, the people and the war. In actual fact, the only important thing for David was that Uriah should go to his house, as he says at the end of their conversation.

In some instances the repetition of 'said' indicates something else than a pause for a reply to be given.

'And he brought him outside and *said*, "Look toward heaven, and number the stars, if you are able to number them". Then he *said* to him, "So shall your descendants be"' (Gen. 15.5). The pause in God's words is intended to enable Abram to look up at the sky and realize that he is unable to count the stars.

'Then he *said*, "Do not come near; put off your shoes from your feet, for the place on which you are standing is holy ground". And he *said*, "I am the God of your father, the God of Abraham, the God of Isaac, and the God of Jacob"' (Exod. 3.5-6). In this case the purpose of the pause is to give Moses time to take his shoes off.

'And she *said* to him, "My father, if you have opened your mouth to the Lord, do to me according to what has gone forth from your mouth, now that the Lord has avenged you on your enemies, on the Ammonites". And she *said* to her father, "Let this thing be done for me; let me alone two months, that I may go and wander on the mountains, and bewail my virginity, I and my companions"' (Judg. 11.36-37). At first Jephthah's daughter accepts her fate and even encourages her father; on second thoughts she decides, nevertheless, to make a request, namely, that she be given two months' delay in order to bewail her virginity.

'Absalom *said* to him, "See, your claims are good and right; but there is no man deputed by the king to hear you". And Absalom *said*, "Oh that I were judge in the land! Then every man with a suit or cause might come to me, and I would give him justice"' (2 Sam. 15.3-4). The first thing that Absalom says is intended for his immediate hearer, as is indicated by its content and from the phrase 'to him' used by the narrator. The second part of what he says, however, seems to be a general statement, not directed at anyone in particular. Absalom is merely expressing the desires of his heart, and his hearer is obviously unable to fulfil them. The narrator accordingly uses 'said', without the phrase 'to him'.

In certain cases the first 'said' is not followed by any speech whatsoever. For example 'And Isaac *said* to his father Abraham, and he *said*, "My father"' (Gen. 22.7). In this instance, the repetition represents irresolution, perhaps nervousness. Isaac wants to ask the question which is bothering him ('Where is the lamb for a burnt offering?'), but he is unsure, begins speaking, then hesitates.

To sum up, narrators in the Bible are quite complex and varied. They generally observe the characters from without, but sometimes also see them from within. They usually watch events as outside observers, but sometimes see things through the eyes of one of the characters. On the whole, they perceive situations from close to, and often hear the characters' conversations, but also occasionally take things in from afar. They generally describe the actual events for us, though in some cases they add their own interpretations and explanations.

Narrators usually speak of the characters and their deeds in a factual tone, but they are not indifferent to them. Their attitudes are expressed in a variety of ways, mostly implicit and inconspicuous. On the whole they keep their distance from the characters, but sometimes their point of view coincides with that of one of them. They frequently hint at things—in delicate and indirect ways—rather than stating them explicitly. The method of the biblical narrator requires a constant mental effort on the part of the reader, involving careful thought and attention to every detail of the narrative.

Chapter 2

THE CHARACTERS

Many of the views embodied in the narrative are expressed through the characters, and more specifically, through their speech and fate. Not only do the characters serve as the narrator's mouthpiece, but also what is and is not related about them, which of their characteristics are emphasized and which are not, which of their conversations and actions in the past are recorded and which are not, all reveal the values and norms within the narrative, and in this respect it makes no difference whether the characters are imaginary or whether they actually existed. The decisions they are called upon to make when confronted with different alternatives, and the results of these decisions, provide undisputable evidence of the narrative's ethical dimension.

The characters can also transmit the significance and values of the narrative to the reader, since they usually constitute the focal point of interest. Their personalities and histories attract the reader's attention to a greater extent than do other components of the narrative (explanations, settings, etc.). They generally arouse considerable emotional involvement; we feel what they feel, rejoice in their gladness, grieve at their sorrow and participate in their fate and experiences. Sometimes the characters arouse our sympathy, sometimes our revulsion, but we are never indifferent to them. We want to know them, to see how they act within their environment, and to understand their motives and desires. We follow their struggles to fulfil their aspirations and pay particular attention to everything they say, for when they speak to one another they are also addressing us.

When discussing individuals who are considered to have existed in the past, like those in biblical narrative, it should be emphasized that we know them only as they are presented in the narratives, and it is to this alone that we can refer. We know nothing whatsoever about the real nature of the biblical characters, and we have no way of examining how accurately they are represented in biblical narrative. Although we can judge whether a particular character is convincing as a human being, we cannot know whether he or she is an accurate representation of a specific historical person. We cannot tell, for example, if the way David is portrayed in the book of Samuel and at the beginning of the book of Kings, is a more or less faithful description of David as he really was. All we can say is that his character, as it emerges from the narratives in these books, is not uniform, but, because of its complexity and many-faceted nature, is more convincing than the ideal person depicted in Chronicles (where the embarrassing episode of Bathsheba and Uriah is omitted altogether).

Moreover, a character in a work of literature is merely the sum of the means used in the description. Whereas in real life an individual exists whether or not someone bothers to describe him or her, in a work of literature it is the portrayal which creates the character.

The principal techniques used in moulding characters in the Bible will be presented below, encompassing first the direct and then the indirect ways of shaping the characters.

1. *The Direct Shaping of the Characters*

A. *Outward Appearance*

There is no precise, detailed description of the physical appearance of the characters in biblical narratives. Nothing at all is said about the looks of most of the characters in the Bible, and only in a few instances is a brief mention made of the characters' outward appearance. Even in those cases where an account of this kind is given, this is done only in very general terms without mentioning unique features.

The few details which are given about the external appearance of characters are not intended to enable us to visualize them clearly. Neither does the outer aspect of a character give us any indication of the personality, for there is no connection between appearance and nature (in contrast to many works of literature, where the good person is handsome and the bad one ugly, or the reverse). In biblical narrative information about someone's outward aspect serves solely as a means of advancing the plot or explaining its course.

Esau is a hairy man, while Jacob is a smooth man (Gen. 27.11).

These facts are very important for the plot of the narrative, since Jacob impersonates Esau in order to obtain the blessing intended for his older brother. 'Leah's eyes were weak, but Rachel was beautiful and lovely' (Gen. 29.17). Naturally, this information is intended to explain why Jacob loves Rachel and not Leah. Laban wishes to give Leah first, and therefore deceives Jacob. Jacob's love for Rachel also explains his special feelings for her sons, Joseph and Benjamin.

Saul was more than a head taller than any of the people (1 Sam. 9.2; 10.23), and this, it seems, won their affection and loyalty. An indirect reference to Saul's height is to be found in God's words to Samuel, when the latter is in the house of Jesse the Bethlehemite to anoint one of his sons king instead of Saul. When Samuel sees Eliab he thinks that he is the man destined to become king, but God says (1 Sam. 16.7): 'Do not look on his appearance or on the height of his stature, because I have rejected him; for the Lord sees not as a man sees; man looks on the outward appearance, but the Lord looks on the heart'. The indirect allusion to Saul is unmistakable, because only a few verses before God also says of him: 'I have rejected him' (16.1). Thus we find it stated in quite explicit terms, that there is no connection between a person's external appearance and internal qualities. The absence of this connection may well explain why so few references are made to the outer aspect of characters in the Bible.

It is said of Bathsheba, in a cursory, undetailed way, that she is 'very beautiful' (2 Sam. 11.2), and of Tamar, the daughter of David, even more briefly, that she is 'beautiful' (2 Sam. 13.1). In both these instances the woman's beauty is mentioned solely because it plays a central role in the course of events, providing the motivation for David's and Amnon's licentious behaviour.

Abishag the Shunammite is described as being 'very beautiful' (1 Kgs 1.4). The description of her beauty serves, contrary to the instances of Bathsheba and Tamar, to emphasize David's abstinence from sexual intercourse in his old age: 'The maiden was very beautiful; and she became the king's nurse and ministered to him; but the king knew her not'. This indicates David's weakness and impotence, and this picture of an old and ailing king is supported by additional details in this narrative of Adonijah's attempt to take over the reins of government before David's death. David's advanced age (1 Kgs 1.1, 15) limits his ability and desire to act, and is a significant factor in Adonijah's plan to proclaim himself king. Not only does the king's weakness make the question of the succession more urgent, but Adonijah can also assume that the king's lassitude and negligence will prevent him from reacting vigorously to his usurpation of the throne. While Adonijah is basing his plans on his father's weakness and indifference, the prophet Nathan mobilizes all the forces at his disposal in order to overcome the aged king's apathy and force him to make a decision and act to have Solomon appointed his successor.

Absalom's beauty is described in relative detail: 'Now in all Israel there was no one so much to be praised for his beauty as Absalom; from the sole of his foot to the crown of his head there was no blemish in him' (2 Sam. 14.25). The text extols his beauty, stating explicitly that he was the handsomest man in all Israel. In the next verse we are told about his hair, but here the narrator uses a narrative rather than a description. He relates what Absalom used to *do* with his hair: 'For when he cut the hair of his head, as he did at the end of every year, when it was heavy on him, he weighed it and it weighed two hundred shekels by the king's weight' (v. 26). The information about Absalom's beauty and hair is intended both to present him as someone who has been blessed by fate and is admired by everyone ('there was no one so much to be praised'), and also, which is the main point, to indicate his vanity and self-love, traits which play an important part in the course of events leading to his revolt against his father. In addition, Absalom's abundant hair causes his death in the final event.

Mephibosheth the son of Saul was a cripple and for that reason had been unable to go with David when he fled from Absalom (2 Sam. 19.26). In verse 24 of that chapter we read that: 'He had neither dressed his feet, nor trimmed his beard, nor washed his clothes, from the day the king departed until the day he came back in safety'. Here, too, we learn how Mephibosheth grieved over David's flight from what he *did*, or rather did not do, concerning his external appearance.

There are also exceptions, however. David is described as being: 'ruddy, and had beautiful eyes, and was handsome' (1 Sam. 16.12), without these details about his outward appearance playing any defined part in the development of the events associated with him. We should remember, however, that this refers not to just any biblical character but to the person who is one day to be considered the ideal king. It is natural that details will be given about him which are not usually provided concerning other characters. His external beauty may have been one of the reasons for his popularity with the people, though not the principal one. It should be noted that Goliath the Philistine disdained David just because he was: 'but a youth, ruddy and comely in appearance' (17.42).

In some cases the expression on the faces of characters at a certain time is mentioned because it reflects their emotions. After Hannah heard Eli's encouraging words we read: 'and her countenance was no longer sad' (1 Sam. 1.18). Jonadab asks Amnon, who is tortured by his love for Tamar: 'O son of the king, why are you so haggard morning after morning?' (2 Sam. 13.4). The king of Persia asks Nehemiah, who has heard very sad news about the plight of his brethren in Judah: 'Why is your face sad, seeing you are not sick?' (Neh. 2.2).

As is the case with physical appearances, the clothes worn by characters in the Bible are never described in detail. In a few isolated cases one item or another of clothing is mentioned, and this is done solely to advance the plot or indicate the individual's emotional state. In most of the instances in which clothing is specified, we are told what is *done* with it.

We read about Tamar, Judah's daughter in law: 'She put off her widow's garments, and put on a veil, wrapping herself up' (Gen. 38.14). The object of changing her clothes is clear: Tamar does not want Judah to recognize her, and even wants him to think she is a harlot. We hear about special mourning clothes also when Joab addresses the wise woman of Tekoa: 'Pretend to be a mourner, and put on mourning garments' (2 Sam. 14.2). Both for Tamar and for the woman of Tekoa clothes play an important part in the 'show' they put on. The same applies to the Gibeonites, 'with worn-out, patched sandals on their feet and worn-out clothes' (Josh. 9.5).

The equipment worn by Goliath the Philistine is described in greater detail than is customary in the Bible: 'He had a helmet of bronze on his head, and he was armed with a coat of mail, and the weight of the coat was five thousand shekels of bronze. And he had greaves of bronze upon his legs, and a javelin of bronze slung between his shoulders. And the shaft of his spear was like a weaver's beam, and his spear's head weighed six hundred shekels of iron' (1 Sam. 17.5-7). Obviously this account of Goliath's heavy and terrifying armour is not an end in itself but a way of emphasizing the astounding victory obtained by David, who went to battle unarmed, in the name of the Lord of hosts, the God of the armies of Israel. 'Then David said to the Philistine, "You come to me with a sword and with a spear and with a javelin; but I come to you in the name of the Lord of hosts, the God of the armies of Israel, whom you have defied"' (17.45). In order to stress this concept of victory with the help of the Lord and not because of armour, the episode of David's attempt to wear Saul's coat of mail, bronze helmet and sword is related, ending in David's abandoning all the implements of war (vv. 38-39).

Mention is often made in the Bible of the tearing of clothes to signify mourning and sorrow, for example: 'And on the third day, behold, a man came from Saul's camp, with his clothes rent and earth upon his head' (2 Sam. 1.2), or, 'Then David took hold of his clothes, and rent them; and so did all the men who were with him' (v. 11).

We read about Tamar, the daughter of David: 'Now she was wearing a long robe with sleeves; for thus were the virgin daughters of the king clad in garments... And Tamar put ashes on her head, and rent the long robe which she wore...' (2 Sam. 13.18-19). In this case the tearing of the robe has another function in addition to the expression of grief and sorrow. Tamar's long robe also fulfils a symbolic role, indicating, as the narrator states in no uncertain terms, that Tamar is a virgin and the daughter of the king, someone with a very high rank. The tear symbolizes the drastic change which has taken place in her situation: she is no longer a virgin and has also been cast out by Amnon and his servant, in contrast to the treatment which should be accorded a king's daughter.

Elijah's casting of his mantle upon Elisha (1 Kgs 19.19) should also be regarded as a symbolic act. Elisha immediately abandons his work, runs after Elijah and serves him. When Elijah ascends to heaven, Elisha picks up the mantle which has fallen from him and strikes the Jordan with it, just as Elijah had done: 'And when he had struck the water, the water was parted to the one side and to the other'. When the sons of the prophets see this they say: 'The spirit of Elijah rests on Elisha' (2 Kgs 2.15). Thus, Elijah's spirit is transferred symbolically by means of the mantle, both at the first meeting between the two prophets and at their final parting.

Finally, it is said of Mordecai: 'Then Mordecai went out from the presence of the king in royal robes of blue and white, with a great golden crown and a mantle of fine linen and purple' (Esth. 8.15). The apparel described here in considerable detail expresses the heights which Mordecai had reached and symbolizes his victory over his enemy, Haman (who had already been obliged to dress him in royal robes in order to honour him on a previous occasion).

B. Inner Personality

There are two kinds of direct statement about an individual's inner personality: one that refers to character traits and one that relates to mental states. The first kind is what is customarily called direct characterization (in the narrow and precise sense of the word).

Direct characterization often embodies an element of judgment. If a person is defined as being righteous, wicked, wise or foolish, this constitutes both characterization and judgment. Thus, direct characterization, particularly when it refers to the individual's entire personality, can serve simultaneously as a way of evaluating it (though it can also fulfil other functions).

Direct characterization may be voiced by the narrator or by one of the characters. There are not many instances of direct characterization by the narrator in biblical narratives. What is evident is that the trait noted by the narrator is always extremely important in the development of the plot. Furthermore, the quality denoted through direct characterization almost always emerges indirectly, too, through either the actions or speech of the character involved or through both of them.

We read about Noah: 'Noah was a righteous man, blameless in his generation; Noah walked with God' (Gen. 6.9). The men of Sodom are characterized as being: 'wicked, great sinners against the Lord' (Gen. 13.13). The sons of Eli are described as follows: 'they were worthless men; they had no regard for the Lord' (1 Sam. 2.12). Sheba the son of Bichri is also described as: 'a worthless fellow' (2 Sam. 20.1). Nabal is presented as being: 'churlish and ill-behaved' (1 Sam. 25.3), Obadiah is described as a person who: 'revered the Lord greatly' (1 Kgs 18.3), while Job was: 'blameless and upright, one who feared God, and turned away from evil' (Job 1.1).

Apart from these characterizations, which refer to the moral aspects of the individuals involved, there are also accounts of their mental traits and other facets of their personalities.

The narrator tells us that the serpent in the garden of Eden was: 'more subtle than any other wild creature that the Lord God had made' (Gen. 3.1). Jonadab the son of Shimeah, Amnon's friend, is

described as: 'a very crafty man' (2 Sam. 13.3), while the woman
from Tekoa (14.2) and the woman from Abel of Beth-maacah (20.16)
are both said to be wise. Esau is portrayed as being: 'a skilful hunter,
a man of the field', while Jacob was considered: 'a quiet man,
dwelling in tents' (Gen. 25.27). The narrator tells us that the man
Moses was: 'very meek, more than all men that were on the face of
the earth' (Num. 12.3). Saul is described as being: '. . . choice and
fine. There was not a man among the people of Israel finer than he'
(1 Sam. 9.2).

Amongst the instances of direct characterization uttered by the
protagonists, particular attention should be paid to those attributed
to God. Characterization voiced by God has absolute validity, like
that pronounced by the narrator, or perhaps even more so.

God says to Noah: 'For I have seen that you are righteous before
me in this generation' (Gen. 7.1). The angel of the Lord says to
Abraham: 'For now I know that you fear God' (Gen. 22.12). God
says to Solomon: 'Behold, I give you a wise and discerning mind, so
that none like you has been before you and none like you shall arise
after you' (1 Kgs 3.12). God says to Satan: 'Have you considered my
servant Job, that there is none like him on the earth, a blameless and
upright man, who fears God and turns away from evil' (Job 1.8).

When characterization derives from human beings the question
arises whether it reflects the author's 'objective' view or only the
character's subjective one. The author can portray any one character
by putting a description in the mouth of any other, but this does not
mean that whenever this occurs it necessarily reflects the author's
opinion. It will not always be easy to decide whether or not the
author identifies with what the characters say in describing each
other.

There is an additional difficulty in this respect, arising from the
fact that in many instances when one of the persons appears to be
characterizing another, there is in fact no characterization at all.
What one person says about another often does not refer to the real
features, but merely expresses the state of mind, emotions or
attitudes of the speaker. On occasions these statements of 'characterization' are made solely to serve the speaker's ends, thus revealing
more about the individual who says them than about the one they
purport to describe. The following examples will illustrate this.

One of Saul's young men says: 'Behold, I have seen a son of Jesse
the Bethlehemite, who is skilful in playing, a man of valour, a man of

war, prudent in speech, and a man of good presence; and the Lord is with him' (1 Sam. 16.18). In this case it can be assumed that the long description of David given by one of Saul's young men conforms with the author's view. All the qualities mentioned here emerge in the stories about David, and Hushai cites some of them as recognized characteristics of David (2 Sam. 17.8, 10). Although Hushai's intention is purely to use his description of David's nature to instil fear into Absalom's heart, thereby causing him to reject Ahithophel's advice, there is no reason to assume that Hushai does not believe what he is saying about David, nor is there any cause to suppose that the author does not concur with Hushai's opinion.

Saul says to David: 'You are more righteous than I' (1 Sam. 24.17). There is no doubt that this positive description is believed by Saul, and from the context it is evident that the author endorses it too.

Several characterizations are given by various individuals in the narrative of Abigail (1 Samuel 25). One of Nabal's servants says of David and his men: 'Yet the men were very good to us' (v. 15) while the same servant says of Nabal: 'he is ill-natured' (v. 17). Abigail herself says about her husband: 'Let not my lord regard this ill-natured fellow, Nabal; for as his name is, so is he; Nabal (fool) is his name, and folly is with him' (v. 25). The statements made by the servant and Abigail—although intended to dissuade David from killing Nabal and all his household—are undoubtedly considered reliable and accurate by the author.

We can also concur with what David says about the sons of Zeruiah: 'And I am this day weak, though anointed king; these men the sons of Zeruiah are too hard for me. The Lord requite the evildoer according to his wickedness' (2 Sam. 3.39). Similarly, what David says about Ishbosheth, the son of Saul, and his murderers, can be accepted: 'How much more, when wicked men have slain a righteous man in his own house' (4.11).

Tamar says to Amnon: 'And as for you, you would be as one of the wanton fools in Israel' (2 Sam. 13.13). Her object in giving this description is to deter Amnon from raping her, but there can be scarcely any doubt that by placing this statement in Tamar's mouth the narrator's opinion of Amnon is being expressed and conveyed to the reader. Tamar serves as the author's mouthpiece in condemning Amnon. Tamar's definition of Amnon is dependent upon his implementing his threat, but since he does so and torments his sister, her statement is ratified.

In addressing Solomon, David says: 'For you are a wise man' (1 Kgs 2.9), and the Queen of Sheba says to him: 'The report was true which I heard in my own land of your affairs and of your wisdom. . . . and, behold, the half was not told me; your wisdom and prosperity surpass the report which I heard' (10.6-7). These accounts of Solomon's wisdom clearly accord with the narrator's statements, God's words and Solomon's acts revealing his sagacity.

When, however, Shimei the son of Gera calls David, 'man of blood, worthless fellow' (2 Sam. 16.7) this does not reflect the author's view. On the contrary, by defining Shimei's words as a curse—the author does not write: 'And Shimei said', but: 'And Shimei said as he cursed'—the narrator hints that they should not be regarded as a balanced pronouncement. Shimei, who is a member of Saul's family, expresses resentment and anger with David for supplanting the previous royal house. His statement makes it clear how low David had fallen at the time he fled from Absalom, while at the same time indicating that not only Absalom opposed his rule but other groups, loyal to the house of Saul, were antagonistic towards him too. In contrast to these words of hate uttered by Shimei, many episodes in the books of Samuel reveal David's fair and just treatment of Saul and his descendants.

David says of Ahimaaz: 'He is a good man, and comes with good tidings' (2 Sam. 18.27). Adonijah says to Jonathan: 'Come in, for you are a worthy man and bring good news' (1 Kgs 1.42). Although both Ahimaaz and Jonathan had proved in the past that they were worthy men when they succeeded in evading their pursuers and bringing important information from the city of Jerusalem to David in the desert, the intention here is not to characterize the two messengers, who play merely a secondary role in the narrative. What is reflected in these two instances is the speaker's high hopes of hearing good news, while through their words the author creates a sharply ironic contrast between the expectations (of David and Adonijah) and the actual content of the information, which is disastrous for the recipient: Absalom's death (in the case of David) and the anointing of Solomon (in the case of Adonijah).

A special kind of 'characterization' uttered by an individual (which in actual fact is a pseudo-characterization) is that phrased as a metaphor or a simile. In this case the object is not to describe but to arouse or express a particular attitude. Metaphors and similes often serve not only to clarify a particular matter by comparing it with something else (in a simile the comparison is overt, while in a metaphor it is covert), but also to express or arouse an emotional stance vis à vis the matter in hand. The emotions which exist with regard to one side of the comparison are transferred to the other, thus filling the second sphere with the emotions associated with the first.

Abishai the son of Zeruiah calls Shimei the son of Gera, 'this dead dog' (2 Sam. 16.9). This metaphor serves merely to express contempt and scorn, reflecting the speaker's emotional stance and his attempt to arouse the same feelings in David so that he will permit Abishai to execute Shimei.

The same metaphor, in conjunction with another one, is used by David to refer to himself. When Saul is chasing him David says: 'After whom do you pursue? After a dead dog! After a flea!' (1 Sam. 24.14). His object is to indicate his unimportance in no uncertain terms, and thus dissuade Saul from continuing to hunt him.

David is 'characterized' four times by means of the phrase, 'as an angel of God' (this simile is not used in connection with anyone else in the Bible). Achish the king of Gath, says to him: 'I know that you are as blameless in my sight as an angel of God; nevertheless the commanders of the Philistines have said, "He shall not go up with us to the battle"' (1 Sam. 29.9). The wise woman of Tekoa uses the simile twice when addressing David: 'For my lord the king is like the angel of God to discern good and evil'. 'But my lord has wisdom like the wisdom of the angel of God to know all things that are on the earth' (2 Sam. 14.17, 20). Mephibosheth says to David: 'But my lord the king is like the angel of God; do therefore what seems good to you' (19.27).

A common element can be discerned, as in all four cases the speaker who uses the simile 'as an angel of God', wants to flatter David. The sycophantic aspect is particularly evident in the case of Mephibosheth. Even at the best of times he is dependent on the king's mercy, and even more so now, after Ziba has accused him of being disloyal to the king and David believes Ziba. His position is extremely precarious, his life is in the balance and all he can do is to praise and extol the king, reminding him of a previous act of mercy he has shown him and hoping that the king will be equally forgiving this time.

The element of fawning is obvious in the words of the woman of Tekoa too. She uses the simile twice because she has two aims; first of all, she wishes to influence the king to allow Absalom to come back, as she desires (or, more precisely, in accordance with the wishes of Joab, in whose service she is acting); and secondly, she wants to avert the king's anger against her and Joab for deceiving him. She believes that she will achieve both these objectives by using a little flattery, thus obtaining the king's goodwill and inducing him to grant her request.

Achish's flattery is less obvious, but it exists nevertheless. He wants to placate David because of the demand made by the commanders of the Philistines that he be removed from the area of the battle and sent back whence he came. The Philistine commanders fear that David will turn against them in their war with Saul, while Achish reiterates that it is they alone who do not trust David, and as far as he, Achish, is concerned David is as honest and upright as the angel of God. In other words, he wants to prevent David from taking offence at the fact that he is not allowed to participate in the battle against Israel and to stop him leaving Achish's service.

The element of flattery explains the exaggeration in the simile. It is no small matter to compare someone to an angel of God. The simile has no basis in reality, there is a vast chasm between humanity and the divine creatures called angels, and each belongs to a very different sphere. The use of the simile is comprehensible, however, if the object is to ingratiate oneself.

Be that as it may, it is clear that the simile used here does not teach us anything about the king's true nature or about qualities really attributed to him. Like metaphors, similes show more about the person using them than the person they purportedly describe.

In addition to statements about characteristics (which are more or less constant), information about moods (which are transient) serves to create the personality of characters in the narrative. As is the case with traits, moods can also be conveyed by both direct and indirect means. Direct information about characters' moods may be transmitted by the narrator, other characters, or the subjects themselves.

In the previous chapter, several instances were quoted in which the narrator indicated characters' inner states. Such items as: 'And David was angry' (2 Sam. 6.8), 'Then David's anger was greatly kindled against the man' (12.5), and 'He was angry' (13.21), make a considerable contribution to building David's personality, even though they relate to passing emotions. By putting together pieces of information about people's feelings a general picture of their character, or at least of significant aspects of their character, can be formed, particularly if the information relates to the same kind of mood, as is the case with the items about David cited above. If the items relate to different kinds of emotional states, we may discern varying aspects of the individual's character. For example, information reflecting additional sides of David's personality is conveyed, in connection with reports of his moods: 'And afterwards David's heart smote him, because he had cut off Saul's skirt' (1 Sam. 24.5), 'And David was greatly distressed... But David strengthened himself in the Lord his God' (30.6), 'And David was afraid of the Lord that day' (2 Sam. 6.9), 'And David mourned for his son day after day' (13.37), 'And the spirit of the king longed to go forth to Absalom; for he was comforted about Amnon, seeing he was dead' (13.39), 'But the king had compassion on Mephibosheth, the son of Saul's son Jonathan' (21.7). The importance of information of this kind in creating the characters lies in the fact that it reveals to us what is happening in their hearts.

Information is also given about the inner states of characters by one of the other protagonists. There is an important difference here, however, for unlike the omniscient narrator, the other character cannot be absolutely certain about the feelings of others. He can draw conclusions about them from such external signs as speech and behaviour, but cannot go beyond (subjective) interpretation. The character who is doing the interpreting usually notes the final conclusion without describing what it is that has led up to it. In some cases, however, the narrator transmits this information, enabling the reader to check the individual's conclusions. What Joab says to David at the bitter moment when the king is overcome by grief for the death of his son, Absalom, carries a strong flavour of personal interpretation, which is difficult to accept as it stands: 'Loving those who hate you and hating those who love you. For you have made it clear today that commanders and servants are nothing to you; for today I perceive that if Absalom were alive and all of us were dead today, then you would be pleased' (2 Sam. 19.6). Although there is an element of truth in Joab's claim—David loved his son and enemy, Absalom, and did not like his devoted servant and associate, Joab— there is no doubt that it is highly exaggerated and does not reflect the situation as it really was. Joab's biting words were intended to bring David out of the mental depression into which he had sunk as a result of his son's death, since Joab feared that David's human weakness could completely undermine the basis of his rule, which was anyway rather uncertain at that moment. It seems, however, that Joab's speech does reflect his true opinion of the king, though phrased in extravagant terms.

What Joab says is an obvious attempt to reverse the state of affairs, and this is evident in both form and content. The clauses 'Loving those who hate you and hating those who love you' reflect the attempt to stand things on their heads by using an opposing construction (loving—hating; who hate you—who love you), which is intensified by the identity of the syntactical-grammatical structure. In addition to the opposing structure of the two clauses, there is also opposition within each one, between its predicate and object (between 'loving' and 'who hate you' and between 'hating' and 'who love you'). Joab means to say that David's reaction is diametrically opposed to what he should be feeling.

Joab's exaggeration is also manifested in his generalizations. He uses the plural (those who hate you, those who love you) and the verbal noun (hating, loving) instead of a conjugated verb (which focuses more on the specific case as regards time and place, while the verbal noun is more general and amorphous).

The generalization that David loves those who hate him and hates those who love him is undoubtedly unjust. Joab's contention that David's grief for his son is tantamount to declaring that his commanders and servants are of no importance to him is not accurate either. And Joab's 'perception' that 'if Absalom were alive and all of us were dead today, then you would be pleased' (which is what he deduced from David's behaviour), is only partly correct. It is true that David would be happy were Absalom alive, but it is false to state that he would be happy were all his commanders and servants dead.

Joab's interpretations comprise half-truths, according with David's feelings only in part, and reflecting Joab's own feelings to a considerable extent. His feelings of guilt, or at least unease, at having deliberately disobeyed David's order not to harm Absalom are reflected in his aggressive tone and in the accusations he hurls at David. Behind what he says are his feelings of resentment at the fact that David does not like him despite his devotion and the many services Joab has done him (when he speaks of 'those who love you' and 'commanders and servants' Joab is naturally thinking of himself). His words, therefore, reflect his own feelings rather than being an accurate representation of David's.

In some cases, however, the assertions made about the characters' emotional states by other characters are not so tendentious and subjective. 'And why is your heart sad?' (1 Sam. 1.8), Elkanah asks his wife, Hannah. This question provides reliable evidence of Hannah's mood. The same applies to the question Jezebel asks her husband: 'Why is your spirit so vexed?' (1 Kgs 21.5), and to the question God asks Jonah: 'Do you do well to be angry?' (Jon. 4.4). Someone tells Solomon: 'Behold Adonijah fears king Solomon' (1 Kgs 1.51). The prophet Elisha tells Gehazi in connection with the Shunnamite: 'Let her alone, for she is in bitter distress' (2 Kgs 4.27). All these statements are confirmed by the context.

In addition to the above examples concerning the emotions and moods of the characters, there are instances relating to their knowledge and intentions.

Jonathan, Saul's son, says to David: 'You shall be king over Israel, and I shall be next to you; Saul my father also knows this' (1 Sam. 23.17). Nathan says to Bathsheba: 'Have you not heard that Adonijah the son of Haggith has become king and David our lord does not know it?' (1 Kgs 1.11). Solomon says to Benaiah: 'The Lord will bring back his bloody deeds upon his own head, because, without the knowledge of my father David, he attacked and slew with the sword two men more righteous and better than himself' (1 Kgs 2.32).

The character's knowledge or lack of it is important either for the characterization or for the development of the plot. In the last example, for instance, David's lack of knowledge is extremely significant as regards his morality: his ignorance absolves him of all blame in the murder of the two commanders of the army; at the same time David's lack of knowledge places the full responsibility on Joab (characterization of Joab), which is the reason for his assassination at Solomon's order (plot).

When one character notes the intentions of another the former's interpretation may be correct or totally mistaken. For example, the king of Jericho receives a report informing him that two men have come to search out all the land (Josh. 2.2). The princes of the Ammonites tell Hanun their lord their assumption: 'Do you think because David has sent comforters to you, that he is honouring your father? Has not David sent his servants to you to search the city, and spy it out, and to overthrow it?' (2 Sam. 10.3).

In the first example, the intentions of the men who penetrated Jericho, as assumed in the report to the king, accord with Joshua's orders: 'Go, view the land, especially Jericho' (Josh. 2.1). While in the second, the interpretation given by the princes of the Ammonites does not conform with David's purpose, as he himself testifies: 'I will deal loyally with Hanun the son of Nahash, as his father dealt loyally with me' (2 Sam. 10.2). Noting intentions may contribute to moulding the characters, but is no less important in accounting for the plot. In the last example, the inaccurate interpretation leads to anger (first of Hanun and later of David), and, in consequence, even to a bitter war between Israel and the Ammonites.

The evidence given by a character about his or her own emotions or knowledge is of particular interest, because, through introspection, people can know only the inner workings of their own heart and mind. It is, of course, possible for individuals to be mistaken about themselves too, or even to distort things deliberately, but even so, independent evidence of this kind should be accorded the respect it deserves, since in every instance it reveals something of the way people see themselves or want others to see them.

On occasions characters speak about their emotions. Jacob says to Laban: 'Because I was afraid, for I thought that you would take your daughters from me by force' (Gen. 31.31). Hannah explains to Eli: 'For all along I have been speaking out of my great anxiety and vexation' (1 Sam. 1.16). Amnon says of himself: 'I love Tamar, my brother Absalom's sister' (2 Sam. 13.4). Jonah answers God's question by saying: 'I do well to be angry, angry enough to die' (Jon. 4.9).

Sometimes characters refer to their knowledge. Cain answers God's question about his brother Abel by saying: 'I do not know; am I my brother's keeper?' (Gen. 4.9). When David asks if all is well with the young man Absalom, Ahimaaz replies: 'When Joab sent your servant, I saw a great tumult, but I do not know what it was' (2 Sam. 18.29). Jonah says to the sailors: 'For I know it is because of me that this great tempest has come upon you' (Jon. 1.12).

As has been mentioned above, the statements characters make about themselves are not always reliable. The declarations of lack of knowledge made by Cain and Ahimaaz are clearly evasive; for a variety of reasons they do not want to reply to the question put to them, though they know the answer perfectly well. In other cases, however, we can place full reliance on the evidence given by the characters themselves.

A different technique of presenting the inner life of characters directly is by giving their thoughts, calculations and intentions. The narrator usually precedes the characters' thoughts by the verb 'said', and sometimes by the phrase 'he said in his heart', since in ancient times thought was considered to be inner, soundless speech. Although the presentation of the thoughts of characters in the Bible does not reach the dimensions of interior monologue, in some cases their considerations and motivations are given at considerable length. It is true that no internal argument or discussion is given, but on occasions one gains the impression that characters wish to convince themselves that the action they are taking, rather than an alternative course, is the right one.

And the Lord *said in his heart*, 'I will never again curse the ground because of man, for the imagination of man's heart is evil from his youth; neither will I ever again destroy every living creature as I have done' (Gen. 8.21).

Then Abraham fell on his face and laughed, and *said in his heart*, 'Shall a child be born to a man who is a hundred years old? Shall Sarah, who is ninety years old, bear a child?' (Gen. 17.17).

The Lord *said*, 'Shall I hide from Abraham what I am about to do?' (Gen. 18.17).

Then Saul said to David, 'Here is my elder daughter Merab; I will give her to you for a wife; only be valiant for me and fight the Lord's battles'. For Saul *said*, 'Let not my hand be upon him, but let the hand of the Philistines be upon him' (1 Sam. 18.17).

Now David *had said*, 'Surely in vain have I guarded all that this fellow has in the wilderness, so that nothing was missed of all that belonged to him; and he has returned me evil for good. God do so to David and more also, if by morning I leave so much as one male of all who belong to him' (1 Sam. 25.21-22).

And David *said in his heart*, 'I shall now perish one day by the hand of Saul; there is nothing better for me than that I should escape to the land of the Philistines; then Saul will despair of seeking me any longer within the borders of Israel, and I shall escape out of his hand' (1 Sam. 27.1).

Now Absalom in his lifetime had taken and set up for himself the

pillar which is in the King's Valley, for he *said*, 'I have no son to
keep my name in remembrance' (2 Sam. 18.18).

It can be said in conclusion that in biblical narrative information
referring directly to the inner feelings of the characters is often
supplied by either the narrator, other characters or the subjects
themselves. If this information is provided by one of the other
characters rather than the narrator, however, it is not always of real
value for shaping those characters to which it refers (and in this case
fulfils a different function). Even if it does have value of this kind,
direct information does not constitute a continual account of internal
processes, but rather illuminates selected aspects of the inner
workings of the individuals. It undoubtedly makes a significant
contribution to the shaping of the characters, but this object is served
far more effectively by those features of the narrative which cast
indirect light on the nature of the characters.

2. *The Indirect Shaping of the Characters*

Whereas the importance of the direct ways of shaping the characters
lies in their quality (the fact that they are clear and unequivocal),
that of the indirect ways lies in their quantity. This means that there
is more indirect than direct shaping of characters in biblical narrative
and therefore the burden of characterization falls primarily on this
method.

Indirect ways of shaping the characters are to be found in all those
external features, like speech or actions, which indicate something
about the individual's inner state. The reader has to interpret these
details and construct the character's mental and emotional make-up
accordingly, a task which is not undertaken for the reader by the
narrator. Thus, indirect characterization requires a mental effort on
the part of the reader, thereby increasing the active participation in
the narrated events.

A. *Speech*
In the previous section we discussed several instances in which one
person characterizes another directly through speech. Speech is also
an important way of characterizing individuals indirectly. Traits of
both the speaker and the interlocutor are expressed through speech,
or to be more precise, all speech reflects and exposes the speaker,

while it sometimes also brings to light qualities of the person being addressed (or reveals the speaker's opinion of that person). What people say witnesses not only to their thoughts, feelings, etc., but is often slanted to accord with the character, mood, interests and status of their interlocutor.

It is customary today to delineate characters in a narrative by the style of their speech and not only by the content of what they say. A person's style of speaking (or pronunciation) reveals social class and even character or emotional state. Is this means used in biblical narrative too?

Biblical narratives do not contain personal speech styles distinguishing one character from another. The characters' speech is more or less identical with the narrator's style, and, apart from a few exceptions, is marked by its matter-of-fact, restrained and unembellished tone. It reaches us through the author's mediation and is subject to the same stylistic principles which govern the work as a whole, giving it unity.

In addition, it is not customary in biblical narrative to make characters speak haltingly or awkwardly in an attempt to imitate natural speech rhythms precisely. Biblical narrative preserves a distance between polished literary style and imprecise colloquial speech, avoiding broken sentences, meaningless words and incorrect structures.

Nevertheless, it is possible to find disjointed sentences spoken by characters in biblical narrative which can be considered to reflect mental or emotional states. For example, when Ahimaaz is asked by David if all is well with Absalom, he answers: 'I saw the great tumult at sending the king's servant, by Joab, and your servant, and I do not know what' (2 Sam. 18.29). It is obvious that this sentence is not constructed correctly. The lack of fluency may be explained by Ahimaaz's confusion at having to answer an uncomfortable question. He wants to tell the king about the victory in battle but does not want to inform him of his son's death, and does not know how to extricate himself from this predicament. This explanation is not necessarily correct, however, since the confusion in the sentence may simply derive from textual inaccuracy. There are several disjointed or defective sentences in the Bible which have no connection with confusion or any other psychological state.

A rare instance in which agitation is reflected in speech may perhaps be found in 1 Sam. 4.16-17, where the messenger has to

inform Eli of Israel's defeat in battle by the Philistines, the death of
Eli's two sons and the capture of the ark of God. The messenger
begins hesitantly: 'I am he who has come from the battle and from
the battle I fled today'. Eli encourages him to continue: 'What has
happened, my son?' Only then does the man summon up the courage
to go on and deliver his dreadful news.

In some cases the style of speech reflects the individual's wisdom.
What Abigail says to David (1 Sam. 25.24-31) is distinguished by its
figurative language. The words of the woman of Tekoa (2 Sam. 14.4-
20) are peppered with a great many similes. Hushai the Archite also
uses numerous similes and metaphors in giving his advice to
Absalom (17.7-13). Abigail is characterized as being of good
understanding, while the woman of Tekoa and Hushai are wise, and
high-flown speech is appropriate for wise people. This kind of speech
was useful and necessary for attaining the objectives which these
speakers desired, and all three were gifted with the ability to express
themselves eloquently, using an abundance of vivid images.

The speaker's or the interlocutor's social standing is often reflected
in speech. For example, the style of the wise woman of Tekoa when
she addresses the king is unlike that used by the king when he speaks
to her. When the woman comes before the king in order to submit
her request, he speaks to her abruptly, saying: 'What is it?' (2 Sam.
14.5), but when the king wishes to ask her something she says
politely: 'Pray let my lord the king speak' (v. 18). The same
difference in the style of speech is found in verse 12. The woman asks
politely: 'Pray let your handmaid speak a word to my lord the king'.
And he answers her curtly: 'Speak'. Throughout the long dialogue
between the woman of Tekoa and the king she adopts polite forms of
speech, addressing him as 'my lord the king', and referring to herself
as 'your handmaid' or 'your servant'.

Other characters also adopt the same polite style when addressing
the king, even if they themselves are from a high social class. They
use the third person form, address the king as 'my lord the king', and
refer to themselves as 'your servant'. Ittai the Gittite says to David:
'As the Lord lives, and as my lord the king lives, wherever my lord
the king shall be, whether for death or for life, there also will your
servant be' (2 Sam. 15.21). Joab expresses himself as follows: 'Today
your servant knows that I have found favour in your sight, my lord
the king, in that the king has granted the request of his servant' (or
according to the $q^e r\hat{e}$, 'your servant') (14.22). Even the king's sons

and wife take care to adopt a respectful tone: 'And Absalom came to the king, and said, "Behold, your servant has sheepshearers; pray let the king and his servants go with your servant"' (13.24). 'Bathsheba bowed and did obeisance to the king, and the king said, "What is it?" She said to him, "My lord, you swore to your maidservant by the Lord your God. . . . although you, my lord the king, do not know it. . . . And now, my lord the king, the eyes of all Israel are upon you, to tell them who shall sit on the throne of my lord the king after him. . . . when my lord the king sleeps with his fathers"' (1 Kgs 1.16-21).

The peak of respectfulness is embodied in the phrase: 'Let the king live for ever', which occurs in the Bible principally in addressing foreign kings (Dan. 2.4; 3.9; 5.10; Neh. 2.3). Bathsheba also says to David: 'May my lord king David live for ever' (1 Kgs 1.31), but her speech reflects not only customary court style but also a considerable degree of tact and refinement. For after David has promised her that 'Solomon your son shall reign *after me*', that is, after his death, she expresses the wish that her son Solomon should not rule, but rather that king David should live for ever.

Speech reflects the speakers' standing not only when they address royalty. For example, Gehazi, Elisha's servant, says: 'See, my lord has spared. . . Your servant went. . . ' (2 Kgs 5.20, 25). The Shunnamite also uses the same style in speaking to Elisha: 'No, my lord, O man of God; do not lie to your maidservant' (4.16).

Deviations from accepted style are of particular importance. There are two kinds: the polite style, like that described above, used by a speaker whose status is equal to that of the interlocutor; the absence of the polite style when the speaker's status is inferior to that of the interlocutor.

Brothers and sisters tend to address one another with the term, 'my brother', or 'my sister' (Gen. 33.9; 2 Sam. 13.11). During the encounter between Jacob and Esau, however, after the former's return from his extended sojourn in Laban's house, Jacob addresses his brother as 'my lord' and refers to himself as 'his servant': 'Let my lord pass on before his servant' (Gen. 33.14, and many times in chs. 32 and 33). When Moses chides Aaron for making the golden calf his brother replies: 'Let not the anger of my lord burn hot' (Exod. 32.22). In both cases the polite speech indubitably reflects the speaker's feelings of guilt towards his brother and the desire to appease him.

Kings also use the term 'my brother' when addressing one another

(1 Kgs 9.13). Nevertheless, Ahab, the king of Israel, says to the messengers of Ben-hadad the king of Syria: 'Tell my lord the king, "All that you first demanded of your servant I will do; but this thing I cannot do"' (1 Kgs 20.9). Here the polite form of speech reflects Ahab's political inferiority and dependence on Ben-hadad.

As has been noted above, Joab uses the polite forms of the court in addressing the king in 2 Sam. 14.22. He uses a very different tone, however, when he upbraids David for succumbing to his personal grief over the death of his son Absalom: 'Now therefore arise, go out and speak kindly to your servants; for I swear by the Lord, if you do not go, not a man will stay with you this night; and this will be worse for you than all the evil that has come upon you from your youth until now' (2 Sam. 19.7). There is nothing in this vehement speech, full of orders and threats, to indicate that it is addressed to the king.

The same applies to the prophet Nathan, whose form of speech also accords with its content. Nathan addresses the king according to all the rules of the court in 1 Kgs 1.24–27, using the term 'my lord the king' when speaking to him and 'your servant' when referring to himself, but he employs a very different tone when he rebukes David in the matter of Bathsheba and Uriah (2 Sam. 12.1-14).

The correspondence between the style and content of speech reinforces the impact of what is said. In addition, the combination of form and content in deviations from accepted court style carries considerable weight in characterizing the speakers: Joab chides David who is mourning for his son, thus revealing his insensitivity; Nathan rebukes David for sinning, thus indicating his courage and high moral standards.

The content of speech is closely connected with its function, whether this is to express emotion, establish an attitude, spur someone to action or provide information.

The type of speech which is particularly effective in disclosing a person's psychological state is the emotive one. A classic example of this kind of speech, revealing quite clearly what is going on in the speaker's mind, is found in 2 Sam. 18.33 and 19.4 containing David's cry on hearing of the death of his son Absalom. The narrator says: 'And the king cried with a loud voice', that is, he specifies the intensity of the cry, thereby heightening its effect on the reader. Furthermore, the content of the cry is given in detail and at length, without flinching from 'unnecessary' repetition. This cry is extremely moving, conveying the depths of emotional shock endured by the bereaved father. The tremendous impact is achieved primarily by the numerous repetitions: the same cry is given both in 18.33 and in 19.4 and within each verse the words 'my son' and 'Absalom' recur frequently. In 19.4 David's entire cry consists of only these three words, and in 18.33 they constitute most of it: 'My son Absalom, my son, my son Absalom. Would that I had died instead of you, Absalom, my son, my son'.

These repetitions, which do not form a complete sentence, indicate David's groans and his inability to think logically during those moments. All his thoughts are focused on only one subject, and he is incapable of concentrating on anything else. He is able only to repeat over and over again the name which fills his heart, 'Absalom', and the words which express more than anything else his biological and emotional attachment to him, 'my son'. The term 'my son' recurs more often than the name 'Absalom', and also begins and ends both cries. This indicates that despite all that Absalom had done to his father and would undoubtedly have done to him had he been victorious, he remained David's son and David loved him 'as a father the son in whom he delights' (Prov. 3.12).

Amongst all the short exclamations, 'my son Absalom, Absalom, my son, my son', there is one complete sentence: 'Would that I had died instead of you'. This expression is shocking not because the father expresses his desire to die in his son's place, but because of the remoteness from reality it reveals: first of all, David expresses a desire which cannot be fulfilled, and secondly, he addresses Absalom in the second person, ignoring the fact that his son is not there nor will he ever be. David speaks to Absalom as if he were still alive and able to hear what he is saying in the same sentence in which he asks to die in Absalom's stead! This lack of logic undoubtedly shows David's emotional confusion. This sentence also indicates that the short exclamations, 'my son, Absalom, Absalom, my son, my son', which come before and after it, do not refer to Absalom in the third person, but address him directly. If this is so, they embody deep within them the tragic and touching illusion that if David calls his son's name often and loudly enough Absalom might hear... But whereas direct address usually serves to establish interpersonal relations, here its sole function is to convey the feelings locked in David's heart which must find an outlet.

Attention should also be paid to the fact that because of the morpheme '*ab*' (father) in the name Absalom, the phrase 'my *son Ab*salom' establishes a stylistic connection between son and father. The numerous repetitions of the elements 'son' and '*ab*' echo continually in our minds, thus highlighting the bond between father and son as well as the preceding conflict between the two. This resulted from an unfortunate relationship, full of contradictions, in which the father's attitude to the son vacillated between weakness and firmness, while the son treated his father with unbridled aggression.

Speech which is intended solely to express emotions and is not addressed to anyone is rare (this does not refer to inner speech, which is in fact thought). On the other hand, speech which is addressed to someone and which often develops into a dialogue is very common.

Speech directed at someone else is sometimes intended to arouse a certain emotion or attitude in them, and can teach us about both the speaker and the interlocutor. Hushai's first words to Absalom, before the crucial occasion when he gives Absalom his advice, can serve as an example. He first has to win Absalom's confidence, and this is no easy task in view of the fact that Hushai is known to be David's friend. On entering Absalom's presence Hushai decides to demonstrate his recognition of the new king immediately and emphatically and calls out twice: 'Long live the king! Long live the king!' (2 Sam. 16.16). Absalom, quite naturally, is suspicious of him and asks in surprise: 'Is this your loyalty to your friend? Why did you not go with your friend?' (v. 17). Absalom's doubts are indicated principally by his repetition of the words 'your friend'. Hushai answers Absalom's double question with a double reply, or rather, with an answer consisting of two parts. In the first part Hushai says: 'No; for whom the Lord and this people and all the men of Israel have chosen, his will I be, and with him I will remain' (v. 18). He begins by categorically denying the implications of Absalom's question, that it better befitted him to accompany David, his friend. After the denial, Hushai gives his reasons for it. His cunning is indicated by the fact that he does not give his reasons for abandoning David, as the question requires, but explains why he decided to come and remain with Absalom. By emphasizing his lack of loyalty to his friend he would have damaged Absalom's opinion of him, while by stressing his choice of Absalom he enhances it and pleases the ambitious prince.

The reason given in the first part of Hushai's answer has a

religious-national background; he affirms the fact that Absalom has
been chosen king by God, the people, and all the men of Israel. This
triple choice makes Absalom's rule a certainty, and it is only natural
that Hushai will join the person whose rule is no longer unsure.
Hushai seems to imply that his loyalty was not to David the man but
to David the king, and since David is no longer king it is obvious that
Hushai cannot follow him. Henceforth the new king will have his
loyalty.

Since Hushai does not explain precisely why he abandoned David
but rather why he decided to follow Absalom, his words compliment
or even flatter Absalom. It is not because of his hatred for David but
because of his love of Absalom that he has done this. The element of
fawning is evident in the structure of the sentence too. Instead of
starting with subject-predicate, as is customary in the Bible, Hushai
begins with a disjunctive clause: 'Whom the Lord and this people
and all the men of Israel have chosen'. This disjunctive clause
emphasizes the antecedent, Absalom, both because of its exceptional
position at the beginning of Hushai's answer and because of its
length. Absalom is made prominent at the end of the sentence too by
placing the pronouns referring to him at the beginning of the two
short clauses, 'his will I be, and with him I will remain'.

The same tendency to focus on Absalom is obvious in Hushai's
second reason: 'And secondly, whom should I serve? Should it not be
his son? As I have served your father, so I will serve you' (v. 19).
Hushai builds his reply to Absalom in two parts, clearly marking the
twofold construction by means of the phrase 'And secondly'
providing evidence of careful and systematic thinking. The second
reason, which is more personal in its nature, explains that the loyal
service which has been given to the father is naturally transferred to
the son, the implication being that the son has taken over his father's
position. This is in effect the same reason David instructed Hushai to
use when he told him to go to Absalom and cause Ahithophel's
advice to be rejected, only in a different form: 'Say to Absalom,
"Your servant, O king, I will be; I have been your father's servant in
time past, and now I will be your servant"' (2 Sam. 15.34).

A comparison of the phrases David tells Hushai to use with those
Hushai actually employs is illuminating (although there appear to be
some minor textual errors in David's sentence). David begins and
ends with the words 'your servant', and 'servant' also appears in the
middle of the sentence, thus placing the emphasis on the servant,

Hushai. Hushai is also emphasized through the threefold repetition of the word 'I', which indicates that David's first thought is for Hushai and the impression he will make on Absalom. In Hushai's version, however, the emphasis is placed more on Absalom himself: both the first word, 'whom', and the last, 'you', hint at Absalom, while the phrase 'his son' in the middle of the sentence refers explicitly to him. Hushai also makes his speech more convincing by using rhetorical devices. He opens with a rhetorical question ('Whom should I serve?'), which he himself answers ('Should it not be his son?'); his comparison ('As I have served your father, so I will serve you') is also more effective than David's straightforward statement of fact ('I have been your father's servant in time past, and now I will be your servant'). David provides Hushai with the general outline, but the final formulation is Hushai's.

Hushai's speech reflects not only his own good sense, but also Absalom's personality, at least as seen by Hushai. Absalom regards himself as being more important than anyone else, and is therefore easily influenced by flattery. Hushai adapts his words to his hearer's personality, but is careful not to overdo things and to conceal his fawning.

The same features which are found in the speech of Hushai also appear in the advice he gives Absalom (discussed below, pp. 223-37). In both cases he begins with a negation, uses a clearly bi-partite structure, which is clearly marked as such by Hushai himself, employs rhetorical devices as well as carefully concealed flattery and avoids placing emphasis on himself. The parallel features in Hushai's speeches on both occasions indicate that what he says reflects characteristic and significant aspects of his personality.

Absalom's reply to Hushai is not given here. Nevertheless, the fact that he later summons Hushai to proffer his advice proves that the latter did succeed in gaining the prince's confidence.

A considerable part of what is said by characters in biblical narrative falls into the category of directive speech, intended to impel someone to action, and characterized by the imperative form. In rare cases individuals will address themselves in this form (inciting themselves to act), but it is usually directed at someone else, whether as a command or as a request (whether the speaker issues a command or attempts to persuade depends on the status of the speaker and the interlocutor). The request is sometimes directed to God (a prayer of petition).

The importance of this kind of speech lies in the fact that it reveals the speakers' intentions and aspirations and through them their characteristics.

Abraham's hospitable nature is reflected not only in his invitation to the three men who appear at the entrance to his tent but also in the language in which he couches it (Gen. 18.3-5). He phrases things in such a way that his guests gain the impression that it is not Abraham who is doing them a favour, but they who are doing him one by condescending to rest and eat with him. Abraham also minimizes the effort involved in preparing the food; he offers them just a little bread and water, though in fact he provides tasty veal, butter, milk and cakes. Abraham also uses polite terms abundantly: the Hebrew *nā'* (please) three times, 'your servant', etc.

Sarah demands that Abraham send Hagar and Ishmael away, using the blunt term 'cast out', and referring to them contemptuously as 'this slave woman and the son of this slave woman' (in contrast to the phrase she uses when she speaks of her own son, 'with my son, with Isaac'), thus shedding light on her personality (Gen. 21.10). It is true that God uses the identical terms rather than Hagar's and Ishmael's names when referring to them, thereby verifying their objective status; but God's words are devoid of the disdain evident in Sarah's, since the term 'this' is not used and He also says that He will 'make a nation' of the lowly 'son of the slave woman' (whom He also calls 'the lad') (vv. 12-13).

A valuable contribution to the shaping of the characters is made by their (verbal) reactions to things that are said to them. However, these reactions are not always recorded.

When a person issues a *command* (to someone of lower status) the speech is generally one-sided and does not develop into a dialogue. In these cases, it is usually only the implementation of the command which is recorded, for example: 'So the servants of Absalom did to Amnon as Absalom had commanded' (2 Sam. 13.29). There are exceptions to this rule, however.

On the one hand, there are instances when the person who receives the order hesitates or is unwilling to implement it. This is Jacob's reaction to his mother's command that he impersonate Esau in order to obtain his brother's blessing: 'Behold, my brother Esau is a hairy man, and I am a smooth man. Perhaps my father will feel me, and I shall seem to be mocking him, and bring a curse upon myself and not a blessing' (Gen. 27.11-12). Jacob's resistance does not derive from ethical values but rather from the fear that the deception will be discovered and the outcome be disastrous.

When God orders Moses to go to Pharaoh and bring Israel out of Egypt, Moses replies: 'Who am I that I should go to Pharaoh, and bring the sons of Israel out of Egypt?' (Exod. 3.11). Like many other leaders in the Bible, Moses is not overjoyed about accepting the exalted position, expressing his doubts as to his ability and suitability. This reveals his modesty, a trait which is noted explicitly in Num. 12.3: 'Now the man Moses was very meek, more than all men that were on the face of the earth'.

There are, on the other hand, several instances when the individual of lower status who receives the order explicitly agrees to undertake it. King Solomon forbids Shimei the son of Gera to leave the borders of Jerusalem, and Shimei answers: 'What you say is good; as my lord the king has said, so will your servant do' (1 Kgs 2.38). This clear assent is reported for the purpose of pointing up Shimei's later infringement of the order.

When a request is made (by someone who is inferior or equal to the person to whom it is addressed), the answer is usually recorded. Abigail sets out to meet David in order to ask him not to kill Nabal and all the members of his household. David replies: 'Blessed be the Lord, God of Israel, who sent you this day to meet me! Blessed be your discretion, and blessed be you, who have kept me this day from bloodguilt and from avenging myself with my own hand! For as surely as the Lord the God of Israel lives, who has restrained me from hurting you, unless you had made haste and come to meet me, truly by morning there had not been left to Nabal so much as one male' (1 Sam. 25.32-34). Not only does David accede to Abigail's request, he also praises her for preventing him from shedding blood. David indirectly admits that he had been about to wrong Nabal and his household and blesses God for sending Abigail to him, as well as Abigail herself and her discretion. ('Blessed be the Lord. . . Blessed be your discretion, and blessed be you'). David's words reveal his inherent nobility, his readiness to admit his mistake and his absolute trust in God and His supervision. These qualities are also revealed on other occasions, such as when David reacts to the rebuke of Nathan the prophet with the simple phrase: 'I have sinned against the Lord' (2 Sam. 12.13). David is prepared to admit his error and to express his repentance, acknowledging the fact that he sinned with regard to Bathsheba and Uriah.

When the aged Barzilai says: 'Here is your servant Chimham; let him go over with my lord the king; and do for him whatever seems good to you' (2 Sam. 19.37), David answers: 'Chimham shall go over with me, and I will do for him whatever seems good to you' (v. 38). In his reply, David uses Barzilai's exact phrases, apart from the fact that he naturally omits the polite expression 'your servant' and 'my lord the king'. The repetition of Barzilai's expressions, without even changing the pronoun 'you' (the Hebrew expression is 'in your eyes') from the second to the first person indicates that not only will the request be granted, but Chimham will get the treatment which seems good to Barzilai himself (which is more than he has requested). In the Hebrew text the phrase 'with me' (*'itti*) occurs at the beginning of the sentence and the pronoun 'I' is emphasized (by being given separately even though it is included in the form of the verb), indicating that David will personally attend to the matter. David is grateful to Barzilai for having helped him when he was in need. This gratitude is also evident in the instructions David gives to Solomon on his death bed: 'But deal loyally with the sons of Barzilai the Gileadite, and let them be among those who eat at your table; for with such loyalty they met me when I fled from Absalom your brother' (1 Kgs 2.7).

Much of the speech in biblical narrative is informative, that is, its object is to obtain or provide knowledge. In addition, it often contributes to the shaping of the characters.

God asks Adam: 'Have you eaten of the tree of which I commanded you not to eat?' (Gen. 3.11), and Adam answers: 'The woman whom Thou gavest to be with me, she gave me fruit of the tree, and I ate' (v. 12). This reply discloses Adam's tendency to absolve himself by placing the blame on others, on the woman, who gave him fruit from the tree, and on God Himself, who gave him the woman.

A far more negative light is shed on Cain when he answers God's question: 'Where is Abel your brother?' by saying: 'I do not know; am I my brother's keeper?' (Gen. 4.9). His reply is a barefaced lie, and in addition he is brazen enough to counterattack by addressing a cynical question to God.

Abraham on the other hand, is revealed in all his fineness of soul when he answers his son's question: 'Behold, the fire and the wood; but where is the lamb for a burnt offering?' with the evasive reply: 'God will see to the lamb for a burnt offering, my son' (Gen. 22.7-8).

This response reveals Abraham's delicacy (he tries to avoid hurting his son unnecessarily), honesty (he is reluctant to lie to his son) and deep religious feeling (he places absolute trust in God).

The way in which characters convey information often sheds light on their nature. The selection or formulation of pieces of information by one of the characters sometimes differs substantially from the actual facts as transmitted to the reader at first hand in the narrative.

When Ahab the king of Israel desires the vineyard of Naboth the Jezreelite he addresses him as follows: 'Give me your vineyard, that I may have it for a vegetable garden, because it is near my house; and I will give you a better vineyard for it; or, if it seems good to you, I will give you its value in money' (1 Kgs 21.2). Naboth refuses and the king goes into his house 'vexed and sullen'. Jezebel his wife asks him why he is so angry and he tells her what happened: 'Because I spoke to Naboth the Jezreelite, and said to him: "Give me your vineyard for money; or else, if it please you, I will give you another vineyard for it", and he answered, "I will not give you my vineyard"' (v. 6).

The two accounts are more or less alike, but there are differences and these are highly significant. In contrast to the 'law of the king' which states: 'He will take the best of your fields and vineyards and olive orchards' (1 Sam. 8.14), it transpires from the conversation that the king of Israel cannot simply take a vineyard belonging to one of his subjects but must beg the subject to give it to him. Ahab justifies his request by explaining to Naboth that he wants the vineyard in order to convert it into a vegetable garden, because it is near his house. In order to persuade Naboth to agree, Ahab offers him another vineyard, and not just any vineyard but 'a better vineyard', and if Naboth prefers to receive its value in cash, Ahab will give it to him.

When he recounts all this to his wife, Ahab omits to say that he explained to Naboth for what purpose he wanted the vineyard and that he also offered him a better one. He does say that he gave Naboth the possibility of choosing either money or another vineyard, but he reverses the order (first the money, then the vineyard), and instead of the polite form 'if it seems good to you', he uses the simple phrase, 'if you wish'. These changes indicate that when Ahab spoke to Naboth he degraded himself, but when he recounted the episode to his wife, who was the daughter of the king of the Sidonians, he tried to conceal this.

There is also a difference between Naboth's actual answer to Ahab's request and the version Ahab tells Jezebel. In his answer, Naboth hints at the reasons for refusing to give up his vineyard: 'The Lord forbid that I should give you the inheritance of my fathers' (v. 3). This points to a religious as well as an emotional element, the Lord and the bond with the land of his forefathers. Ahab fails to mention Naboth's reasons when he tells Jezebel what happened (already beforehand, when Ahab returned home 'vexed and sullen' he had obliterated the religious element from his memory: 'I will not give you the inheritance of my fathers'), making Naboth's refusal appear to be mere stubbornness: 'I will not give you my vineyard' (v. 6).

B. *Actions*
A person's nature is revealed by deeds; action is the implementation of character, and individuals are disclosed through their deeds no less than through their words. Since one's inner nature is embodied in external behaviour a narrator can present the characters in action rather than spelling out their traits. In biblical narrative deeds do in fact serve as the foremost means of characterization, and we know biblical characters primarily through the way they act in varying situations.

The characters' actions are also the building blocks of the plot, though the protagonists should not be regarded merely as a means for getting the story going. The narrative is concerned not only with the events which occur but also with the people involved. While the plot plays a central role in biblical narrative, the individual within it is no less important than the events.

It can be said that the actions which comprise the plot interrelate with the characters: the individuals are a function of the events, and vice versa. In other words, just as the characters serve the plot, the plot serves the characters, illuminating them and contributing to their characterization. Moreover, just as the characters' personalities influence the course of events, the course of events affects the personalities of the characters.

The technique of building a character through deeds confronts the reader with a problem, however. For it is in the nature of this technique to refrain from revealing to us what are the internal motives which give rise to the actions and as in real life, we have to build hypotheses about people's motives. These hypotheses will be based on our knowledge of other actions and things said by the same person, as well as on our understanding of human psychology.

It is, for example, very difficult to understand the reasons for many of David's exploits. Why did he bring Michal back to him after she had become the wife of Paltiel the son of Laish? Was it because of love, because he had wed her at the price of a hundred foreskins of the Philistines, or perhaps because she was the daughter of the former king (2 Sam. 3.14-16)? Why did David execute Rechab and Baanah, the two men who killed Ish-bosheth, the son of Saul (4.8-12)? Was it because he was enraged at the cold-blooded murder, as he claimed, or was it for political reasons (to win over the tribes of Israel)? Mephibosheth, the son of Jonathan, the son of Saul, was brought by David to Jerusalem and granted the right to eat at his table (ch. 9). Was this an act of generosity for Jonathan's sake, as David said it was, or rather a way of keeping an eye on this descendant of the previous king? Why did David forgive Shimei the son of Gera, who had mocked and cursed him virulently, and why did he tell him he would not die (19.22-23)? Was this genuine magnanimity or was David guided by political considerations (improved relations with the tribe of Benjamin and Saul's family)? Why did David decide to appoint Amasa commander of his army instead of Joab, despite the fact that Amasa had previously commanded Absalom's army against David? Was this also a matter of political expediency (the support of the tribe of Judah) or was it because of his personal hatred of Joab, who had slain his son Absalom and demanded of the bereaved father in blunt and brusque terms to overcome his deep grief without further ado (ch. 19)?

We cannot answer these questions. Various motives may have combined to lead to these actions. Be that as it may, David's deeds quite often give rise to questions, his intentions are frequently ambiguous, and his character appears to be enigmatic. Despite the fact that there is more information in the Bible about David than any other figure or perhaps just because of this, it is extremely difficult to fathom the depths of his personality, though questions about intentions and motives arise with regard to other characters too.

People's actions in daily life are hardly mentioned at all in biblical narrative, and we do not usually hear about the minutiae of their day-to-day routine. We meet the biblical characters primarily in special and unusual circumstances, in times of crisis and stress, when they have to undergo severe tests.

Whenever simple, daily tasks are mentioned this is important in shedding light on the character. It is not usual to find it explicitly stated in biblical narrative that the protagonist ate or drank, but in the case of Esau we are told that after Jacob his brother gave him the mess of pottage: 'Esau ate, drank, rose, went away and despised his birthright' (Gen. 25.34); Esau is characterized by these verbs as a man of action for whom immediate pleasure and the material things of life are most important.

We read that Jehu: 'went in and ate and drank' (2 Kgs 9.34) immediately after giving the order to have queen Jezebel thrown out of the window: 'And some of her blood spattered on the wall and on the horses, and they trampled on her' (v. 33). Despite the gory murder and the blood splashed around Jehu goes off to eat and drink as if nothing has happened.

When it is reported that someone does not eat, this also contributes to the shaping of the character. Every year, when they went up to the house of the Lord at Shiloh, Peninnah would provoke Hannah. Hannah would not answer Peninnah but: 'wept and would not eat' (1 Sam. 1.7). Hannah's sorrow is deep, but is expressed through weeping and the failure to eat rather than by a counter-attack; in other words, it is directed inward.

After Naboth has refused to sell his vineyard, king Ahab returns to his house 'vexed and sullen.... And he lay down on his bed, and turned away his face, and would eat no food' (1 Kgs 21.4). The king is in a bad mood, he has been deeply wounded by the refusal, but takes no action other than lying down, turning his face away and refusing to eat.

We read that: 'the boy Samuel was ministering to the Lord under Eli' (1 Sam. 3.1). When he was lying down in the temple of the Lord at Shiloh God appeared to him. After this: 'Samuel lay until morning; then he opened the doors of the house of the Lord' (v. 15). Why are we told that Samuel opened the doors in the morning? Ostensibly this is an unimportant fact, but in effect it is a way of characterizing Samuel. The tremendous event—the revelation of God—does not turn his head (even though 'the word of the Lord was rare in those days', 'there was no frequent vision'), he does not become conceited but continues fulfilling his duties as usual.

Every now and again we read that someone rose early in the morning. This fact is usually noted in order to show that the person concerned hastened to undertake a certain task. Thus, for example, this is what Abraham does after God tells him to obey Sarah and drive Hagar and Ishmael away, and again after God instructs him to sacrifice his son, Isaac: 'So Abraham rose early in the morning' (Gen. 21.14; 22.3). Abraham does not postpone the unpleasant task.

As has been stated above, it is rare to find routine tasks mentioned in biblical narrative. Since only important and exceptional deeds are generally recounted, the question arises whether unusual actions, which are more or less unique occurrences by their very nature, are sufficient to indicate characteristic traits of the protagonists. Only if someone repeats the same deed or similar ones several times is it possible to learn about the disposition and, in consequence, the character, while one single action need not necessarily show anything apart from a passing impulse.

Would it be right to consider Cain an inveterate murderer, for example, because he committed one murder? Should Aaron be regarded as weak-willed because he gave in to the people and made them a golden calf? Is the nature of Jael, the wife of Heber the Kenite, indicated by the fact that she drove a stake through Sisera's temple when he was lying tired in her tent? Does the rape of Tamar betoken Amnon's character? Does Lot's reception and protection of the two angels who came to Sodom—to take a positive example— prove that he is a hospitable person?

In real life not everything people do is characteristic of them, but this is not the case in a literary work of art, or at least in a short story. In this respect, the length of the work is of decisive importance: because there is no room in a short story to describe the various deeds and repeated actions of any one character single actions necessarily serve to define the person. The short story chooses to relate the particular action which is characteristic of the individual and can exemplify what is considered to constitute the essential nature. We remember Cain as someone who murdered his brother, and Amnon as the person who violated his sister. If the author had wanted us to see them in a different light we would have been told about other (or additional) things they did.

In a longer narrative, on the other hand—and it makes no difference whether this is one long one or several short ones in which the same character appears—it is possible to relate different actions illustrating the same tendency or characteristic.

Abraham obeys God's commands several times, even when they are extremely difficult to accept. At an advanced age he leaves his country, his kin and his father's house in order to go to an unknown land (Gen. 12.1-5). He is circumcised when he is ninety-nine years old (17.24). He sends his son Ishmael into the desert (21.14). And he goes to sacrifice his son Isaac as a burnt offering (ch. 22).

Samson, whose strength and heroism are revealed on numerous occasions and through various deeds, is shown to be weak because he succumbs twice to the blandishments of a woman. On the first occasion, he reveals the solution of the riddle he has set the Philistines to the woman of Timnah, who 'wept before him and pressed him hard for seven days' (Judges 14); and on the second, he tells Delilah, 'who pressed him hard with her words day after day', the secret of his great strength and how he could be made weak (ch. 16).

We are also told how Joab the son of Zeruiah, twice kills the commanders of an opposing army by treachery: he first kills Abner the son of Ner (2 Sam. 3.26-27) and then Amasa (20.9-10). Joab's hard and callous character ('These men, the sons of Zeruiah, are too hard for me', David says after Abner's murder) is also evinced in the slaying of Absalom even though he knows how much pain this will cause David.

The narrator occasionally uses a different method to make it clear to us that a specific deed is characteristic of a certain individual, by stating explicitly that this action was regularly performed by the person concerned. This is the case with Elkanah, who used to go '*year by year*' to Shiloh to worship and sacrifice to the Lord (1 Sam. 1.3, 7), reflecting his religious devotion. It is said of Absalom that '*at the end of every year*' he cut the hair of his head and weighed it (2 Sam. 14.26), proving his exaggerated self-love. The narrator tells us that at the end of the feast which Job's sons made, 'he would rise early in the morning and offer burnt offerings according to the number of them all; for Job said, "It may be that my sons have sinned, and cursed God in their hearts". Thus Job did *continually*' (Job 1.5), illustrating how upright and God-fearing he was.

A great deal can be learned about people from the decisions they make. Because it involves choosing between alternatives, decisions reveal a person's scale of values, showing us the outcome of the struggle between desires, emotions and spiritual values, whether ethical, religious or social. The characters in biblical narrative often have to choose between conflicting values or ethical precepts on the one hand and the desire for power, vengeance, or the pleasures of the flesh, on the other. We learn about the characters' decisions indirectly, drawing our conclusions from the outcome (the deeds) about the reasons (the decisions) which preceded and gave rise to them.

For example, when Jonah is commanded by God to go to Nineveh and prophesy, he can decide whether to obey or not. His decision to flee to Tarshish (namely, in the opposite direction) reveals that personal prestige is more important to him than God's directives or the chance to save the lives of a great many people. While he is on board ship a great storm blows up, whereupon all the sailors pray and throw the cargo into the sea. Jonah can follow suit, but decides to go and sleep in the inner part of the ship, thus revealing his indifference to life.

When the sailors realize that Jonah is the reason for the fearful storm, they can choose to kill him in order to save their lives. They decide, however, to ask Jonah himself what should be done with him. After he tells them that they should throw him into the sea they first try to row for shore and only after they find out that they cannot and that the sea is becoming even rougher, do they decide to throw Jonah into the sea. These decisions indicate that the sailors' moral values are more powerful than their instinct for survival, that they hold such a high regard for the life of their fellow-man that they are prepared to endanger their own lives in order to save his (and only when there is no doubt that the choice is between Jonah's death and everyone's do they decide to sacrifice one man in order to save many).

When Nehemiah hears of the plight of his brethren in the land of Judah and the city of Jerusalem he is faced with several alternatives. He can limit himself to expressing his regret, he can mourn and pray to God, or he can send help to the land of Judah. What Nehemiah decides to do is to ask permission of the king of Persia, whose cupbearer he is, to go to Jerusalem and rebuild its walls himself. This decision proves that Nehemiah's sense of solidarity with his people is stronger than his natural tendency to preserve his own comfort and position as well as his life (by making this request he ran the risk of enraging the king and causing his dismissal or even execution).

Both actions and inaction bear evidence of a person's character. The failure to act sometimes results from a deliberate decision to refrain from action and sometimes from weakness and passivity. It is impossible, however, to draw conclusions about someone's character simply because no report is given of actions. The author carefully selects the incidents to be related about any individual, and what is chosen is always just a fraction of what could be revealed. If more is left out than is included in every narrative, how much more is this the case in a short story. Nevertheless, the narrative on occasions directs the reader's attention, whether overtly or covertly, to someone's inaction, and in this case it can be assumed that this is significant. This way of characterization will be illustrated by means of the figure of David.

In view of the fact that throughout his life David is active, even energetic, his inaction with regard to his children is remarkable. In connection with Adonijah we read: 'His father had never displeased him by asking, "Why have you done thus and so?"' (1 Kgs 1.6), and the Septuagint makes a similar statement in connection with Amnon (2 Sam. 13.21). These comments indicate that David was lax and negligent when it came to educating his children. The same is insinuated at the end of the episode of Amnon's rape of Tamar: 'When king David heard of all these things, he was very angry' (v. 21). The information that David heard all this and was very angry arouses the expectation that he will take action of one sort or another, but we are not told that he did anything in this respect. The narrator's silence is significant here. Because it is stated that David heard all this and was very angry, the absence of any action is conspicuous.

Absalom is permitted to return to Jerusalem from Geshur, not at David's initiative but at Joab's. Although David agrees to let Absalom return to Jerusalem he refuses to see him for a long time, which indicates that he does not know his own mind. Once again, no decision is made one way or another until Absalom takes the initiative and Joab intervenes once again (ch. 14).

David also appears to be irresolute when it comes to determining which of his sons should succeed him. He apparently never made a decision on this point, and if he did, never mentioned it in public or did anything to implement it. He would probably have accepted Adonijah's *fait accompli* had not pressure been exerted on him by Nathan and Bathsheba to appoint Solomon his heir. In this case too David is led by others (1 Kings 1).

David's attitude to his children is characterized by a lack of understanding as well as inaction, and it can be said that his relationship with them is composed of both incomprehension and weakness. He fails to realize what Amnon is plotting when the latter feigns illness and persuades David to send Tamar to him (2 Sam. 13.5-7). David also accedes to Absalom's entreaties that Amnon accompany him to the sheepshearing, not sensing Absalom's hatred for Amnon, or if he does, ignoring the danger in letting Amnon go with Absalom (vv. 23-29). Similarly, David allows Absalom to go to Hebron and pay his vow, never imagining for a moment that Absalom plans to proclaim himself king there, despite the fact that Absalom had been preparing his revolt for a long time right under David's nose (15.1-9).

In some instances, people's gestures are mentioned. This is done because they have expressive value and indicate something about the inner state of the person involved.

After being violated by her brother Amnon, Tamar puts ashes on her head and tears her long robe, 'and she laid her hand on her head' (13.19). This gesture clearly serves as an expression of deep pain and sorrow.

After Naboth has refused to give him his vineyard, Ahab returns home, 'And he lay down on his bed, and turned away his face' (1 Kgs 21.4). The movement of turning his face to the wall indicates the king's sorrow and depression.

When Ezra hears of the mixed marriages of the people of Israel he rends his garments and his mantle, pulls hair from his head and beard and sits appalled (Ezra 9.3). All these actions are clear expressions of grief and anguish.

Another way of shaping the characters is through the judgment by one of the participants of an action performed by another (as distinct from judgments relating to personality). This way of moulding the characters sheds light on both the person judged and the one making the judgment, while at the same time enabling the former to react (either by word or by deed) and thus to reveal still more.

Amongst the judgments of actions pronounced by the characters, a special place should be allotted to those made by a prophet. Because of his special standing as God's emissary, whatever a prophet says carries particular weight, and it can be assumed that the author identifies fully with the prophet. There are abundant examples of this, such as Samuel's condemnation of Saul's actions, Nathan's of David's, Elijah's of Ahab's, etc.

Even though, in the following example, the judgment of the action is not made by a prophet, there is no doubt that it reflects the author's opinion. Before Tamar is raped by Amnon she refers to the deed as wanton folly, pleading: 'Do not do this wanton folly' (2 Sam. 13.12). Afterwards she says: 'For this wrong in sending me away is greater than the other which you did to me' (v. 16). Since she herself is the victim of the actions she is condemning, her statement is particularly effective, making a powerful impression on the reader.

Whereas the judgments made by Samuel, Nathan and Elijah occur after the actions to which they refer, those of Tamar are made beforehand with the object of preventing the deed. The same applies to what Abigail says about the act of vengeance which David intends to undertake: 'And when the Lord has done to my lord according to all the good that he has spoken concerning you, and has appointed you prince over Israel, my lord shall have no cause of grief, or pangs of conscience, for having shed blood without cause' (1 Sam. 25.30-31).

The characters' personalities are revealed by their reactions to the judgments. Both Saul and David accept the condemnations made by Samuel and Nathan and confess their sins. Saul says, 'I have sinned; for I have transgressed the commandment of the Lord and your words' (1 Sam. 15.24), and David says, 'I have sinned against the Lord' (2 Sam. 12.13). This self-condemnation reveals both the negative and the positive aspect of the character. The admission of having sinned naturally proves that the individual has not behaved as required, but also indicates contrition and an inner change (though in Saul's case this occurred after a great many evasions).

Saul's and David's reactions cause the reader to feel sympathy for them. They sinned, but they also regretted what they had done; we feel for them in their hour of emotional need and respect them for their strength and readiness to confess. The change which occurs in their personality is, therefore, accompanied by a shift in the reader's attitude towards them. Nevertheless, this shift is not enough to obliterate completely our negative attitude towards them as a result of their sins. The duality in the character's personality, which is reflected in the admission of sin—transgression and repentance—is paralleled by duality in the reader's attitude—condemnation and sympathy.

The admission of sin does not always, however, have the same significance and effect. In the case of Shimei the son of Gera, who declares: 'For your servant knows that I have sinned' (2 Sam. 19.20), we tend to suspect that his admission is the result of cold calculation aimed solely at advancing his interests rather than indicating any genuine inner change. The first thing Shimei says when he falls at David's feet is: 'Let not my lord hold me guilty or remember how your servant did wrong on the day my lord the king left Jerusalem; let not the king bear it in mind' (v. 19). Despite the fact that Shimei mentions his guilt, he phrases things in such a way as to make it evident that he is not afflicted by remorse and that his prime object is to persuade the king to overlook his sins. Since Shimei's motive is not honest repentance his admission of guilt smacks of hypocrisy, adding another negative aspect to his character and making the reader even less sympathetic towards him.

C. *Minor Characters*

The ways of characterization mentioned above occur both in life and in literature. A way of characterization which occurs only in literature is that achieved through minor characters.

Subsidiary characters have a part to play in the network of interpersonal relations in both speech and acts, such as when one character conducts a dialogue with another or acts in some way towards him or her. This relationship exists in real life too, and has been discussed above. In addition, however, the minor characters play a structural role in literature, paralleling and highlighting the main ones, whether through correspondence or contrast. The positive or negative parallel between the primary and secondary characters is not enough to shape the characters, but it provides emphasis and colour. The minor characters serve as a background against which the personalities of the main ones stand out.

It is not always possible to make a clear and unequivocal distinction between a primary and a secondary character. In this context it is better to refer less to two completely different categories than to a continuum, since there are distinct disparities in the level of 'secondariness' of the subsidiary characters. On the one hand, there are such characters as the messenger or courier, who fulfil only a minor technical role in the structure of the plot, such as the anonymous person who escapes from Sodom and informs Abram that Lot has been taken captive by Ched-or-laomer and the kings who were with him (Gen. 14.13); while on the other, there are subsidiary characters who have such an important function that it is difficult to decide whether they are secondary or primary, particularly since a character who is secondary in one narrative may become primary in another. Joshua appears as a minor character in the Pentateuch, but is the principal one in the book of Joshua. In the narrative of David and Abigail (1 Samuel 25) there is no doubt that David is the main figure. But what about Abigail? Should she be regarded as a principal or a subsidiary character? We may be able to fix criteria for deciding this, but it is more important to determine what roles the characters fulfil in relation to one another, since it is these which emphasize the various features of their personalities.

In the narrative of Bathsheba (2 Samuel 11) aspects of David's character are contrasted with those of Uriah, who serves as the 'normative hero', that is, as the representative of desired values. Because Uriah displays such noble characteristics as honesty and unflinching loyalty, David's treacherous, dishonest and unprincipled behaviour is accentuated. The contrasting traits of David and Uriah parallel the opposing structural roles they fulfil within the narrative, which is based on the clash between them over a woman.

When the rumour that Absalom has killed all the king's sons reaches Jerusalem David believes it, whereas Jonadab the son of Shimeah realizes that only Amnon has been killed: 'For Amnon alone is dead, for by the command of Absalom this has been determined from the day he forced his sister Tamar' (13.32). Through Jonadab, the son of Shimeah, David's blindness and lack of understanding of the relations between his sons, and particularly of Absalom's character, motives and intentions, is emphasized.

Jonadab, the son of Shimeah, who is astute and discerning, also appears as a foil to his friend Amnon (13.5). Amnon is tormented by his love for Tamar and cannot find a remedy for his ills. Unlike his brother Absalom, he is unable to plan matters himself and has recourse to Jonadab (who has noticed that Amnon is upset) to contrive an excuse for a private meeting between him and the object of his desire. Jonadab uses his brain, Amnon his brawn.

The negative behaviour of the prophet Jonah is emphasized by the positive conduct of the sailors, who feature as a collective minor hero (Jonah 1). Through her normal reaction ('Do you still hold fast your integrity? Curse God, and die'), Job's wife stresses Job's unusual stand in maintaining his faith despite the heavy blows which have struck him (Job 1 and 2).

There is a marked correspondence between Absalom and Adonijah, who both covet the throne and express their aspirations in concrete actions. We are told that Absalom got himself a chariot and horses, and fifty men to run before him (2 Sam. 15.1), and that Adonijah prepared for himself chariots and horsemen, and fifty men to run before him (1 Kgs 1.5). Chariots, horsemen and runners were considered a distinct symbol of kingship, as is manifested by the fact that they are the first items mentioned in the 'king's law' in 1 Sam. 8.11: 'He said, "These will be the ways of the king who will reign over you: he will take your sons and appoint them to his chariots and to be his horsemen, and to run before his chariots"'. Both Absalom and Adonijah attempt to seize the crown, both prepare themselves adherents and establish a *fait accompli* (their proclamation as king). Both start their rebellion by sacrificing a great number of beasts in the presence of guests, and both bring disaster on themselves in the final event as the result of their lust for power. The narrator draws our attention to the parallel between the two brothers by saying of Adonijah: 'He too was a very handsome man; and he was born next after Absalom' (1 Kgs 1.6).

Sometimes several of the elements of characterization referred to above function together, emphasizing or intensifying one of the principal character's traits. The narrator portrays Abigail, for example, by stating explicitly: 'The woman was of good understanding' (1 Sam. 25.3), and David says to her: 'Blessed be your discretion' (v. 33). Her sagacity is also evinced indirectly in her speech to David, which is distinguished by both its content and its form, as well as in her actions—going out quickly to meet David and giving him a generous gift. Her wisdom is particularly apparent against the background of the foolish behaviour of her husband Nabal (who is a minor character).

Job is also characterized in a variety of ways, some of them extremely powerful. The narrator presents him as 'blameless and upright, fearing God and turning away from evil' (Job 1.1), using *four* terms to emphasize his righteousness. God reiterates this direct characterization, even twice (1.8; 2.3), adding: 'There is none like him on the earth' (also twice) and: 'He still holds fast his integrity'. These expressions of direct characterization are uttered by the narrator, who is the supreme authority, and by God, who is above every authority.

The narrator also evaluates Job's conduct: 'In all this Job did not sin or charge God with wrong' (1.22), later repeating: 'In all this Job did not sin with his lips' (2.10). Job's prodigious piety is also demonstrated by what he himself says: '*It may be* that my sons have sinned, and cursed God *in their hearts*'. ('It may be', namely, it is not at all certain that they sinned; 'in their hearts', namely, only in their thoughts, not even in speech.) 'Naked I came from my mother's womb, and naked shall I return; the Lord gave, and the Lord has taken away, blessed be the name of the Lord'. 'You speak as one of the foolish women would speak. Shall we receive good at the hand of God, and shall we not receive evil?' (1.5, 21; 2.10). Similarly, Job's *practice* of sacrificing burnt offerings for his sons at the end of the days of feast (1.5), is recorded to prove his righteousness. And finally, his wife serves as a foil to offset his unusual nature.

Why does the narrative use so many ways of characterization in order to illustrate one of Job's features? The answer is that this underscores the question which the narrative tackles, namely, whether everyone, even the *most righteous* man, does good only in order to receive a reward. (This is the problem of the narrative, whereas the poetic part of the book deals with another issue.)

To sum up, just as the narrator makes very few direct statements about the characters' personalities, the protagonists themselves make very few such pronouncements. In this respect there is complete coordination between the narrator and the characters. The protagonists are characterized primarily by indirect means, namely, by their speech and actions. This approach resembles the one we adopt in real life, where we usually draw conclusions about people's personalities from what they say and do. In this respect it can be said that the dominant technique used for shaping the characters in biblical narrative is 'realistic'. We should not, however, ignore the fact that a work of literature can never imitate reality precisely, neither in its content nor in its techniques of characterization, and therefore it is not surprising to find that every now and again the author deviates from the way people are characterized in real life.

It is in the nature of the indirect method that characters are not defined comprehensively, but that their personalities emerge gradually from the totality of their appearances and actions during the course of the narrative. The indirect approach cannot make it clear to us at the outset of the narrative what the character's nature is, and this will not be fully evident until the end, when we are able to review and combine all the relevant facts. The use of the indirect method entails that the individual's character is depicted dynamically. While direct characterization, which determines an individual's nature in definite terms, embodies a static view of the person, indirect characterization, which is based on both words and deeds, tends to regard personality as being mobile. In many biblical narratives a person's character is not regarded as constant, but as something continually shifting and changing, even though stable components can be discerned. Character is existential rather than essential, since it is revealed in actual and transient real-life situations. Accordingly, epithets relating to biblical characters do not refer to aspects of their personalities but to their origin—nation, tribe, city or geographical region (Uriah the Hittite, Ehud the son of Gera the Benjaminite, Jesse the Bethlehemite, Barzilai the Gileadite, etc.). In other words, the epithets serve to identify and not to characterize people. In terms of language, this view of human nature is typified by a minimum of adjectives (illustrating aspects of personality) and a high percentage of verbs (relating to speech and deeds).

The dynamic view of personality is connected with the wider issue of types of literary characters. A distinction is usualy made between flat (one-dimensional) and round (three-dimensional) characters. There are two aspects to this distinction which often overlap one another but are by no means identical. On the one hand, a flat character is defined as having one single feature, while a round one is complex and has several traits. On the other hand, a round character is perceived changing and developing while flat ones remain static however often they may appear. There is an obvious connection between these two aspects: a changing character cannot be simple and have just one feature, but a complex character need not develop at all in the narrative.

In short stories, like most biblical narratives, there is virtually no technical possibility of gradual development. We often feel, neverthe-less, that those characters who appear in many episodes change profoundly in the course of their lives. How great is the difference between the young Jacob who steals the blessing intended for Esau his brother, and the Jacob, who, after twenty years of suffering in exile, begs his brother to accept his 'blessing'; between the innocent lad Samuel, who does not realize that the voice calling him is the voice of God, and the old Samuel, who gives orders to king Saul and rebukes him angrily when Saul does not obey him; between the young David, who storms out angrily to wreak his terrible vengeance on Nabal the Carmelite, and the old king, who flees from Jerusalem on foot for fear of his son Absalom and listens to the curses of Shimei the son of Gera with humility and acceptance.

Sometimes the change is rapid and sudden, in which case it can be presented within one short narrative. For example, Ahab, who wanted Naboth's vineyard and had him executed on false charges, hears the reprimand of the prophet Elijah and as a result repents his deed: 'And when Ahab heard those words, he rent his clothes, and put sackcloth upon his flesh, and fasted and lay in sackcloth, and went about dejectedly' (1 Kgs 21.27). We cannot say that his repentance is neither deep nor genuine, for God himself provides evidence of Ahab's humility: 'Have you seen how Ahab has humbled himself before me? Because he has humbled himself before me, I will not bring the evil in his days' (v. 29).

The other aspect of the characters, namely, their complexity, should be perceived as a continuum of possibilities extending between the two extremes rather than just two contingencies, either flat or round. The main characters are usually more complex and the minor ones simpler.

Abraham's greatness is revealed when he argues with God about the destruction of Sodom, but he does not arouse our admiration when he asks Sarah to say she is his sister, so that he may prosper and his life may be spared. Saul, the first king, is an able and admirable man (because of his modesty, amongst other things), but from various episodes we realize that he suffers from a deep emotional disturbance. The prophet Elijah is portrayed as a brave and zealous warrior of the Lord, but is, nevertheless, subject to such deep depression that he wishes to die. The Bible, as is well-known, does not obscure its heroes' weaknesses, and so even such characters as Abraham, Moses and David are depicted not as ideal people but as human beings with both good and bad in them.

There is no doubt that the most complex, deep and multi-faceted character in the Bible is David. We meet him in a large variety of situations, revealing different—and sometimes contradictory—aspects of his personality. David the statesman is entirely different from David the father. On the one hand, he appears as a balanced and calculating individual, while on the other, he reveals passionate emotions and fierce desires. He has a deep belief in God, alongside his belief in his own powers and those of his adherents. He is able to subdue his own will to God's, while nevertheless acting boldly and aggressively to get what he wants. A rich palette is used in portraying him, and because of his diverse qualities his personality is prominent against the background of the host of characters surrounding him, all simpler than he.

Few of the characters in biblical narrative are depicted extensively and in detail, most being sketched in with only a few lines. Nevertheless, they are convincingly real and human, and have unique features.

The characteristics attributed to biblical figures are not only unique, however, but are also general human traits. The characters embody various aspects of human nature and therefore have considerable representative force and general significance. Because of the way they are portrayed, combining both universal and individual features, biblical characters can fulfil their functions within the world of the narrative as carriers of the plot as well as making their way straight to the reader's heart as the bearers of a message.

Chapter 3

THE PLOT

If the characters are the soul of the narrative, the plot is the body. It consists of an organized and orderly system of events, arranged in temporal sequence. In contrast to life—where we are invariably confronted by an endless stream of incidents occurring haphazardly and disparately—the plot of a narrative is constructed as a meaningful chain of interconnected events. This is achieved by careful selection, entailing the omission of any incident which does not fit in logically with the planned development of the plot.

The plot serves to organize events in such a way as to arouse the reader's interest and emotional involvement, while at the same time imbuing the events with meaning.

An isolated incident receives its significance from its position and role in the system as a whole. The incidents are like building blocks, each one contributing its part to the entire edifice, and hence their importance. In the building which is the plot there are no excess or meaningless blocks. The removal of one may cause the entire structure to collapse or at least damage its functional and aesthetic perfection.

The units which comprise the plot are of different kinds or, more precisely, of different sizes. The smallest narrative unit is the one which contains one incident, whether an action or an event. An action occurs when the character is the subject (the logical, not necessarily the syntactical, subject) of the incident, and an event occurs when the character is the object.

The combination of several small units of this kind creates larger ones, scenes and acts. Some narratives consist of only one act, but most are composed of several.

Various kinds of connections and relations exist between the units comprising the narrative system, thereby creating the structure of the plot. The principal relations between the various units are those of cause and effect, parallelism and contrast.

The plot in its entirety has a clear beginning and end. Incidents which are appropriate to serve as starting and finishing points, such as birth and death or the imposing of a task and the reward for its fulfilment, are chosen from the unlimited reservoir of events. Consequently, we do not feel that the story we are reading is unfinished or incomplete. The beginning and end of the narrative are sometimes denoted by explicit introductions and conclusions.

Between the starting and finishing points the plot evolves along a line of development which creates a certain pattern. One can often discern a line which gradually ascends to a climax, and then descends to a state of relaxation. There are, however, other patterns of plot development, such as a sudden turn constituting an unexpected change in the line of development.

At the centre of the plot there is almost always a conflict or collision between two forces, whether these be two individuals, a person and his or her inner self, a person and an institution, custom or outlook, or an individual and a superhuman force, such as God or fate.

Several narratives, each one a complete unit in its own right, combine with one another in the Bible to create an extensive block, and thus the single narrative becomes one component of a greater narrative whole. The unity of the greater narrative whole is determined by the ways in which the individual ones are connected and by the nature of the relations between them. The individual narrative usually acquires additional significance when it serves as a constituent element of the wider whole.

The extensive blocks combine to form books, and the books to constitute comprehensive compositions, bringing before us the vast canvas of history from the creation of the world to the Babylonian exile (from Genesis to 2 Kings), and from Adam to the period of restoration (Chronicles and the books of Ezra and Nehemiah). Within these large compositions, which partially overlap with one another, the individual narratives are embedded in more or less chronological order and in accordance with an overall historical and religio-ethical view. It is this view which grants these vast compositions their unity even though they are composed of many different elements.

Thus, units exist at various levels, starting with the smallest, containing one incident, and including the vast composition, which comprises several books. Each unit, at every level except for the last, serves as a component of the one above it and each plays a part and obtains significance in accordance with its position within the great hierarchical structure.

1. *The Single Narrative*

A. *The Units of the Plot*

The smallest narrative units—the incidents—almost always have multiple purposes in biblical narrative, at the same time serving as components of the plot, as a means of characterizing the protagonists and as ways of expressing meaning. Since there are very few elements in biblical narrative whose task is solely to characterize individuals or express meaning, these functions devolve primarily onto those units which also comprise the plot.

It should be noted that speech as well as incidents almost invariably serves a number of purposes. For example, when Abigail says to David: 'My lord shall have no cause of grief, or pangs of conscience, for having shed blood without cause or for my lord taking vengeance himself. And when the Lord has dealt well with my lord, then remember your handmaid' (1 Sam. 25.31), her words serve as an element in the plot, because they cause a change in David's intention to destroy Nabal and his household, as a way of characterizing Abigail, indicating her perspicacity, and as a means of expressing the significance of the narrative, negating David's intention to shed blood and take the law into his own hands.

The order in which the small narrative units are arranged is both temporal and causal. In other words, the incidents succeed one another in a chronological as well as a causal sequence, one incident being the outcome of the previous one and the cause of the one that follows it.

There are, nevertheless, events which are not complete links in the tight causal chain of the narrative, serving solely as the cause of another incident and not as the result of a previous one. Thus, what the snake says to the woman in the narrative of the Garden of Eden (Genesis 3) causes her to eat the fruit of the forbidden tree, but the snake's words are not themselves the outcome of any previous incident.

Sometimes the chain of incidents bifurcates, one event having two results, either of which can set off a separate chain of occurrences. For example, the fact that the ark of God is captured by the

Philistines (1 Samuel 4) has two results, each one developing into an independent causal chain; one is the death of Eli, leading to Samuel's promotion to the rank of judge and leader, while the other is the removal of the ark to the land of the Philistines and the resultant series of disasters which strikes them, and eventually leads to the ark's return to the land of Judah. Both these chains coincide and combine again when David, anointed and supported by Samuel, brings the ark of God from Kiriath-Jearim in the land of Judah to his city, Jerusalem.

On some occasions the causal connection between the events is noted explicitly by means of such words as 'because' and 'for', while on others it is not mentioned at all and the reader must grasp the causal relation for himself. The second method is used far more frequently in biblical narrative, most incidents being connected by the letter *'waw'* ('and').

There are very few events in biblical narrative which have neither a causal nor a sequential role to play in the chain of the narrative. The task of those incidents, which are not essential to the structure of the plot and could be omitted, is to emphasize aspects, expand situations, illuminate characters, deepen significance, etc. Because there are so few of them, the biblical narrative is not diffuse but is cohesive, concise and very tightly constructed.

The unit created by the combination of several events—the scene—is defined through the characters participating in it. When all or some of the characters change a new scene starts.

In biblical narrative the number of characters involved at any one time is very small, usually not more than two. Even when the total number of characters in a narrative is greater, only a very limited number of active characters appear in each scene (sometimes there are additional 'silent' characters in the background, who do not take an active part in what is happening). As a result, the reader's attention is not distracted but is concentrated on a few focal points within the scene.

Since there are rarely more than two active characters in any one scene, virtually all conversations are duologues. Although in some conversations one of the participants is not an individual but a group, as in the case of Lot and the men of Sodom, for example (Gen. 19.4-9), these should also be regarded as duologues, because the group of people is in fact a collective figure.

In two instances it is possible to distinguish separate voices emerging from within a group of people participating in a conversation.[1] In one case, it is stated explicitly: in the book of Nehemiah (5.1-5) the cry of the people is reported, and the content of the cry is divided between several voices which the narrator precedes each time with the phrase: 'For there were those who said'. In the second instance, the separate voices are not noted explicitly, but it is possible to discern them intermingling with one another. Saul, who is searching for the lost asses, asks, 'Is the seer here?' and the maidens give him a very long and complicated answer containing unnecessary repetitions. The reader gains the impression that this is not one answer but many, given by different maidens, all trying to respond and supply information: 'He is. Behold, he is just ahead of you. Make haste; he has come just now to the city, because the people have a sacrifice today on the high place. As soon as you enter the city, you will find him, before he goes up to the high place to eat. For the people will not eat till he comes, since he must bless the sacrifice. Afterward those eat who are invited. Now go up, for you will meet him immediately' (1 Sam. 9.12-13). In spite of the separate voices the conversations in both cases must still be regarded as bilateral.

In the narrative of the Garden of Eden, after the fruit of the forbidden tree has been eaten, there is a conversation with four participants: God, the man, the woman and the snake (Gen. 3.8-19). This must be considered as a series of bilateral conversations, since God addresses each of the other three characters separately in succession, receiving an answer from only two of them.

The conversation between Hamor, Shechem and the sons of Jacob in the narrative of the rape of Dinah can perhaps be regarded as multilateral (Gen. 34.8-18). Jacob's sons appear here as a collective character (Jacob is present but does not participate in the conversation). Hamor starts by asking that Dinah be given to his son in marriage. Shechem speaks after him, promising to accept any demand provided Dinah is given to him. Finally the sons of Jacob speak, and their reply is intended for both Hamor and Shechem. Thus, there are three participants (one of them collective) in this conversation, two of whom belong to the same side and therefore obtain a common answer from the other side. There is, nevertheless, a certain difference between the words of Hamor and of Shechem.

1. S. Talmon, *Darkei Hasippur Bamikra* (Jerusalem, 1964), pp. 45ff. (Hebrew).

Although their aim is the same (to obtain Dinah), their motives are different. Hamor, being the prince of the Hivites, speaks of establishing close ties between the two ethnic groups: 'Make marriages with us; give your daughters to us, and take our daughters for yourselves. You shall dwell with us; and the land shall be open to you; dwell and trade in it, and get property in it' (vv. 9-10). Shechem's motives, on the other hand, are of a personal nature: 'Ask of me ever so much as marriage present and gift, and I will give according as you say to me; only give me the maiden to be my wife' (v. 12).

A genuine multilateral conversation takes place at one point in the narrative of Absalom's revolt (2 Sam. 19.19-23). There are three characters who participate: king David, Shimei the son of Gera and Abishai the son of Zeruiah. The first to speak is Shimei, who asks the king to forgive him for insulting him when he fled from Jerusalem. Then Abishai interrupts, stating that Shimei should be put to death for cursing the Lord's anointed. David first replies to Abishai, rebuking him: 'What have I to do with you, you sons of Zeruiah, that you should this day be as an adversary to me?' and then answers Shimei, giving him his oath: 'You shall not die'.

In several narratives the scenes are organized in such a way as to show the parallel, contrasting or sequential relations between them quite clearly. For example, in the story of the Garden of Eden (Genesis 3) the scenes are organized in the following way:

> the snake and the woman
>
>   the woman and the man
>
> GOD   and the man
>
> GOD   and the woman
>
> GOD and the snake
>
> GOD   and the woman
>
>   GOD   and the man

This is a chiastic and concentric structure[2] with a forward and

_____

2. A distinction should be made between a ring or envelope structure (A. . . . A), a concentric structure (A,B,x,B,A) and a chiastic structure (A,B,B,A).

backward motion: snake, woman, man—man, woman, snake, woman, man, indicating the continuity between the scenes. God appears five times, the woman four times, the man three times and the snake twice, reflecting the relative importance of the characters in this narrative. Nevertheless, the man's special importance is indicated by the fact that he is the first and the last character to whom God speaks.

In the first part the snake appears as the initiator, the woman as the link (tempted and tempter) and the man as objective. The reversed order of the second part fits the concept of measure for measure: the sin of eating gives rise to the punishment of eating ('In the sweat of your face you shall eat bread'), the woman's tempting of the man leads to the man's supremacy over the woman ('. . . and he shall rule over you'). Thus, the structure accords with the content, reinforcing its impact.

A different order of scenes is found in the story of Isaac's blessing (Gen. 27.1-28.5).[3]

(1) Isaac—Esau	(2) Rebekah—Jacob	(3) Isaac—Jacob
(4) Isaac—Esau	(5) Rebekah—Jacob	(6) Isaac—Jacob

The symmetrical construction is very apparent. Of the four characters in the narrative no more than two encounter one another at any one time, and although all are from the same family, they belong to two opposing camps: Isaac and Esau on one side, Rebekah and Jacob on the other (see also 25.28). In scenes 1 and 4 the members of one camp meet, in scenes 2 and 5 the members of the other, and only in scenes 3 and 6 do members of the opposing camps meet (the two principal contestants, Jacob and Esau, do not meet at all). Scene 3 is the cardinal one: at this point the tension reaches its height and Jacob obtains the blessing from his father. In scene 6 the conflict is resolved: Isaac and Jacob meet again, but this time in order to part, since by sending Jacob away from home the dangerous encounter between him and his brother rival will be avoided.

There is also symmetry in the order in which the parents and the sons appear. The parents appear according to the following order:

Isaac Rebekah Isaac   Isaac Rebekah Isaac

while the sons appear in this order:

Esau Jacob Jacob   Esau Jacob Jacob

3. J.P. Fokkelman, *Narrative Art in Genesis* (Assen, 1975), pp. 97ff.

Isaac is the dominant parent, but Rebekah enters the picture each time in order to arrange matters. Jacob appears twice as often as Esau, indicating that he gains the upper hand.

The construction of the scenes is not only symmetrical but also chiastic:

(1) Isaac—Esau

      (2) Rebekah—Jacob

            (3) Isaac—Jacob

            (4) Isaac—Esau

      (5) Rebekah—Jacob

(6) Isaac—Jacob

In both the two central scenes, 3 and 4, Isaac encounters one of his sons and blesses him, and there is clearly a contrastive parallel between these two scenes. They are surrounded by scenes 2 and 5, in which the mother plans the steps of her favourite son. They, in turn, are encompassed by scenes 1 and 6, which open and close the series and in which Isaac sends his son out. There is a difference between the two, however, regarding which of the sons is sent and to what purpose. This difference embodies the development of the plot between the initial and final situations. In both these scenes, 1 and 6, Rebekah appears in a subordinate role, first listening to what Isaac says to Esau, and later advising Isaac about Jacob. The symmetrical structure reflects the family relationships: there are two parents and two sons, and each parent prefers a different son. The chiastic structure accords with the reversal in the situation as a result of the switch (in the central scenes) between the two sons.

In the narrative of the birth of Samuel (1 Sam. 1.1–2.11) we find the following arrangement of scenes according to the conversations conducted within the narrative:

(1) Elkanah—Hannah   (2) Eli—Hannah (after Hannah's prayer)

(3) Hannah—Elkanah   (4) Hannah—Eli (before Hannah's prayer)

Once again the symmetrical construction is obvious, the events prior to Samuel's birth paralleling those after it. Before and after the birth Elkanah speaks to Hannah, his wife, on the first occasion, in order to console her for the fact that she has no son, and on the second, to give his assent to her remaining at home so as to tend to her son until he is weaned. Before and after the birth Hannah speaks to Eli, on the first occasion, in order to tell him that she has prayed for a son, and on the second, to present her baby to him. Hannah prays twice to God, on the first occasion, to make a request, and on the second, to thank and praise Him. The similarity in form here emphasizes the difference in content caused by the birth of Samuel.

Since she is the central figure, Hannah appears in every scene, but while in the first two she is spoken to (Elkanah and Eli initiate the conversation), in the last two she is the one to start the exchange (she addresses Elkanah and Eli). This is another way of reflecting the shift in her situation. This change also explains the fact that on the first occasion Hannah's prayer precedes her conversation with Eli, while on the second her prayer occurs after she has talked to him, at the close of the scene.

A different construction is found in the narrative of the reconciliation between David and Absalom (2 Samuel 14), in which four characters participate: David, Absalom, Joab and the wise woman of Tekoa. There is a bitter conflict between David and Absalom, and Joab and the woman of Tekoa want to heal the rift and get the two to meet and make their peace with one another.

In this narrative also two characters appear in each scene:[4]

(1) Joab—the woman of Tekoa
   (2) the woman of Tekoa—David
      (3) David—Joab
         (4) Joab—Absalom
            (5) Absalom—Joab
               (6) Joab —David
                  (7) David —Absalom

What distinguishes this arrangement is the fact that the second figure in each pair is the first in the following one. The woman of Tekoa, who is the second figure in the first scene, is the first in the second scene; David, who is the second figure in the second scene, is the first in the third scene, and so on. The pinnacle is the last scene, when David and Absalom finally meet. Joab appears at the start of the series and in several other scenes, as fits his role as initiator of matters and mediator between father and son. A period of two years separates the fourth and the fifth scenes from one another. This is also the axis of the structure, since the same characters appear in scenes 4 and 5, and in scenes 3 and 6, and there is considerable similarity between scenes 2 and 7 (the woman of Tekoa represents

4. A. Schulz, *Erzählungskunst in den Samuel-Büchern* (Münster, 1923), p. 7.

Absalom's interests). In addition to the linear order, therefore, there
is also a chiastic order here:

(2) The woman of Tekoa—David
                    (3) David—Joab
                                    (4) Joab—Absalom
                                    (5) Absalom—Joab
                    (6) Joab—David
(7) David—Absalom

The chiastic structure exists not only in the order of the scenes but
also in the order in which the characters appear within each of the
corresponding ones. To understand the significance of the chiastic
structure here attention should be paid to the fact that Absalom
appears on both sides of the turning-point (4—5), being the second
the first time and the first the second time. This means that from
being manipulated he becomes a manipulator: Absalom, who was the
object of the efforts to bring him back to Jerusalem, despite the fact
that he was guilty of the murder of his brother, now becomes the one
to initiate matters and make demands. Accordingly Joab, who was
originally sent by David to Absalom, is now sent by Absalom to
David. And just as at the beginning the woman of Tekoa got David to
summon Joab to him (2—3), now Joab gets David to summon
Absalom to him (6—7); in both cases the summons is the expression
of the king's readiness to be reconciled (whether partially or fully)
with his son.

In most of the narratives it is possible to discern different parts or
blocks, which are somewhat similar to the acts in a play. The acts are
sometimes delimited by the location of the incidents, and sometimes
by the time at which they occur, each act taking place at a different
time or place. For example, the narrative about Abraham's servant
and Rebekah (Genesis 24) is clearly divided into two large acts, with
a prelude and a conclusion. The prelude takes place in Abraham's
house before the servant sets out on his journey, the conclusion in a
field in the Negeb, when the servant returns with Rebekah; the two
main acts take place in Mesopotamia, one beside the well and the
other in Bethuel's home. The narrative of the war between Ahab, the
king of Israel, and Ben-Haddad, the king of Syria (1 Kings 20), is
divided into two main acts separated by the words: 'And it happened
at the return of the year' (v. 26), indicating that a period of about a
year separates one act from the other.

In many instances, however, the division into acts is based on the subject matter, namely, on the central topic in the various parts of the narrative (the division by subject matter often accords with the division by place or time). For example, the narrative of the revolt against Athaliah (2 Kings 11) consists of five acts dealing with the following subjects: 1. the slaying of all the members of the royal family, except for Joash, by Athaliah; 2. the preparation of the revolt by Jehoiada; 3. the implementation of the revolt and the proclamation of Joash as king; 4. the slaying of Athaliah; 5. the making of the covenant between the Lord, the king and the people.

The narrative of Jacob's dream (Genesis 28) comprises two acts.[5] The first deals with Jacob's preparations for sleep and his dream, while the second relates his awakening and his reactions to the dream. There is a clear parallel between the two acts, which is made manifest by the use of the same words and roots:

(11) And he happened upon a certain *place*, and stayed there that night, because the sun had set. And he *took* one of the *stones* of the *place*, he *put* it under his *head* and lay down in that *place* to sleep.

(16) Then Jacob awoke from his sleep and said, 'Surely the Lord is in this *place*; and I did not know it'.

(17) And he was afraid, and said, 'How awesome is this *place*. This is none other than the house of God, and this is the gate of *heaven*'.

(12) And he dreamed that there was a ladder *standing* on the earth, and its *head* reached to *heaven*; and behold, the angels of God were ascending and descending on it.

(18) So Jacob rose early in the morning, and he *took* the *stone* which he had *put* under his *head* and *put* it up for a *standing* pillar and poured oil on its *head*.

(13) And behold, the Lord *stood* upon it. . .

(19) He called the name of that *place* Bethel. . .

(15) Behold, I am *with* you and will *keep* you wherever you go, and will *bring you back*

(20) Then Jacob made a vow, saying, 'If God will be *with* me, and will *keep* me in

5. J.P. Fokkelman, *Narrative Art in Genesis* (Assen, 1975), pp. 46ff.

to this land; for I will not
leave you until I have done
that of which I have spoken
to you.

this way that I *go*, and will
give me bread to eat and
clothing to wear.

(21) So that I *come back* to my
father's house in peace,
then the Lord shall be my
God.

(22) And this *stone*, which I
have *put* up for a *standing*
pillar, shall be God's house;
and of all that thou givest
me I will give a tenth to
thee'.

What is hinted at by so many repetitions of words and roots in the
two acts of the narrative? The word 'place' recurs three times in the
first act, and three times in the second. As if by chance, Jacob
happens on a *place* on his way from Beer-Sheba to Haran and
decides to spend the night there. But after the revelation he
recognizes and pronounces the *place* to be not just a place but the
house of God, the gate of *heaven*, which should be called Bethel
(House of God). In that place Jacob *took* a *stone*, just any stone, and
put it under his head. Jacob *takes* the same *stone* in the second act
and *puts* it up for a standing pillar, commemorating and symbolizing
the ladder he saw in his dream. The ladder was *standing* on the earth,
and the Lord *stood* upon it, and therefore Jacob puts the stone up as a
standing pillar, vertical like the ladder, between heaven and earth.[6]
The *head* of the ladder reached to *heaven*, and therefore Jacob pours
oil on the *head* of the stone-pillar which he had put under his *head*:
here is the encounter between heaven and earth, between man and
God.

God promised in the first part to be *with* him, to *keep* him
wherever he went and to *bring him back* to this land, to which Jacob
responds in the second part by making a vow that if God is *with* him,
will *keep* him on the way in which he was going and *bring him back*
in peace to his father's house, then the stone which he had put up for
a standing pillar shall be God's house, and as a sign of his gratitude
Jacob will give God a tenth of all that God gave him. Thus, there is

6. The words translated 'standing', 'stood' and 'standing pillar' are all of
the same root in Hebrew.

here a highly significant increase in the level of importance: the simple stone becomes first a pillar, and then the house of God.

The parallelism of the structure emphasizes that Jacob's actions are the counterpart of the appearance of God, and Jacob's vow echoes God's promise. God is the initiator, and man responds accordingly.

The narrative of the ten plagues (Exodus 7–12) is divided into ten acts (corresponding with the ten plagues) organized in the following way: 3/3/3/1.[7]

A	*B*	*C*	
Blood	Murrain	Hail	Slaying of
Frogs	Pestilence	Locusts	the Firstborn
Lice	Boils	Darkness	

For the first two plagues in each triad God instructs Moses to inform Pharaoh in advance, while for the third of each triad there is no prior notice. The command to inform Pharaoh in advance is worded in similar form each time:

First plague, Triad A: 'Go to Pharaoh in the morning, as he is going out to the water; stand there to meet him' (7.15).

First plague, Triad B: 'Rise up early in the morning and stand before Pharaoh, as he goes out to the water' (8.20).

First plague, Triad C: 'Rise up early in the morning and stand before Pharaoh' (9.13).

Second plague, Triad A: 'Go in to Pharaoh and say to him' (8.1), without citing time or place.

Second plague, Triad B: 'Go in to Pharaoh and say to him' (9.1), also without citing time or place.

Second plague, Triad C: 'Go in to Pharaoh' (10.1), again without citing time or place.

As stated above, the third plague of each triad is not preceded by any warning, and God tells Moses to act straightaway to bring it about.

7. M. Greenberg, 'The Redaction of the Plague Narrative in Exodus', *Near Eastern Studies in Honor of William Foxwell Albright* (Baltimore and London, 1971), pp. 243-52.

In the first triad (in the first two plagues) the magicians of Egypt can do the same things by their secret arts as Moses and Aaron did.

In the second triad (in the first two plagues) the *discrimination* between Egypt and the Israelites is stated explicitly: 'But on that day I will set apart' (8.22), 'But the Lord will make a distinction' (9.4).

In the third triad (the first two plagues) the particular severity of each plague is stressed by the phrases: 'such as never has been in Egypt from the day it was founded until now' (9.18); 'such as had never been in all the land of Egypt since it became a nation' (9.24); 'as neither your fathers nor your grandfathers have seen, from the day they came on earth to this day' (10.6); 'such a dense swarm of locusts as had never been seen before, nor ever shall be again' (10.14).

What does this special structure express? Whereas the plagues in general are intended to show God's greatness and strength, while punishing Egypt, each triad is unique in the way this central idea is evinced.

The first triad presents God's greatness and power by confronting them with the art of the magicians of Egypt. Although they can bring the plagues too, they cannot dispel them. This idea is expressed explicitly in the third plague, when as a result of their failure the Egyptian magicians admit: 'This is the finger of God' (8.19).

In the second triad God's greatness is indicated by His ability to discriminate between the Israelites and the Egyptians: 'But on that day I will set apart the land of Goshen, where my people dwell' (8.22). Thus, God's control over the forces of nature is so complete that he can bring disaster to one part of the land while protecting another area nearby.

In the third triad God's immense power is reflected by the unparalleled potency of the plagues, the like of which had never been seen before. The concept of the discrimination between the Israelites and the Egyptians is also expressed in this triad, although without the use of the verb 'set apart': 'Only in the land of Goshen, where the people of Israel were, there was no hail' (9.26); 'They did not see one another, nor did any rise from his place for three days; but all the people of Israel had light where they dwelt' (10.23).

The third triad is far longer than the first two, since each unit devoted to one plague is almost as long as the two parallel units in the first two triads combined. The length corresponds with the increased severity of the plagues.

The tenth plague is the most serious of all. Its impact is the greatest and consequently the unit describing it is far longer than those devoted to the other plagues. This plague is brought about by God Himself through direct action (not through Moses): 'For I will pass through the land of Egypt that night, and I will smite all the firstborn in the land of Egypt, both man and beast; and on all the gods of Egypt I will execute judgments: I am the Lord' (12.12). All the concepts mentioned in the previous triads appear in the tenth plague. Moses' supremacy over the magicians of Egypt is cited in the verse: 'The man Moses was very great in the land of Egypt, in the sight of Pharaoh's servants and in the sight of the people' (11.3). Of this plague it is also said: 'such as there has never been, nor ever shall be again' (v. 6), and also: 'that you may know that the Lord makes a distinction between the Egyptians and Israel' (v. 7). Thus, the tenth plague is the zenith in every respect, and this is reflected in the structure of the narrative.

A different structure occurs in the narrative of Elijah and Ahaziah, king of Israel (2 Kings 1), which is divided into three acts.

In the first act (vv. 2-8) it is reported in brief that Ahaziah fell through the lattice in his upper chamber and lay sick and that he sent messengers to ask Baalzebub, the god of Ekron, whether he would recover from that sickness. In the second act (vv. 9-15) we are told that three times the king sends 'a captain of fifty with his fifty', while in the third act (vv. 16-17) Elijah stands before the king and delivers his message: 'Thus says the Lord, "Because you have sent messengers to inquire of Baalzebub, the god of Ekron,—is it because there is no God in Israel to inquire of his word—therefore you shall not come down from the bed to which you have gone, but you shall surely die"'.

The number three is very prominent in this narrative. In the second (middle) act we find three parallel events—each time a captain of fifty is sent to Elijah—but there is, nevertheless, some development between each one. The first captain of fifty commands Elijah: 'Come down'; the second commands: 'Come down quickly', while the third begs the man of God for his life, and succeeds in bringing him to the king. This development embodies the significance underlying this narrative structure: the power of the man of God is far greater than that of the king and his cohorts. Nothing can be achieved by means of commands based on display of military strength. The use of stronger language is of no avail either, and all the soldiers lose their lives. The only approach which achieves anything is that of request or entreaty, signifying recognition of the supremacy of the man of God.

Three times—twice in the first act and once in the third act—it is said: 'Is it because there is no God in Israel... Therefore you shall not come down from the bed to which you have gone, but you shall surely die'. We first hear these words, which are intended for the king, when the angel of God transmits them to Elijah, then when they are conveyed to the king by his messengers, who heard them from Elijah, and the third time when Elijah himself communicates them to the king. This triple repetition focuses attention on this prophecy, stressing its role as the main point of the narrative. (Further emphasis of the prophecy is achieved in the narrative by other stylistic devices: putting the first part as a rhetorical question: 'Is it because there is no God in Israel?'; phrasing the second part as a disjunctive clause: 'From the bed to which you have gone you shall not come down';[8] and the metonymic-concrete portrayal of falling sick as going (up) to a bed and of being healed as coming down from it.)

The structure of the acts in the narrative of Job displays conspicuous symmetry. The introduction, giving details of the protagonist (1.1-5), precedes a scene in heaven, consisting of a conversation between God and Satan (1.6-12); this is followed by a scene on earth, dealing with the disasters which befall Job and his reaction to them (1.13-22); after this there is another scene in heaven, comprising an additional conversation between God and Satan (2.1-6); this is succeeded in turn by a further scene on earth, once again concerning a disaster which afflicts Job and his reaction to it (2.7-10); and finally, we are told about the appearance of Job's three friends, bringing the prologue to an end.

Similar symmetry is found in the act depicting the four disasters. The first and third calamities are caused by man (the Sabeans and the Chaldeans), while the second and fourth are caused by nature (fire from heaven and a great wind). Several expressions recur three or four times: 'and I alone have escaped to tell you'; 'While he was

8. Literally: 'The bed to which you have gone up, you shall not come down from it'.

yet speaking, there came another. . .' The cumulative effect of the disasters is expressed through these repetitions: each tragedy follows hard on the heels of the other, the blows fall in rapid succession, and there is no relaxation or opportunity to recover. The fourth calamity is the worst of all: in each instance, 'the young people' (*hann^e'ārîm*) are killed, but whereas in the first three they are Job's servants, in the fourth they are his children.

The second scene in heaven is very similar to the first as regards both content and language. This similarity, however, merely emphasizes the difference, since on the first occasion Satan obtains permission to harm anything that belongs to Job but not Job himself, while on the second Satan is given license to injure Job too, though not to take his life. This is a clear case of intensification. The fifth affliction, which affects Job's body, is considered to be worse than the previous four, which affected his property and his family.

There is also a parallel between what is said about Job's reactions at the end of the two acts concerning the catastrophes. On the first occasion the narrator says: 'In all this Job did not sin or charge God with wrong' (1.22); and the second time he says: 'In all this Job did not sin with his lips' (2.10). Once again, the similarity emphasizes the difference. Not only are the words 'or charge God with wrong' omitted on the second occasion, thereby weakening the statement about Job's firm stand, but the expression 'with his lips' is added. If it is said that Job did not sin with his lips, should this be regarded as a hint that he harboured sinful thoughts in his heart?[9] This interpretation is supported by the fact that the Job narrative distinguishes between sinning in one's heart and sinning with one's lips, as is indicated by 1.5: 'For Job said, "It may be that my sons have sinned, and cursed God in their hearts"'. It can, therefore, be said that despite the obvious parallels, there are evident differences which indicate significant development.

Sometimes the relation between the acts of the narrative is not a parallel or intensificatory-parallel one, as in the previous examples, but a contrastive one. The narrative of the tower of Babel (Gen. 11.1-9), for example, consists of two acts, constructed in such a way as to contrast with one another. In the first (vv. 1-4) the people act, while in the second (vv. 5-9) God acts. In the first, the people wish to build a city and a tower reaching up to heaven, while in the second God

9. *Bab. Talmud, Baba Batra*, 16a and also the Targum.

descends to earth in order to see the city and the tower. In the first, there is unity of language, and the people wish to preserve their unity by dwelling in the same place, while in the second God confuses their language and scatters them throughout the earth. This construction of the narrative is emphasized by the fact that the same words and roots are used in both acts:[10]

One language and few words	One people and one language
Let us. . . . let us	Let us
Build	And they left off building
Make a name	Its name was called Babel
Lest we be scattered abroad upon the face of the whole earth	He scattered them abroad over the face of all the earth

This structure supports the content of the narrative, dealing as it does with action and counteraction while at the same time bringing into prominence the immense difference between the two sides, man and God.

There is also a contrastive structure between the two central acts in the narrative of Elijah and the prophets of Baal on Mount Carmel (1 Kings 18). In these acts the confrontation between Elijah and the prophets of Baal, held on the basis of equal conditions, is presented: 'Let two bulls be given to us; and let them choose one bull for themselves, and cut it in pieces and lay it on the wood, but put no fire to it; and I will prepare the other bull and lay it on the wood, and put no fire to it. And you call on the name of your god, and I will call on the name of the Lord' (vv. 23-24). The parallel is also evident in the implementation (vv. 26-37):

And they took the bull. . . and they prepared it	And he cut the bull in pieces
And they called on the name of Baal	And he said: 'O Lord, God of Abraham, Isaac, and Israel
'O Baal, answer us'	Answer me, O Lord, answer me
For he is a god	Thou, O Lord, art God'

This parallel, however, merely stresses the contrast. For whereas in the act depicting the prophets of Baal (vv. 26-29) 450 people participate, in the corresponding act Elijah is on his own. And whereas the prophets of Baal use a variety of devices in order to

10. M. Buber and F. Rosenzweig, *Die Schrift und ihre Verdeutschung* (Berlin, 1936), pp. 214-17.

attain their aim, calling on the name of Baal from morning until noon, limping about the altar, even cutting themselves with swords and lances until they bleed, Elijah simply makes one short prayer. Nevertheless, the prophets of Baal are not answered, while Elijah is. This, after all, was the object of the entire 'contest': 'The God who answers by fire, he is God' (v. 24).

There are additional differences between the two contrastively parallel acts. Not only can the prophets of Baal choose the bull they prefer, but Elijah also gives instructions to pour a large amount of water on his burnt offering and on the wood until even the trench around the altar is full. Nevertheless, the fire which descends at Elijah's request is so powerful that it consumes not only the burnt offering and the wood but also the stones, the dust and the water in the trench. In this way the omnipotence and undeniable supremacy of God is offset against Baal's ineffectualness.

B. *The Stages of the Plot*

The situation existing at the beginning of the action is presented in what is usually called the exposition. This serves as an introduction to the action described in the narrative, supplying the background information, introducing the characters, informing us of their names, traits, physical appearance, state in life and the relations obtaining among them, and providing the other details needed for understanding the story.

In many cases it is unnecessary to communicate preliminary information of this kind, since the facts serving as background to the story are known to the audience. This is probably the reason why background information that seems indispensable to the present-day reader is often lacking in biblical narratives. The reader or listener in biblical times could draw the background material from the traditions known to him about persons and events from the past, or even from the realities of his own life and culture, whereas the contemporary reader often encounters serious difficulties in understanding the story precisely because this information is absent.

In some cases the facts cited in the exposition, or the way they are presented, hint at later developments in the plot. For example, at the beginning of the narrative of Cain and Abel (Genesis 4), the two protagonists are introduced to the reader and information is given about them in chiastic fashion:

> And she conceived and bore *Cain*
> And again, she bore his brother *Abel*
> Now *Abel* was a keeper of sheep
> And *Cain* was a tiller of the ground

This structure hints at the contrast and conflict between the two brothers, which is immediately made clear in the verses which follow, also arranged chiastically:

> *Cain* brought to the Lord an offering of the fruit of the ground
> And *Abel* brought of the firstlings of his flock and of their fat portions
> And the Lord had regard for *Abel* and his offering
> But for *Cain* and his offering he had no regard.

Eli's two sons are mentioned at the beginning of the narrative of the birth of Samuel, though they play no part in the actual narrative: 'Now this man used to go up year by year from his city to worship and to sacrifice to the Lord of hosts at Shiloh, where the two sons of Eli, Hophni and Phinehas, were priests of the Lord' (1 Sam. 1.3). The fact that Eli's two sons are mentioned at this point appears to indicate that Samuel, whose birth is recounted in this narrative, will eventually take their place, and that it is he, not they, who will inherit Eli's position. This is proved in the following chapter (2), when the decline of Eli's sons is recounted *alternately* with Samuel's ascent.

There are two basic methods in organizing narratives for bringing expositional material to the reader's knowledge. One is to concentrate all preliminary information at the beginning, and the other is to reveal it gradually in the course of the narrative. For although the expositional information refers to the situation existing at the outset of the action, or even to previous events, it is by no means necessary to locate it at the beginning of the narrative. Both methods are represented in biblical narrative. When deferred to later phases, the expositional information may be disseminated either directly by the narrator or indirectly by means of the characters.

An example of background information about the setting which is placed at the beginning is found in the narrative of Jacob and Rachel: 'for out of that well the flocks were watered. The stone on the well's mouth was large, and when all the flocks were gathered there, the shepherds would roll the stone from the mouth of the well and water the sheep, and put the stone back in its place upon the mouth of the well' (Gen. 29.2-3).

Another example occurs in the narrative of the conquest of Jericho: 'Now Jericho was shut up from within and from without because of the people of Israel; none went out and none came in' (Josh. 6.1).

Again, in the narrative of Saul and the medium at Endor: 'Now Samuel had died, and all Israel had mourned for him and buried him in Ramah, his own city. And Saul had put the mediums and the wizards out of the land' (1 Sam. 28.3).

In many instances the characters are introduced at the beginning of the narrative:

Now Sarai, Abram's wife, bore him no children. She had an Egyptian maid whose name was Hagar (Gen. 16.1).

Now Jephthah the Gileadite was a mighty warrior, but he was the son of a harlot. Gilead was the father of Jephthah. And Gilead's wife also bore him sons, and when his wife's sons grew up, they thrust Jephthah out, and said to him: 'You shall not inherit in our father's house: for you are the son of another woman'. Then Jephthah fled from his brothers, and dwelt in the land of Tob; and worthless fellows collected round Jephthah, and went raiding with him (Judg. 11.1-3).

There was a certain man of Ramathaim-Zophim of the hill country of Ephraim, whose name was Elkanah the son of Jeroham, son of Elihu, son of Tohu, son of Zuph, an Ephraimite. He had two wives; the name of the one was Hannah, and the name of the other Peninnah. And Peninnah had children, but Hannah had no children (1 Sam. 1.1-2).

There was a man of Benjamin whose name was Kish, the son of Abiel, son of Zeror, son of Becorath, son of Aphiah, a Benjaminite, a man of wealth; and he had a son whose name was Saul, a handsome young man. There was not a man among the people of Israel more handsome than he, from his shoulders upward he was taller than any of the people (1 Sam. 9.1-2).

And there was a man in Maon, whose business was in Carmel. The man was very rich; he had three thousand sheep and a thousand goats. He was shearing his sheep in Carmel. Now the name of the man was Nabal, and the name of his wife Abigail. The woman was of good understanding and beautiful, but the man was churlish and ill-behaved; he was a Calebite (1 Sam. 25.2-3).

There was a man in the land of Uz, whose name was Job; and that man was blameless and upright, one who feared God and turned away from evil. There were born to him seven sons and three daughters. He had seven thousand sheep, three thousand camels, five hundred yoke of oxen and five hundred she-asses, and very many servants; so that the man was the greatest of all the people of the east (Job 1.1-3).

It might perhaps be claimed that in the instance of Jephthah the verses recounting his being thrust out by his brothers, his fleeing to the land of Tob and his going out raiding with the worthless fellows who had collected round him belong less to the exposition than to the part of the narrative dealing with the action proper. This contention could be based on the fact that these verses do not contain elementary information about the initial situation, but refer to specific happenings and even include direct speech ('You shall not inherit in our father's house; for you are the son of another woman'). Nevertheless, the verses under consideration do in fact constitute part of the exposition, because the events of Jephthah's past mentioned in them do not appertain to the subject treated in the narrative, which is Jephthah's victory over the Ammonites. In this instance, moreover, the exposition is also clearly marked off from the main part of the narrative by the phrase *wayhî miyyāmîm* ('After a time', or more literally, 'It was after many days'), just as in the case of Job the delimitation of the exposition is indicated in a formal way by the phrase *wayhî hayyôm* ('Now there was a day').

In view of the well-known economy of expression characteristic of biblical narrative, however, and the tendency to include only essential details, the question arises—why are events from Jephthah's past mentioned in the exposition? The answer seems to be that in this way the plight of the people and leaders of Gilead is emphasized. The elders of Gilead appear to be in such a precarious position that they have to beseech a man who is the son of a harlot, who has been driven out of his home and has become chief of a band of worthless fellows, to lead the war against the Ammonites. They even have to promise the outcast to make him head and leader of the people of Gilead. By stressing the almost hopeless situation at the outset, the subsequent victory, or God's act of deliverance, is made more glorious and impressive.

It should be emphasized that in general no information is included in the exposition which does not have a definite function in the development of the action (with the exception perhaps of the genealogies, which seem unimportant to us but were of considerable significance to the people in biblical times).

For instance, in the last two examples (Nabal and Job), the material circumstances of the heroes are described in some detail. In the case of Nabal his great wealth makes his parsimony and inhospitality to David and his men stand out more conspicuously. In this connection attention should be paid to the way the facts are organized within the exposition. It is evident from the examples given above that a more or less similar pattern is often found, consisting of an opening phrase such as 'there was a man', followed by details concerning his dwelling-place or tribe, his name and finally his traits, family, possessions, etc. Not all these details are always given, but the order in which they are arranged is generally invariable. In the case of Nabal, however, the order is different. Details about his property come before his name (and the name of his wife and their traits). Nabal's wealth is probably given pride of place in order to hint at its significance for the central theme.

In the case of Job the description of his vast property has a dual function: on the one hand, his possessions should be regarded as a reward for his righteousness, according to the doctrine of retribution, while on the other, the loss of all his possessions in one day serves as a test of his virtue. The reference to Job's seven sons and three daughters also fulfils a twofold purpose: first they are regarded as Job's reward and subsequently they are the instrument of his trial. In the exposition concerning Nabal no sons or daughters are mentioned because they have no function in the action of the story.

It should also be noted that in most cases where details concerning characters or background are communicated at the beginning of the narrative, they connect *immediately* and organically with the account of the events themselves. In other words, there is a direct and smooth transition from the exposition to that part of the narrative which is concerned with the actual developments.

For instance, following the information in the exposition that Sarai, Abram's wife, bore him no children and that she had an Egyptian maid whose name was Hagar, it is stated immediately: 'And Sarai said to Abram, "Behold now, the Lord has prevented me from bearing children; go in to my maid, it may be that I shall obtain children by her"' (Gen. 16.2).

Similarly, immediately after informing us that a man of Benjamin named Kish had an excellent son whose name was Saul, the narrator continues: 'Now the asses of Kish, Saul's father, were lost. So Kish said to Saul his son, "Take one of the servants with you and arise, go and look for the asses"' (1 Sam. 9.3).

The information included in the exposition at the beginning of the narrative thus serves as a natural point of departure for the action itself. Instances such as the one mentioned above, where we learn at the beginning of the narrative of Saul and the medium of Endor, that Samuel had died and that Saul had put the mediums and the wizards out of the land (1 Sam. 28.3), are exceptions to the rule, because here the exposition is followed by many facts concerning the action which have no direct bearing on either Samuel's death or the fact that the mediums and wizards were put out of the land. Only at a later point in the narrative are we informed that Saul himself had recourse to a medium, requesting her to conjure up Samuel, and that she replied: 'Surely you know what Saul has done, how he has cut off the mediums and the wizards from the land' (1 Sam. 28.9).

We are informed twice of the fact that Saul cut off the mediums and the wizards from the land, once by the narrator in the exposition and once by the medium, resulting in redundancy (Samuel's death is also recorded twice, here and in 25.1). Repetitions of this kind occur quite often in biblical narrative. It is indeed rare for information that does not occur in the main part of the story to be included in the exposition. In most cases details concerning characters and background which appeared in the exposition at the beginning are reiterated in the body of the narrative, mentioned by either the author or one of the characters.

What is the object of these repetitions? There is no single answer to this question and each instance should be examined on its merits. In many cases, however, the repetition serves to stress some matter of importance in the story. The double reference to Saul's removal of the mediums and wizards from the land, in the example under consideration, brings into focus the sharp contrast between Saul's act in the past and his present undertaking, when he secretly makes use of the services of a medium himself. The contrast points up the desperate condition in which Saul finds himself and the steep decline in his fortunes.[11]

Information contained in the exposition is also repeated in the

11. M. Weiss, 'The Craft of Biblical Narrative', *Molad* (1962), pp. 169-70 (Hebrew).

narrative of Jacob and Rachel (Genesis 29). The narrator informs us at the outset that only when all the flocks had been gathered would the stone be rolled away from the mouth of the well to water the sheep. The same is recounted by the shepherds themselves: 'We cannot until all the flocks are gathered together, and the stone is rolled from the mouth of the well; then we water the sheep' (Gen. 29.8).

Here, too, the repetition serves to draw the reader's attention to an important point. Immediately after the shepherds' words we are told: 'When Jacob saw Rachel, the daughter of Laban his mother's brother, and the sheep of Laban his mother's brother, Jacob went up and rolled the stone from the well's mouth and watered the flock of Laban his mother's brother' (Gen. 29.10). It is stated three times that Laban is his mother's brother, implying that it was Jacob's love for his mother's relatives (the very close relationship between Jacob and his mother is made clear more than once in the previous chapters) that caused him to go up and roll the stone single-handed from the mouth of the well.

Thus, it can be concluded that rather than supplying knowledge required for understanding the story—which is also usually conveyed in subsequent sections of the narrative—the information in the exposition frequently serves to emphasize matters of importance or to hint at implied meanings.

As stated above, information about the characters and the background may be communicated in the body of the narrative only, as is the case in a great many instances.

In the narrative of the wooing of Rebekah (Genesis 24), for example, we make Rebekah's acquaintance not at the beginning but only when she appears near the well where Abraham's servant is stationed. The moment the servant sees her she is introduced by the narrator: 'behold, Rebekah, who was born to Bethuel the son of Milcah, the wife of Nahor, Abraham's brother, came out with her water jar upon her shoulder. The maiden was very fair to look upon, a virgin, whom no man had known' (Gen. 24.15-16).

This method of presenting characters is similar to the way we get to know people in real life. We sometimes obtain preliminary information about people before we actually meet them (corresponding to the exposition at the *beginning* of the narrative), but in most cases we learn about them through having direct contact with them. The biblical narrator frequently makes use of this technique of introducing people and mentioning background details *in their proper place*, that is, at the point when they are discerned by the chief characters or become important as regards the development of the plot.

Thus, the narrator informs us that Eglon, the king of Moab, was a very fat man at the precise moment that Ehud, the son of Gera, who had come to present the tribute, saw him and observed his physical appearance (Judg. 3.17). We hear that there was peace between Jabin, the king of Hazor, and the house of Heber the Kenite at the point in the narrative when we are told that Sisera fled to the tent of Jael, Heber's wife. We understand from this that Sisera had no reason to fear or suspect Jael (Judg. 4.17).

Similarly, only after Saul's death do we learn that he had a concubine named Rizpah, the daughter of Aiah, when Ishbosheth, Saul's son, reproaches Abner, the commander of the army, for having gone in to his father's concubine (2 Sam. 3.7). As a result of this rebuke Abner decides to go over to David and transfer Saul's entire kingdom to him.

In the narrative of David and Bathsheba the new characters are not introduced at the beginning either. We meet them in the course of the story, at the same time that David does. As a result of this technique we see Bathsheba at the same moment that David first catches sight of her and we realize that she is beautiful together with David: 'he saw from the roof a woman bathing; and the woman was very beautiful' (2 Sam. 11.2). The word order here corresponds with the order of the process of perception: first David sees a woman bathing, and then discovers that she is very beautiful. This does not mean that Bathsheba is beautiful only in David's subjective view. The narrator tells us about Bathsheba's beauty as an objective fact, but we become aware of it together with David and through his eyes.

This also applies to the woman's name. Her identity is a mystery to us, as it is to David observing her from his roof. Only when her name is revealed to David does it become known to us: 'And David sent and inquired about the woman. And one said: "Is not this Bathsheba, the daughter of Eliam, the wife of Uriah the Hittite?"' (2 Sam. 11.3). The anonymous servant who tells David of her identity and family relations gives us the information at the same time.

This technique fits in with the overall design of the narrative, in which Bathsheba has no status of her own, performs no actions and does not take part in any conversations. In fact, she does not speak at all, except for the two words *hārâ 'ānokî* ('I am with child'), which are important to David no less than to her. She is completely passive and her feelings are not described, whether directly or indirectly. Contrary to Hannah and Abigail, who are introduced at the beginning of the narratives concerning them (1 Samuel 1 and 25), Bathsheba does not attain independence or assume importance in her own right in this narrative, any more than do Eglon or Saul's concubine in the instances just mentioned.

In many cases a combination of the two methods is used: part of the information about the characters and the background is imparted at the beginning and part at later stages of the narrative.

In the narrative of Jacob and Rachel (Genesis 29) the narrator informs us at the beginning that only when all the flocks were gathered would the shepherds roll the stone from the mouth of the well (vv. 2-3). Rachel, who plays a passive role in this story, is introduced only in the course of the narrative, when she comes to the well with her father's sheep and is seen by Jacob (vv. 9-10). The narrator does not tell us that she is beautiful when she first appears, stating only that she is the daughter of Jacob's mother's brother. Consequently, it is not her beauty that inspires Jacob to roll the stone away from the well single-handed but, as noted above, the fact that she is a relative of his mother's. Rachel's beauty is mentioned only when Jacob asks for her hand and expresses his willingness to serve seven years for her. The reference to her beauty at this point explains why Jacob fell in love with Rachel and not with her sister Leah, whose eyes were weak (vv. 17-18).

In the narrative about Samuel's call (1 Samuel 3) we are informed at the beginning: 'The word of the Lord was rare in those days; there was no frequent vision' (v. 1). Afterwards it is stated that: 'Samuel did not yet know the Lord and the word of the Lord had not yet been revealed to him' (v. 7). In this instance the narrator gives us general background information at the beginning of the narrative and specific background information later on. The general information serves to explain why neither Samuel nor Eli understood that the voice calling Samuel was the voice of the Lord. The specific information clarifies why Samuel did not understand even the third time that it was the Lord, not Eli, who had called him (whereas Eli understood by this time), and that is why the information is located at this point, between God's second and third call to Samuel.

The narrative of David and Goliath (1 Samuel 17) has two distinct blocks of exposition. The first is located at the outset and provides general background information about the battle between Israel and the Philistines, particularly as regards the geographical and topographical positions of the two hostile camps. This block passes quickly into a detailed description of Goliath and his arms.

The second block of exposition, introducing David and his family is placed after the account of Goliath's insulting challenge and the panic it aroused in the camp of Israel. It has often been observed that this introduction is largely superfluous, since we have already made David's acquaintance in the previous chapter, where his physical appearance is described at the very moment that Samuel sees him for the first time (1 Sam. 16.12) and in approximately the same terms as are used at the point when Goliath catches sight of him (1 Sam. 17.42). This redundant introduction of David (which is missing in codex B of the Septuagint) is usually explained as being due to the fact that the narrative about David and Goliath in chapter 17 was originally independent of the stories in chapter 16 concerning David's anointing and his entering Saul's service in a musical and military capacity.

The problem which concerns us here, however, is a different one. Assuming that the narrative of David and Goliath was indeed originally independent and that it was therefore necessary to include an introduction of David in it, the question arises why this was not placed at the beginning. According to the present arrangement, there is an abrupt break in the thread of the narrative at the conclusion of the passage dealing with Goliath (v. 11), and a new start is made when David and his family are introduced. This break could easily have been avoided. It would have been far more 'natural' and the transitions much smoother if the narrative had started with the necessary expositional information about the protagonist, his father and his three elder brothers who followed Saul to battle, had continued with Jesse's instruction to take a supply of food to his brothers in the army, and had told about Goliath, his physical appearance, military equipment and challenge to Israel only at the moment when he was seen by David, who had come to find his brothers in the Israelite camp.

What is gained by the way the narrative material is arranged, though at the expense of the smooth and uninterrupted flow of the story, is that the frightening and paralysing effect of Goliath's appearance is presented in a much bolder and impressive way. This is achieved because Goliath's appearance is the first topic treated both extensively and as a primary and independent subject, and not as something subsidiary to David's performance (as in vv. 23ff.). Moreover, by placing the description of Goliath at the beginning and delaying the introduction of David to a later stage, the reader is kept aware of the tense situation for a relatively long stretch of narration time, and is made to sense the persisting atmosphere of panic and powerlessness among the Israelites, until the hero, who is to fight the terrifying enemy, finally appears on the scene.

The same purpose, namely, keeping the reader constantly aware of the threat posed by Goliath, is also served by verse 16, which is effective because of the combination of its content and its position in the text. This verse crops up rather unexpectedly in the middle of the passage devoted to David and his family, or to be more precise, between the exposition and the beginning of the action concerning David and his relatives. It informs us that: 'For forty days the Philistine came forward and took his stand, morning and evening'.

This presentation of Goliath and his impact upon Israel is clearly intended to enhance David's triumph over the Philistine champion.

Thus, in several instances expositional information is placed at the beginning of the narrative; when this is so, the information is usually repeated in one way or another during the course of the story, with the result that a certain point receives emphasis. In some cases the information is imparted only during the unfolding of the story, at the natural point in the development of the plot, in which case it may refer to a passive or minor character. In a number of instances, moreover, part of the information is conveyed at the beginning and part in the course of the narrative, in accordance with the function it has to perform in each particular case.

The plot develops from an initial situation through a chain of events to a central occurrence, which is the prime factor of change, and thence by means of varying incidents to a final situation. If we were to sketch the line connecting these two situations, with its ups and downs, we would have a graphic depiction of the plot.

We usually find the classic pattern in biblical narrative: the plot line ascends from a calm point of departure through the stage of involvement to the climax of conflict and tension, and from there rapidly to the finishing point and tranquillity. This line of development is found, amongst other places, in the narrative of the sacrifice of Isaac (Genesis 22).

This narrative begins by posing the question which constitutes the basis of the tension. The narrator informs us that God is testing Abraham, and the reader begins to wonder whether Abraham will pass this difficult trial and whether he will sacrifice his only son, born to him after so many years of waiting. The narrative gradually brings the reader to the climactic point. First we are told about Abraham's preparations for sacrificing his son, how he sets out on his journey and all that happens until he reaches the designated spot. Here the narrator relates in detail everything Abraham does in order to fulfil the divine command: he builds the altar, arranges the wood, binds Isaac and places him on the wood. The narrative reaches its peak when Abraham puts out his hand and takes the knife in order to slay his son. The turning point comes at the very moment that the tension reaches its height: an angel of the Lord calls to Abraham from heaven, and at the very last moment the terrible deed is prevented. From here the line of the plot descends rapidly. Abraham hears the angel's reassuring words, sees a ram and sacrifices that instead of his son, and after the angel speaks to him again, Abraham returns to his young men and they all go home together. Everything appears to be the same as before, but as a matter of fact a very great change has occurred, though it is an internal one: Abraham has actually come through an extremely difficult test, having proved his readiness to sacrifice his dearest treasure to God, and this makes the final situation completely different from the initial one.

The plot of the book of Esther is far longer and more complicated than that of the sacrifice of Isaac. At the centre of the Esther narrative is the clash between the two opponents, Mordecai and Haman. Haman decides to kill all the Jews in the kingdom and obtains the king's agreement for this, while Mordecai attempts to avert the disaster with Esther's help. The conflict between the two rivals will reach its peak, it is to be expected, at the banquet which Esther has arranged. The decision is postponed, however. Haman erects the gallows on which he intends to hang Mordecai and the tension increases. The turning point occurs at the second banquet, when the king grows angry with Haman and orders him to be hanged. Esther is given Haman's house, Mordecai is appointed the king's minister instead of Haman and the Jews are given license to smite their enemies.

The book of Esther contains a sub-plot alongside the main one. After Esther has been made queen and before Haman is appointed minister to the king, Mordecai discloses to Ahasuerus that two of his eunuchs have been plotting to assassinate the king, and this is recorded in the book of chronicles. On the night between the first and the second banquets the book is read to the king, who commands that Mordecai be honoured and that Haman be the one to implement this. The great honour done to Mordecai, and the humiliation of Haman this involves, take place shortly before the turning-point in the main plot and both presage and reinforce it. This turning-point is the central issue of the plot of the book of Esther.

In both the examples given above the pattern of the plot is characterized not only by a line which ascends to the decisive point and descends from it rapidly, but also by a turning point in the development of the plot, occurring at the place where the tension reaches its height. These changes of direction in the plot are not rare in biblical narrative.

For example, in the narrative of Jacob's return home after working for Laban for twenty years (Genesis 31–33), emphasis is placed on the fact that Jacob is very apprehensive at meeting Esau because of the deception he used in the past in order to obtain Isaac's blessing. Esau wanted to kill him then (27.41) and Jacob was forced to flee abroad. While he is returning, Jacob hears that Esau is coming towards him with four hundred men, and he is so terror-stricken that he decides to divide all his belongings into two camps, for: 'If Esau comes to the one company and destroys it, then the company which is left will escape' (Gen. 32.8). Jacob also prays to God to save him from his brother, as well as sending many flocks to him as a present, leaving a space between each flock, in the hope that Esau's anger will be assuaged before the encounter with Jacob. Despite all these actions, Jacob is extremely anxious on the last night before the meeting, as is evident from the episode of his struggle with a man till dawn. In the morning Jacob sees Esau coming with the four hundred men and, fearing the worst, also divides his wives and children into two camps. Then he approaches Esau, bowing himself to the ground seven times as he does so. At the crucial moment Esau runs towards him, but, contrary to expectations, falls on Jacob's neck and embraces and kisses him (33.4). It transpires that Esau no longer harbours resentment and the brothers are reconciled.

Another example of a turning point of this kind can be found in the narrative of David and Abigail (1 Samuel 25). David, angered by Nabal's reply, sets out with four hundred armed men in order to attack Nabal. Abigail, Nabal's wife, goes out to meet David in an attempt to prevent him from wreaking his vengeance, bearing many gifts. Just before the decisive meeting the narrator returns to David and tells us his thoughts: 'Now David had said, "Surely in vain have I guarded all that this fellow has in the wilderness, so that nothing was missed of all that belonged to him; and he has returned me evil for good. God do so to David and more also, if by morning I leave so much as one male of all who belong to him"' (vv. 21-22). The communication of David's intentions at this moment shows us clearly how the story line is developing towards a climax of violent revenge. David has made up his mind to destroy everything that belongs to Nabal, even giving his decision the force of an oath. At the meeting between David and Abigail, which is recounted immediately afterwards, Abigail succeeds in altering David's plan, and this serves as the turning point of the story. David relinquishes his ideas of vengeance and Nabal is punished by God.

Another structural feature of several biblical narratives which determines the pattern of the plot is that of the illusory conclusion. In contrast to the previous examples, where the story line gradually rises to a climax and then descends rapidly to the serene conclusion, here the narrative does not end after the gradual ascent and the rapid decline but rises once more to another pinnacle, only then descending to the genuine conclusion.

A structure of this kind can be found in the narrative of Isaac's blessing (Genesis 27). Jacob pretends to be Esau in order to obtain his father's blessing, and the question is, will his deception succeed or will it be discovered? The uncertainty on this point is the primary cause of suspense in this narrative. Jacob himself expresses this uncertainty already at the planning stage: 'Perhaps my father will feel me, and I shall seem to be mocking him, and bring a curse upon myself and not a blessing' (v. 12). The tension rises when Jacob goes to his father and says hesitantly: 'My father' (v. 18). It is further heightened when Isaac asks him: 'Who are you, my son?' and Jacob answers with a blatant lie: 'I am Esau your first-born' (v. 19). The suspense increases even more when Isaac expresses surprise that his son has returned from hunting so quickly, and reaches its peak when Isaac feels his son in order to ascertain: 'Are you really my son Esau or not?' (v. 21). After the physical examination at close quarters has not resulted in the deception being discovered (even though the voice arouses Isaac's suspicions), and particularly after Isaac has given

Jacob the desired blessing, the tension drops and tranquillity is achieved. But the narrative does not end here. No sooner has Jacob gone out than Esau enters, and the suspense increases once more. Calmness is achieved again only after Jacob has left home and physical distance has been established between the brothers. Complete serenity, however, is attained only after the final reconciliation between Jacob and Esau, twenty years later.

A similar line of development with a renewed ascent after the descent to the point of calmness can also be found in the book of Job. The tension in this narrative derives from the uncertainty as to whether Job will pass the trial. The suspense reaches its height with the reports of the four calamities which befall him, especially the last one (the death of all his children at one fell swoop). Job's response, indicating his firm stand and continuing righteousness, leads us to the point of relaxation (end of chapter 1). At this point, with the proof that Job has preserved his integrity, the narrative could come to an end. The plot flares up again, however, when an additional disaster overtakes Job. Once again he emerges successfully from his trial, but the final tranquillity is not attained until the last chapter of the book, when God restores Job's fortunes, giving him twice as much as he had beforehand (42.10).

On occasions the plot of biblical narratives is built in such a way as to create ironic situations. This is dramatic irony, which derives from the fact that the character knows less than the reader, or unknowingly does things which are not in his or her own best interests, or from the course of events leading to results which are the reverse of the character's aspirations.

Irony is sometimes embodied in an event and sometimes in an utterance of one of the characters. Even when it is spoken, however, we are not dealing with verbal irony here (for verbal irony see below, p. 210), since the ironic expression is used knowingly and with forethought and the individual concerned is not aware of the irony of what he or she says. The character speaks in all innocence, while the author, who is after all responsible for the way the character phrases the words, gives them an ironic flavour.

Dramatic irony has a variety of functions, such as expressing criticism, stressing a shocking event or emphasizing a tragic situation, to name but a few. Dramatic irony sometimes serves as a vehicle for the view that justice rules the world and that everyone receives just deserts, in contrast to the distorted view held by the character concerned.

To illustrate this, examples of dramatic irony will be given from three narratives: David and Bathsheba,[12] Absalom's revolt and the story of Esther.

When Uriah answers David's question: 'Why did you not go down to your house?' by saying: 'The ark and Israel and Judah dwell in booths; and my lord Joab and the servants of my lord are camping in the open field; shall I then go to my house, to eat and to drink, and to lie with my wife? As you live and as your soul lives, I shall not do this thing!' (2 Sam. 11.11), he is not aware of the ironic sting in his words (assuming that Uriah does not know what happened between his wife and David while he was absent from Jerusalem). To all intents and purposes Uriah simply compares his conditions with those of his comrades in the field, declaring that he will not enjoy any privilege which they cannot share. The sting, however, lies in the fact that an implicit comparison is made between his behaviour and David's. Uriah asserts that he will not go to lie with his wife, and that is precisely what David has been doing! The emphasis of the personal pronoun in the Hebrew ('Shall *I* then go') implies: *I* will not go to lie with my wife, but *you* lay with my wife. What David did is, of course, far more serious than what Uriah refuses to do, because Uriah does not wish to lie with his own wife, while David lay with Uriah's.

The reader senses the additional (ironic) meaning in what Uriah says because of the many ways his words are emphasized. First of all, Uriah's refusal is stated not once but twice. Secondly, on the first occasion it is expressed not as a declarative sentence but as a rhetorical question, which is a clearly emphatic device. Thirdly, the second time the refusal is phrased as an oath, which is another way of reinforcing its content.

Uriah uses the phrase 'this thing', which is vague and ambiguous, and because of its indefinite nature both denotes the deed which Uriah will not do—the 'thing' which is mentioned explicitly—and hints at what David actually did, the 'thing' which is implied (cf. vv. 25, 27). The subtle irony reaches its zenith when Uriah swears by David's life, namely, by the life of the man who did just what he will not do. It is true that it was quite common to swear by the king's life,

12. M. Perry and M. Sternberg, 'The King through Ironic Eyes—The Narrator's Devices in the Story of David and Bathsheba and Two Excursuses on the Theory of Narrative Text', *Hasifrut* 1 (1968/69) (Hebrew).

but David's life is mentioned here twice: 'As you live, and as your soul lives. . . ' and this double expression is unique in the Bible, drawing our attention to the irony of Uriah's oath.

It is also ironic that it is by his honesty and adherence to his principles, his lord and his comrades that Uriah brings about his own undoing. The fact that Uriah is the bearer of his own death-warrant is particularly poignant in its irony. It is also ironic that the king's wrath at the great number of his servants killed in the battle at Rabbah of the Ammonites can be assuaged by the news that his servant Uriah the Hittite is also among the dead. It would be thought that information of this kind would depress someone's spirits still more.

In all these instances the irony serves to give prominence to David's culpability. David is guilty of having sentenced Uriah to die because of his loyalty, of having made him the bearer of his own death-warrant and of allowing his anger to be mollified by the news of Uriah's death. The irony seems to indicate that not only did David sin, but that he did it with unmitigated cynicism.

A distinctly ironic situation is also created when David unknowingly passes sentence on himself when he thinks that he is condemning the rich man who, according to the prophet Nathan, took the poor man's ewe-lamb away from him (2 Sam. 12.5-6).

We also find several instances of irony in the narrative of Absalom's revolt. Absalom asks for David's permission to go to Hebron to pay his vow, and David's reply: 'Go in peace' (2 Sam. 15.9) certainly has no ironic intent. There is irony in it, nevertheless, because Absalom's designs are by no means peaceful, and because the outcome of that journey is not peace but disaster, for both David and Absalom. These are, in fact, the last words David ever says to Absalom. In this case, too, the irony serves to express concealed and indirect criticism. David does not know that Absalom's intentions are not peaceful, but should he not have known? Should not the king have suspected his son, who had made himself a chariot and horses and fifty men to run before him, and who for years had risen early and stood by the way of the gate in order to steal the allegiance of anyone coming to the king for justice? David's naïvety and lack of insight into Absalom's character are simply astonishing here, just as they were on a previous occasion, when Absalom planned his revenge on Amnon for several years and David remained blithely unaware. On that occasion, too, David agreed to Absalom's request to let Amnon go with him, and then also blessed him before he went (13.25-27).

In the last examples irony serves to stress the *extent* of the disaster as well as to criticize. The function of the irony in 2 Sam. 18.27 is also to give prominence to the depth of the tragedy: 'And the watchman said, "I think the running of the foremost is like the running of Ahimaaz the son of Zadok". And the king said, "He is a good man, and comes with good tidings"'. A few minutes later it transpires that the 'good tidings' are the news of his son's death.

Ahimaaz does in fact bring good tidings. He begins by saying, 'All is well', and then goes on to report: 'The Lord. . . . has delivered up the men who raised their hand against my lord the king' (v. 28), and he is not the one to tell the king that his son is dead. There is evident irony here, because the news of Absalom's death, which is brought immediately afterwards by the Cushite, completely overshadows Ahimaaz' information about the victory in battle. The good news simply momentarily postpones the bad, which is the main point as far as David is concerned. The fact that first good tidings are delivered heightens the irony, since for an instant it seems that David's expectations were justified. The crucial, bad news also casts an ironic light on Ahimaaz' first words 'All is well', which appear to confirm David's anticipation of good tidings (though Ahimaaz himself had no intention of speaking ironically). In this instance the irony is far more subtle than in the similar one in 1 Kgs 1.42: 'And Adonijah said, "Come in, for you are a worthy man and bring good news"', where an immediate and obvious contrast is created between the expected good tidings and the bad news which is in fact delivered.

In all these examples, the (dramatic) irony derives from the fact that there is a contrast between the situation as perceived or hoped for by the character involved and the actual state of affairs. In the last examples, the actual situation is known to the reader but not to the character, and therefore the reader is immediately aware of the irony of what is said.

The irony of fate, which is a kind of dramatic irony, is encountered in the circumstances of Absalom's death. Absalom, who took such extraordinary pride in his hair, eventually dies because of it. 'Absalom was proud of his hair, and therefore was hung by his hair', said the Rabbis (Mishnah, *Sota* 1.8), regarding this as a manifestation of the principle of just deserts.

The same kind of irony presents itself in the fact that Absalom, who set up a memorial for himself in the Valley of the King during his lifetime, is thrown after his death into a great pit in the forest (2 Sam. 18.17-18).

The function of the irony in these cases is to highlight the connections between cause and consequence, between the individual's aspirations and what actually happens, and between character and fate.

There are several instances of dramatic irony in the book of Esther, all of them aimed at Haman and serving to make him appear ridiculous. The irony begins with Haman being joyful and glad of heart at being invited to Esther's banquet and boasting of the honour involved: 'Even queen Esther let no one come with the king to the banquet she prepared but myself. And tomorrow also I am invited by her together with the king' (Esth. 5.12), never imagining that Esther is a member of the Jewish people he hates so much and that she is related to Mordecai, his mortal enemy.

Haman's mistaken assumption that there is no one whom the king would like to honour more than himself (6.6) also gives rise to a highly ironic situation. Haman himself causes Mordecai to be greatly honoured, and in addition he, Haman, has to implement it, leading Mordecai on the king's horse through the streets of the city, and calling out: 'Thus shall it be done to the man whom the king delights to honour' (6.11).

An ironic situation is also created through the king's mistaken supposition that Haman intends to assault the queen in his presence and in his own house when in actual fact Haman is merely pleading with Esther to spare his life (7.7-8). Once again the victim of the error is Haman.

Similarly, there is considerable irony in the fact that Haman is himself hung on the gallows he has prepared for Mordecai (7.9-10), as well as in the fact that the person who inherits Haman is none other than his rival, Mordecai. Through his plan to kill all the Jews, Haman in effect causes his own death and the promotion of Mordecai the Jew. This ironic course of events reflects the view that there is justice in the world, that the wicked are punished and the righteous rewarded.

As stated above, the narrative reaches a point of calmness at the end, the tension drops, the story-line descends and life returns to its former pace and daily routine.

The conclusion is clearly marked in many biblical narratives. For example, if we are told at the beginning or during the course of a narrative that someone leaves home and goes elsewhere, it is frequently stated at the end of the narrative that the person returns home, thus giving the reader the feeling that the incident is over.[13] A few examples are given below.

In 1 Sam. 16.1-13 we are informed that Samuel goes to Bethlehem in order to anoint David king there. At first Samuel thinks that one of Jesse's other sons is meant to be king, but in the end he anoints the right one. The incident ends at this point, and then we find the concluding phrase: 'And Samuel rose up, and went to Ramah'.

The tale of Saul's visit to the medium at Endor is told in 1 Samuel 28. The woman summons up Samuel's spirit, Saul is greatly alarmed by what Samuel says and falls full length on the ground, and finally the woman gives Saul and his servants food in order to strengthen them. The narrative ends with the statement: 'Then they rose and went away that night'.

We are told of the revolt of Sheba the son of Bichri in 2 Sam. 20.1-22. The narrative ends with Sheba's death, and the concluding words are: 'And they retired from the city, every man to his tent, and Joab returned to Jerusalem to the king'.

This ending occurs in a slightly different form on several occasions, when, instead of noting the fact that someone went, it is said that he was sent off. Thus, at the end of the narrative about Abram and Sarai in Egypt (Gen. 12.10-20) we read: 'And Pharaoh gave men orders concerning him; and they sent him on the way, with his wife and all that he had'. Similarly, at the conclusion of the narrative of the great assembly summoned by Joshua at Shechem (Josh. 24.1-28) we find: 'So Joshua sent the people away, every man to his inheritance'.

We sometimes come across a combination of both types of ending, when it is stated that someone is sent off and also goes. The narrative of Jethro's visit to Moses in the wilderness (Exodus 18) concludes with the words: 'Then Moses sent his father-in-law away, and he went his way to his own country'. The narrative of the Syrians, who were struck by blindness at Elisha's request and led by him to Samaria (2 Kgs 6.8-23) also ends with the phrase: 'he sent them away, and they went to their master'.

13. I.L. Seeligmann, 'Hebräische Erzählung und biblische Geschichts-schreibung', *Theologische Zeitschrift* 18 (1962).

In other cases the end is indicated by the statement that two people (or groups) who met during the course of the narrative separate again. Sometimes their parting is denoted by the assertion that both went their own way. For example, the narrative about Balak, who brought Balaam in order to curse Israel, ends with the words: 'Then Balaam rose, and went back to his place; and Balak also went his way' (Num. 24.25). A similar conclusion ends the narrative recounting the battle between Saul and the Philistines: 'Then Saul went up from pursuing the Philistines; and the Philistines went to their own place' (1 Sam. 14.46); the narrative of Saul's war against the Amalekites: 'Then Samuel went to Ramah; and Saul went up to his house in Gibeah of Saul' (15.34); and the narrative of the meeting between Saul and David in the wilderness of Ziph: 'So David went his way, and Saul returned to his place' (26.25).

It should be noted that in several instances concluding phrases like those cited above occur not at the end of the narrative but at the end of a stage in it, that is, at the end of an act or scene.

For example, after God's revelation to Moses from the burning bush, when Moses is charged with going to Pharaoh and bringing the Israelites out of Egypt, we read: 'Moses went back to Jethro his father-in-law' (Exod. 4.18). This does not mark the conclusion, however, because the verse continues: 'and said to him, "Let me go back, I pray, to my kinsmen in Egypt"', and then we are told how Moses discharges the mission which he had been given at the revelation.

In the narrative of the birth of Samuel we find: 'They rose early in the morning and worshipped before the Lord; then they went back to their house at Ramah' (1 Sam. 1.19). The words, 'then they went back to their house at Ramah', occur at the end of the stage in the narrative when Hannah prays for a son and before the stage when the son she has longed for is born.

At the conclusion of the narrative of Absalom's revolt we are told of David's return from Transjordan to Jerusalem. At this stage of the narrative the meetings between David and various characters are depicted. The encounter between David and Barzilai the Gileadite ends with the words: 'And the king kissed Barzilai and blessed him, and he returned to his own home' (2 Sam. 19.39), marking the end of one scene but not of the entire narrative.

Another way of indicating the conclusion of a narrative is by noting the death of the protagonist. An ending of this kind is found in the narrative about Gideon: 'And Gideon the son of Joash died in a good old age, and was buried in the tomb of Joash his father, at Ophrah of the Abiezrites' (Judg. 8.32); in the narratives concerning the kings: 'And Solomon slept with his fathers, and was buried in the city of David his father; and Rehoboam his son reigned in his stead' (1 Kgs 11.43); and in the narrative of Job: 'And Job died, an old man, and full of days' (Job 42.17).

In all these cases, and in others like them, there is an obvious tendency to bring the narrative to a clear and unequivocal end. The explicit statement that the principal character has gone on his or her way, returned home or died clarifies to the reader that the narrative is concluded or that a stage in the plot has terminated.

2. *Collections of Narratives*

The narrative books of the Bible are not mere compilations of unconnected stories but, as is well-known, are made up of sequences of narratives, which combine to constitute wider structures. What is the nature of these combinations and to what extent are the narratives integrated within the wider structures?

There appear to be a variety of connections between the individual narratives, some of them external and most of them internal.

The simplest external connection is established by means of the letter *waw* (and), being either conjunctive or consecutive. For example, 'And Adam knew Eve his wife' (Gen. 4.1) at the beginning of the narrative of Cain and Abel, or: 'And Abram went up from Egypt' (Gen. 13.1) at the start of the narrative recounting the parting of Abram and Lot. We often find the phrase, 'And it came to pass', as a means of connecting two narratives (Gen. 6.1) or such expressions as, 'After these things' (Gen. 15.1), 'At that time' (Gen. 21.22), 'After the death of Moses' (Josh. 1.1), 'After this' (Judg. 16.4), 'In those days' (Judg. 19.1). These connective formulae and others like them often occur at the beginning of biblical narratives.

The question arises, however, whether this is merely a technique for establishing an external connection or whether these connective formulae indicate internal relations between the narratives so joined. Many biblical narratives are contiguous but are not linked by any connective formula, so that when these are used they probably hint at a closer, more substantive association. The nature of this substantive link or what is expressed by it should be examined in each individual case.

For example, the narrative of the sacrifice of Isaac begins with the words: 'After these things' (Gen. 22.1), hinting at a substantive connection between this narrative and what has been recounted beforehand about the birth of Isaac when Abraham was already one hundred years old, the great feast that Abraham made 'on the day that Isaac was weaned', and the sending away of Abraham's other son, Ishmael. The testing of Abraham, which is recounted in the narrative of the sacrifice of Isaac, is given added poignancy against the background of these facts, which are conveyed in the preceding chapter. After years of waiting for a son, who is finally and miraculously born to Abraham and Sarah in their old age, after the joy of bringing him up and after the other son has been sent into the wilderness and Isaac is the only son left at home, 'after these things' Abraham is commanded to sacrifice this son as a burnt offering!

The expression 'And after this' (2 Sam. 13.1) connects the narrative of David and Bathsheba with that of Amnon and Tamar. The parallel between these two narratives is evident, since in both sexual sin leads to murder. The explicit link together with the thematic parallel hint at the view, which is expressed in Nathan's rebuke (2 Sam. 12.10-11), that the disasters which befall David within his own house are the punishment for his sin.

The same connective formula appears at the beginning of the narrative of Absalom's revolt (2 Sam. 15.1), and there can be no doubt of the causal connection between David's anger with Absalom for the murder of Amnon (the king's anger and the efforts to appease him form the subject of ch. 14) and Absalom's revolt against his father (chs. 15–19).

Another kind of link is created by one narrative beginning with the same subject or words with which the previous one ended. For example, the narrative concerning Abram in Egypt (Gen. 12.10-20) concludes with the words: 'And they sent him on the way, with his wife and all that he had'. The following narrative, which deals with the parting of Abram and Lot (Genesis 13) starts with the phrase: 'And Abram went up from Egypt, he and his wife, and all that he had'.

The narrative of Saul and Amalek (1 Samuel 15) concludes with the information that Samuel did not see Saul again until the day of his death, 'but Samuel grieved over Saul. And the Lord repented that he had made Saul king over Israel'. The narrative of the anointing of David comes immediately afterwards (1 Sam. 16.1-13), starting with the words: 'And the Lord said to Samuel, "How long will you grieve over Saul, seeing I have rejected him from being king over Israel?"' That narrative ends with the phrase: 'And the spirit of the Lord came mightily upon David from that day forward. And Samuel rose up, and went to Ramah'. The same subject (the spirit of the Lord) begins the following narrative, which tells how David is brought to Saul's house to play to him: 'And the spirit of the Lord departed from Saul. . . '

The combination of isolated narratives into one extensive block can lead to duplication or even inconsistencies. In some cases of duplication or contradiction, there is explicit or implicit reference within one narrative to the parallel or opposing one.

The narrative of Isaac, Rebekah and Abimelech the king of Gerar (Genesis 26) bears a great resemblance to that of Abram, Sarai and Pharaoh the king of Egypt (Gen. 12.10ff.). Not only in both narratives is the wife presented as the husband's sister so that he will not be killed in the strange land (as in Genesis 20 in the narrative of Abraham, Sarah and Abimelech the king of Gerar), but both begin with the words 'And there was famine in the land'. In the second narrative, however, the words 'besides the former famine that was in the days of Abraham' are added, making it quite clear that despite the considerable similarity between them, each narrative recounts different events.

In the verse, 'Now David was the son of this an Ephrathite of Bethlehem in Judah, named Jesse, who had eight sons' (1 Sam. 17.12) the word 'this' seems out of harmony as regards both sense and grammar. Its function, however, is to hint to the reader that David and Jesse, who are presented here in the narrative of David and Goliath as new characters, are the same individuals who were introduced in the previous chapter concerning the anointing of David and his being brought to play before Saul. The succeeding passage, 'And David went back and forth from Saul to feed his father's sheep at Bethlehem' (v. 15) also serves to connect the narrative of David and Goliath, in which David is with his father at Bethlehem, with the preceding one, in which David is with Saul, acting as his armour-bearer. On the other hand, no attempt is made to resolve the discrepancy deriving from the fact that in the narrative of David and Goliath Saul does not know David (17.55-58), while in

the previous one David found favour in Saul's sight and Saul loved
him greatly (16.21-22).

An internal connection is often established between narratives
because they share the same principal character. When this is so,
each narrative deals with a different exploit of the protagonist. The
chief character accords unity to the separate narratives, not only
because he features in all of them but also because the permanent
aspects of his personality are reflected in them all. Thus, a cycle of
stories is created, presenting different episodes from the hero's life in
chronological order, whether a few central events or the entire span
of his life from birth to death (though the Bible does not contain a
complete and continuous sequence covering the life of any one
character). Examples include the cycles of narratives about Abraham
in Genesis, about Samson in Judges and about Elijah in Kings.

In these sequences, the narratives are arranged in linear fashion,
though in others they are also organized in a circular way, as is the
case with the narratives about Jacob. The first few of these narratives
deal with Jacob and Esau in Canaan, the next few concern Jacob and
Laban in Haran and the last ones tell about Jacob and Esau in
Canaan once more. The narratives about Jacob in Canaan are
separated from those about him in Haran by the incident at Beth-El,
and the narratives concerning him in Haran are separated from those
about him in Canaan by the episode of Penuel (and of Mahanayim,
which parallels it). These episodes resemble one another:[14] Jacob
stayed in Beth-El, 'because the sun had set' (Gen. 28.11), and when
he left Penuel, 'The sun rose upon him' (Gen. 32.31). At both places
Jacob is granted a revelation of God at night, in both of them God
blesses him and Jacob names both of them on the basis of the
revelation he has experienced. Thus, the following structure is
obtained in the series of narratives about Jacob:

Canaan
            Beth-El
                        Haran
            Penuel
Canaan

A bridge is sometimes constructed between the separate narratives
in a sequence through keywords (see below p. 212) whose reiteration

14. J.P. Fokkelman, *Narrative Art in Genesis* (Assen, 1975), pp. 208ff.

hints at a substantive connection between the various narratives, at a unifying line and at the significance of the overall plot.

For example, in the sequence of narratives about Abraham the following words and roots recur: go forth, bless, defend, afflict, righteousness and justice.[15]

The word 'fire' occurs as a key word in the series of narratives concerning Elijah. It features in the narrative depicting Elijah's contest with the prophets of Baal on Mount Carmel (five times), in the narrative of God's revelation to Elijah at Horeb (three times), in the narrative about the captains of fifty sent to Elijah by Ahaziah (five times) and in the narrative of Elijah's ascent to heaven (twice). In each case the fire concerned is not of the ordinary variety but is the fire of God; in most instances it comes from heaven and in the last one it takes Elijah up to heaven. This fire 'consumes' a bull, wood, an altar and even people, and symbolizes the terrible, awe-inspiring and destructive power of God, whose prophet Elijah is.

Contrasting with the word 'fire', the word 'water' occurs frequently (11 times) in the narratives concerning Elijah, as well as words akin to it, such as 'river' (seven times), 'dew' and 'rain' (eight times), and 'drink' (seven times). In addition to the verb 'drink', the verb 'eat' features frequently in the narratives about Elijah, both in the sense of eating bread (or meat) and of being consumed by fire. These words create one complex which is patently related to the famine and drought depicted in these narratives, but is not restricted to this subject and encompasses all Elijah's activities.

Each narrative in a cycle is an independent unit containing a complete story, while at the same time constituting a link in the overall pattern and contributing its share to the creation of the overall plot. This, however, is often very loosely bound and does not always comprise a close network of cause and effect, being based more on the principle of chronology than on that of causality.

There is greater unity in the block of narratives in 2 Samuel 11–20. These narratives which are concerned with David and the members of his family are so closely interconnected that they cannot be considered a cycle any more. Although each narrative contains an independent story, focusing on a different event or person, they are linked by having an overall plot with a fairly tight causal structure.

15. M. Buber, and F. Rosenzweig, *Die Schrift und ihre Verdeutschung* (Berlin, 1936), pp. 226ff.

The story begins with David's sin of adultery with Bathsheba. In order to obscure this sin, David causes Uriah's death (the war against Rabbah of the Ammonites serves as the background of this narrative, accounting for both Uriah's protracted absence from home and the circumstances of his death). David's sins give rise to Nathan's rebuke as well as to a series of disasters which constitute David's punishment: first the death of the child born to David and Bathsheba, then the rape of Tamar by Amnon, and then Absalom's murder of Amnon. Because of the murder Absalom is obliged to flee to Geshur. With the help of the wise woman of Tekoa, Joab succeeds in obtaining David's consent to Absalom's return to Jerusalem, although several years pass before the king agrees to be reconciled with his son. The tense relations between father and son give rise to Absalom's revolt against David, and the narrative of Absalom's uprising, which itself displays both complex and logical development of the plot, ends with Absalom's death and David's return to his throne in Jerusalem.

The cohesive plot of this block of narratives derives not only from the fact that the events in each narrative are the logical outcome of those in the previous one, but also from the fact that the thematic structure of the narratives is analogous: as with David, so with Amnon and Absalom (and also, to some extent, with Adonijah) sexual transgression gives rise to murder.[16]

David	+ Bathsheba	→ The killing of Uriah
Amnon	+ Tamar	→ The killing of Amnon
Absalom	+ David's concubines	→ The killing of Absalom
(Adonijah	+ Abishag)	→ The killing of Adonijah

This analogous structure reflects the view embodied in these narratives and operating as a unifying factor: David is forced to see how the same vices of lust and violence to which he succumbed re-emerge in his sons, causing disaster and great suffering. Thus, the principle of measure for measure, or rather, sons' measure for father's measure, operates here. David's sons follow in his footsteps, but the punishment imposed on them is presented as being simultaneously their father's.

This block of narratives, which is marked by a considerable degree of unity, is itself embedded within a wider narrative framework

16. J. Blenkinsopp, 'Theme and Motif in the Succession History (2 Sam XI 2ff.) and the Jahwist Corpus', *Supplements to Vetus Testamentum* 15 (1966).

which includes all the narratives about David. These, in turn, combine with other complexes of narratives to form the books of Samuel, just as the narratives concerning Abraham are part of the narratives of the patriarchs, which combine with others to form the book of Genesis. Within these broad structures there is no tight, well-constructed plot development as regards the internal causal connections between all the components, yet there is considerable unity, both because of the same outlook which underlies them and because of shared literary characteristics (such as style and ways of narration). There are also threads which connect narratives belonging to different blocks and cycles.

For example, in the narrative of Absalom's revolt, there are two passages (2 Sam. 16.1-4; 19.24-30) which tell of Mephibosheth and Ziba his servant. These passages are connected with what has been related beforehand in chapter 9 about the kindness David showed Mephibosheth, Jonathan's lame son, and the task David gave Ziba of tilling the land which used to belong to Saul for Mephibosheth. Chapter 9 is itself linked to the narratives recounting the relations between David and Jonathan (1 Samuel 19-20), and thence to the complex of narratives about David and Saul. Chapter 9 opens with the words: 'And David said, "Is there still any one left of the house of Saul, that I may show him kindness for Jonathan's sake?"'. And further on in the same chapter we read: 'And the king said, "Is there not still some one of the house of Saul, that I may show the kindness of God to him?"' and also: 'And David said to him, "Do not fear; for I will show you kindness for the sake of your father Jonathan"'. The emphasis on kindness in this context should be compared with 1 Sam. 20.14-15, where Jonathan says to David: 'Show me the kind love of the Lord. . . and do not cut off your kindness from my house for ever'. Chapter 9 of 2 Samuel is also connected with 2 Sam. 21.1-14, which tells of David's relations with Saul's descendants, and with 2 Sam. 4.4, where Jonathan's son is mentioned for the first time and the way in which he became a cripple is recounted.

A typical example of the various layers of narrative structures in the Bible can be found in the book of Judges. The narrative of Samson and Delilah (Judg. 16.4-31) is complete in itself and also has a tight plot structure. In the exposition we are told that Samson loved a woman in the valley of Sorek whose name was Delilah. This woman asks Samson three times for the secret of his strength and the way he can be subdued and three times Samson gives her a false answer. Three times she says: 'The Philistines are upon you, Samson!' and three times he shows that he has retained his strength. On the fourth occasion, however, after Delilah has used her feminine wiles, Samson succumbs and discloses the truth, as a result of which he is captured by the Philistines and blinded. Nevertheless, in the dénouement Samson's strength returns to him and in his death he succeeds in slaying thousands of Philistines, more than the number he killed during his life.

This narrative is a link in the cycle concerning Samson which consists of more or less independent narratives relating the hero's various exploits, starting with his birth and ending with his death. The unity of this series of narratives is achieved by the personality of the protagonist—who appears in all of them as an elemental, unpolished type of man with immense physical strength, ruled solely and unreservedly by his passions and emotions—as well as by the historical and geographical background which is common to all of them.

The cycle of narratives about Samson is combined with the other narratives about the judges, which together comprise the book of Judges. This is not simply a collection of narratives concerning the various judges, but has a considerable degree of unity and cohesion, primarily because of the outlook which characterizes it. This view, which is stated explicitly in chapter 2, maintains that the Israelites abandoned God and worshipped Baal; as punishment God sent them an enemy in the form of one of the neighbouring nations; the Israelites cried to the Lord, who sent them a judge in order to save them from the enemy, and then all over again. The book of Judges is built so that the narratives about the various judges are embedded within this general scheme, illustrating and detailing the stage in the cycle of events at which the judge rescues the Israelites suffering under the enemy's yoke. The chronological system which governs the book of Judges, according to which the land was at peace for forty years (once for eighty years and once for twenty) after each great judge, also contributes to the book's unity.

Yet the entire book of Judges is merely part of an extensive corpus which relates all history, from the creation of the world (Genesis) to the Babylonian exile (the book of Kings). Threads connect the various books which constitute this extensive corpus. For example, in the book of Samuel Joab says: 'Who killed Abimelech the son of Jerubbesheth? Did not a woman cast an upper millstone upon him from the wall, so that he died at Thebez?' (2 Sam. 11.21), and the details of this incident are recounted in the book of Judges (9.50-54). The extensive corpus is also characterized by a single world-outlook, which regards the course of history as the embodiment of the relationship between the one God, the creator of the world, and His chosen people, the people of Israel.

Chapter 4

TIME AND SPACE

A narrative cannot exist without time, to which it has a twofold relationship: it unfolds within time, and time passes within it. The narrative needs the time which is outside it in order to unravel itself by stages before the reader. Because of the consecutive nature of language, which is the means by which works of literature are conveyed, the narrative cannot be absorbed all at once and is communicated through a process which continues in time; in order to follow the development of the plot a certain amount of time is needed. The narrative also requires internal time, because the characters and the incidents exist within time. Everything that changes during the course of the narrative as well as everything that remains static exists within time.

This twofold link with time has significant implications for the nature, possibilities and limitations of the narrative as well as for the way it is interpreted. As far as external time is concerned, the fact that the narrative is disclosed to us successively makes it impossible for us to grasp the full significance of the first word until we have reached the last. Literature resembles music in this and differs from the plastic arts, such as painting and sculpture, which can be grasped in their entirety at one instant. Unlike music, however, which can convey several tunes together, the narrative cannot describe simultaneously different events which occurred at the same time. This constitutes one of the major limitations of the narrative form, and an attempt will be made below to indicate how the biblical narrators endeavoured to overcome it.

Since the narrative is revealed to the reader gradually, the author can exploit the reader's temporary ignorance in order to heighten interest and tension. The author similarly uses the narrative's dependence on external time to construct and organize the units comprising the narrative, such as the words, collocations, sentences and paragraphs, so that their length is varied, thereby preventing monotony. The author chooses the words, builds the sentences and constructs the paragraphs, paying careful attention to their size so as to create a dynamic rhythm, which is also a function of time.

The author also makes use of internal time, in both the qualitative and the quantitative aspects.

Time within a narrative is completely different to physical, objective time. Objective time is continuous and flows evenly, without interruptions, delays or accelerations (provided the speed of the measuring mechanism remains constant), advancing in a straight line and an orderly fashion from the past via the present to the future. It is also irreversible.

This does not apply to narrated time, which is subjective and expands or contracts according to the circumstances; it is never continuous, being subject to gaps, delays and jumps, nor does it display the meticulous division into past, present and future. By moving backwards and forwards in time, arousing memories from the past and future expectations, the different periods are made to mingle with one another. Narrated time is not uniform or regular and its directions and speed often change.

Time is like clay in the potter's hand as far as the author is concerned, he moulds it as he pleases, making it an integral part of the form of the work as a whole. The shaping of time within the narrative is functional and not random or arbitrary, making a genuine contribution, in coordination and cooperation with the other elements, to the character, meaning and values of the entire narrative. Apart from its role within the narrative itself, such as providing emphases or implying connections between separate incidents, narrated time can fulfil direct functions for the reader, such as creating suspense or determining attitudes.

Internal time is an invaluable constituent of the structure of the narrative. Sections in which time passes quickly alternate with passages in which it goes slowly or even stands still. Thus, the structure of the narrative is determined by the changing speeds of time and, in particular, by means of the gaps—the empty areas of time—between the episodes.

The author makes no attempt whatsoever to portray a continuum of time which proceeds unwaveringly and at an unchanging pace. Since the decision as to what to include and what to omit, what to convey rapidly and on what to dwell at length, is closely bound up with the importance of the various subjects, the character of time as it is shaped within the narrative will be of great value in any attempt to analyze and interpret the narrative.

Because the author can arrange time with complete disregard for the laws governing physical time, events from the past or even the future are sometimes introduced into the narrative outside their chronological order. This is a means of hinting at connections and meanings which must be taken into account in trying to understand the narrative.

Thus, the nature, structure and meaning of the narrative are determined to a considerable extent through the shaping of internal time, while at the same time emphases and climaxes are established.

Despite the central position occupied by time in the fabric of the narrative, the reader does not usually pay attention to it and takes it for granted. It exists solely as background and infrastructure. Although it is indispensable and constant, and the entire narrative rests upon it, its existence is not apparent. Even when explicit denotations of time occur within a narrative, they seem to be of only marginal importance. It will become clear, however, that a close scrutiny of the factor of time provides us with a key for penetrating to the very heart of the narrative.

1. *The Shaping of Time*

A. *The Duration of Time*

As mentioned in the foregoing, the narrative has a twofold link with time, with objective time outside it (narration time) and with literary time inside it (narrated time). Literary scholarship has made it clear that the examination of the relations between these two networks of time can be very fruitful. By studying the relation between narration time and narrated time the relative weight of the various sections of the narrative will be clarified, as will their proportions with regard to one another and the narrative as a whole, thereby disclosing the focal points of the narrative. By elucidating the relationship between the two time systems we will be able to see in how much detail matters are presented within the narrative, enabling us to draw conclusions about the meaning of the narrative, its central theme, etc.

Narration time, namely, the time required for telling or reading the narrative, can be determined easily. It might be claimed that the time required by different narrators to tell or by different readers to read a narrative varies, but these differences pale into insignificance alongside the immense disparities between narration time and narrated time. Furthermore, narration time can be assessed in terms of the number of printed words, lines or pages, thereby making it possible to define it in a precise and objective way.

Thus, there is no problem concerning the measurement of narration time. The question of gauging narrated time still holds, however, and we must now inquire whether and how it is revealed.

Language contains two ways of marking time and denoting its various kinds and relationships: a. tenses; b. temporal expressions (year, day, tomorrow, etc.).

The value of tenses for marking time is very limited. Even if we assume that Hebrew tenses do in fact express time and not aspects (a complete or incomplete action), they can indicate time only in the most general and imprecise way. The most that can be inferred from them is that a certain action occurred at some point in the past, but whether this was in the distant past or just a moment ago cannot be defined. The same applies to the future. Tenses denote the relative perspective, such as the past perfect, and this is of some importance in determining the order of events, but they cannot indicate the duration of an event or action, which is needed in order to assess the relation between narration time and narrated time.

Temporal expressions, namely, the nouns, adverbs and prepositions denoting points, periods, relations and the movement or direction of time, are far more important and (particularly when they appear in conjunction with numbers) can mark time precisely as well as defining duration.

There are two kinds of temporal expressions: 1. those denoting duration, 2. those denoting points of time.

Expressions Denoting Duration

> And rain fell upon the earth forty days and forty nights (Gen. 7.12).

> So Jacob served seven years for Rachel (29.20).

> The time that the people of Israel dwelt in Egypt was four hundred and thirty years (Exod. 12.40).

> And Achish said to the commanders of the Philistines, 'Is not this David, the servant of Saul, king of Israel, who has been with me now for days and years' (1 Sam. 29.3).

Expressions Denoting Points of Time

> And he made the camels kneel down outside the city by the well of water at the time of evening, the time when women go out to draw water (Gen. 24.11).

> So Gideon and the hundred men who were with him came to the outskirts of the camp at the beginning of the middle watch, when they had just set the watch (Judg. 7.19).

> Then at the break of dawn Samuel called to Saul (1 Sam. 9.26).

Expressions denoting points of time make a considerable contribution to the sense of narrated time. They cannot indicate duration, however, unless they are connected with one another, establishing internal relations between themselves or with events in the narrative, or if they are supplemented by such prepositions as 'from' and 'to':

> And they abused her all night until the morning. And as the dawn began to break, they let her go. And as morning appeared, the woman came and fell down at the door of the man's house. . . (Judg. 19.25-26).

> And Mephibosheth the son of Saul came down to meet the king; he had neither dressed his feet, nor trimmed his beard, nor washed his clothes, from the day the king departed until the day he came back in safety (2 Sam. 19.24).

> And they called on the name of Baal from morning until noon saying, 'O Baal, answer us!' But there was no voice and no one answered (1 Kgs 18.26).

Time is not denoted in biblical narratives solely by explicit temporal expressions, however, nor even primarily by them. These expressions serve as points of departure for establishing the temporal structure of the narrative, but despite the fact that they occur quite frequently they cannot set up a complete temporal network. They are not all-encompassing, nor do they transmit the sense of real time, which exists and flows incessantly.

The full fabric of time is woven primarily through the events presented in the narrative rather than by direct indications of time. Because they occur within time, the events determine its nature and fill it with content to a considerable extent. Through the developments the course of time becomes tangible and its movement is expressed in a concrete way. The narrative does not present bare time in a direct way, but rather indirectly, through what is contained in it. Although it is impossible in this way to determine duration precisely, the time system created by the presentation of actual events, in combination with explicit temporal expressions, is sufficiently clear to enable it to be compared with external, narration time. There are events whose duration is more or less constant, such as pregnancy; but even when duration can be assessed only approximately, this does not prevent us establishing the relationship between narration time and narrated time. As has been noted above, precise assessments of time are not required in order to attain significant results.

The speed of narrated time varies frequently, as compared with narration time, whose progress is steady and fixed. Narrated time is sometimes faster, sometimes slower than narration time, and sometimes the two are virtually coterminous. The nature of the relationship between them should not be limited to these three possibilities alone, however, but should rather be regarded as a continuum, ranging from total immobility to mercurial speed.

When do we find total immobility, that is, the absolute cessation of the passage of time in a narrative?

Time stops in two situations: a. when interpretations, explanations, conclusions or evaluations are given by the narrator; b. when depictions are given within the narrative.

Every explanation given by the narrator unlike those by one of the characters causes the flow of time to stop. In more precise terms, it does not cause time to stop but creates a divergence outside the sphere of time. By introducing interpretations and explanations the narrator is placed at a distance from the flow of events, above time, and it is from this point, not from within, that he or she views occurrences. The various kinds of interpretations and explanations have been discussed above (in the chapter on the narrator) and there is no need to repeat them.

Depictions cause narrated time to stop (while narration time continues as before), since they describe a (static) situation rather than an event. Although we remain within the world of the plot (which is not the case with interpretations and explanations), because the depictions present a picture of the way people, places, things, etc. look, they hold up the progress of the action; and while we are looking at that picture time stops within the narrative. Depictions of the outward appearance of the characters have been discussed in Chapter 2, and the descriptions of places will be dealt with below in the section on space.

The interpretations, explanations, and evaluations given by the narrator as well as the depictions are both infrequent and brief. As a result, there are very few instances in which time stops, and these are short and of little impact. This is what gives biblical narrative its characteristic dynamic nature and its almost incessant, rapid motion.

Unlike the elements noted above, conversations occur frequently in biblical narrative, and consequently leave their mark on it to a considerable degree.

In many cases the conversation constitutes the bulk of the narrative, overshadowing the actual narration and serving as the principal means of conveying the developments. This is the case, for example, in the narrative of the Garden of Eden (Genesis 3), and that of Saul and the asses (1 Sam. 9.1–10.16), which are based primarily on conversations. In some instances the whole story is communicated through conversations, and the narrator merely provides a frame. This is the case, for example, in the narrative of David's banishment from the Philistine camp before the battle at Gilboa (1 Samuel 29) and in the episode of the messengers who run to David after Absalom's death (2 Sam. 18.19-32).

Despite the fact that conversations account for a considerable part of most biblical narratives, they are not long. The characters generally express themselves in a succinct style and the dialogues usually contain no more than two or three rounds. There are only a few exceptions, such as the conversation between David and the wise woman of Tekoa (2 Sam. 14.4-20), which contains no less than fifteen utterances. The woman speaks eight times and David seven, and in addition the woman speaks at considerable length. In a few instances speech is reported extensively, constituting what amounts to an oration, as in Rabshakeh's address (2 Kgs 18.19-25, 28-35), which occupies fifteen verses in all.

Conversations fulfil two principal functions in biblical narrative. On the one hand, they serve as a vehicle for the development of the plot, since they do not usually convey thought and contemplation but deal rather with actions, generally focusing on the future. They are often concerned with plans and aspirations or with attempts to persuade and influence. On the other hand, conversations serve to illuminate the human aspect, revealing such psychological features as motives and intentions, points of view and approaches, attitudes and reactions. The narratives cited above, concerning the Garden of

Eden, Saul and the asses, David's banishment from the camp of the Philistines and the episode of the messengers, as well as many others, serve as examples of this. (See also above, in the chapter on the characters, for the contribution made by conversations to the characterizations of the protagonists.)

In conversations the speed of narrated time approximates that of narration time though it does not correspond to it exactly. Conversations in biblical narrative are never precise and naturalistic imitations of real-life conversations. They are highly concentrated and stylized, are devoid of idle chatter, and all the details they contain are carefully calculated to fulfil a clear function. Moreover, the conversations are sometimes so compressed that the details we want or expect to find in them are missing.

Below are several examples showing that conversations in biblical narrative are far more condensed than those in everyday life or, in other words, that narration time is shorter than narrated time.

> And Absalom used to rise early and stand beside the way of the gate; and when any man had a suit to come before the king for judgment, Absalom called to him, and said, 'From what city are you?' And he said, 'Your servant is of one of the tribes of Israel'. And Absalom said to him, 'See, your claims are good and right, but there is no man deputed by the king to hear you' (2 Sam. 15.2-3).

In this succinct conversation, revealing the cheap way in which Absalom made himself popular with the people, Absalom's interlocutor gives him a reply which would not be possible in reality. Absalom asks: 'From what city are you?' and the answer should be the name of a city, possibly with the addition of the tribe, while here we find what amounts to a telescoping of all the answers given by all the petitioners over time (as we find further on: 'Thus Absalom did to all of Israel who came to the king for judgment').

Moreover, later on in the conversation Absalom would presumably ask the petitioner what was his suit and why he had come to the king for judgment, and the man would tell him the details of his case, explaining how matters had developed and what was the position of each side. All this is omitted from the conversation before us. The man and his suit are of no interest or importance to the subject of the narrative. What is significant, however, is Absalom's reaction, both as a means of characterizing him and as a way of advancing the plot: 'See, your claims are good and right; but there is no man deputed by the king to hear you'. Also what Absalom added: 'Oh that I were judge in the land! Then every man with a suit or cause might come to me, and I would give him justice'. Thus, the conversation contains only what is necessary, after careful selection, for the purposes of the narrative, rigorously excluding all the rest.

An even more telling example of condensation and omission can be found in what Hushai says to Zadok and Abiathar the priests after Absalom has accepted his advice: '*Thus and so* did Ahithophel counsel Absalom and the elders of Israel; and *thus and so* have I counselled' (2 Sam. 17.15). Naturally, in reality Hushai would have had to give the actual advice in detail, but the narrator abbreviates matters in order not to repeat unnecessarily what is already known to the reader, even though it is not known to Zadok and Abiathar. By refraining from repetition the narrator speeds up the pace of the development, as befits a stage in a narrative in which speed is of the essence. The narrator uses the same form of abbreviation, which does not reflect real-life conversation, further on: 'After they had gone, the men came up out of the well, and went and told king David. They said to David, "Arise, and go quickly over the water; for *thus and so* has Ahithophel counselled against you"' (v. 21). This time not only are no details given of Ahithophel's advice, but Hushai's counsel is not mentioned at all, since only Ahithophel's advice is important now in order to impel the king to make haste and cross the water that very night.

A similar technique of avoiding repetition is found in Joab's speech to the wise woman of Tekoa: 'And go to the king, and speak *thus* to him' (2 Sam. 14.3). This time, however, the reader does not yet know to what the 'thus' refers, and this will be made clear only when the conversation between the king and the woman actually takes place. In the previous example, the event itself was first recounted, and was then alluded to through the expression 'thus and so', whereas in the case of Joab and the wise woman of Tekoa the order is reversed because here the decisive point is the actual conversation. This is because that conversation does not serve to give a report, as in the previous instances, but constitutes an attempt to persuade, and future developments are dependent on its outcome.

Conversation is the principal, often the sole component of biblical scenes, which present a specific event occurring at a defined time and place. As has been shown above (p. 34), the scenes do not give the reader an outline of what has happened, but rather create the impression that the events are taking place before the reader's very eyes, as if he or she is seeing and hearing what is happening at that precise instant and consequently becomes emotionally involved. Because scenes portray events in a clear and detailed way, they illuminate the crucial incidents, the crises, climaxes, vital decisions and central activities.

The speed of time within scenes is close to that of narration time because they are based primarily on conversation. When action is included in a scene its duration is longer than narration time: 'When they came to the place of which God had told him, Abraham built an altar there, and laid the wood in order, and bound Isaac his son, and laid him on the altar, upon the wood' (Gen. 22.9). Despite the considerable detail with which Abraham's actions are recounted, there can be no doubt that building the altar, laying the wood, binding Isaac and laying him on the wood took far longer than the time required to read the verse. This is generally the case, though there are exceptions to the rule; in other words, the actions depicted in a scene sometimes occur within a shorter space of time than it takes to read the narrated event. This can be observed in the following verse: 'Then Abraham put forth his hand, and took the knife to slay his son' (v. 10). The action of taking the knife is divided into two operations—putting forth his hand and taking the knife— and is supplemented by the intention of the actor, so that altogether the time it takes to read the verse (narration time) is longer than the duration of the action (narrated time). By this device the reader's complete attention is focused on that action, which constitutes the climax of the narrative.

It is impossible to tell a story which extends over a considerable amount of time by the scenic technique alone, since a scene can depict only a limited period of time. The narrative must establish a connection between these limited segments of time, conveying a sense of continuity and communicating information about developments which happen during the longer sections of time. Summary account fulfils this function in the narrative. The summary passages are generally brief in biblical narratives, which accord more space to scenic representation. In some narratives, however, summary account occupies most or even all of the text, as is the case with Joshua's wars, related in chapter 11 of the book of Joshua.

Time passes far more quickly in summary account than in scenic representation, but is not uniform or unchanging. The differences in the speed of time within summary account are sometimes immense, as is demonstrated by the following examples:

> and he pursued him for seven days (Gen. 31.23).
>
> And Leah conceived and bore a son (29.32).
>
> And Jacob served seven years for Rachel (29.20).

The first example summarizes a period of days, the second a period of months and the third a period of years. This means that the ratio between narration time and narrated time in the first example is approximately 1:200,000, in the second 1:10,000,000 and in the third 1:70,000,000, while in scenic representation (conversation) it is approximately 1:1 (the ratios are based on the Hebrew text).

These figures illustrate the vast differences in the density of the narrative, which is loose when there is a great divergence between narration time and narrated time, and tight when they approximate one another. If we note the variations in narrated time in relation to narration time, ranging from scenic representation to summary account, we will discover the narrative's focal points and the relative importance of its various subjects.[1]

An examination of the narrative of David, Bathsheba and Uriah (2 Samuel 11) reveals that the relations between David and Bathsheba are conveyed through summary, at a fairly rapid pace and with no details. This applies to both the occasions on which this subject is treated, at the beginning and end of the chapter. Everything concerning David and Uriah, however, is conveyed through scenic representation, slowly and at length. David's repeated attempts to persuade Uriah to go down to his house, and Uriah's refusal to do so, as well as the reporting to David of Uriah's death, are all portrayed through detailed scenic representation. This leads us to conclude that David's efforts to conceal the results of his adultery, which eventually lead to the killing of Uriah, constitute the axis of the narrative. David's moral depravity is depicted even more through his actions in connection with Uriah than with Bathsheba. The conclusion that the main point of the narrative is what David does to Uriah is strengthened by Nathan's rebuke (2 Sam. 12.7-10). Nathan does not mention the adultery, but accuses David of smiting Uriah the Hittite with the sword and taking Uriah's wife to be his

---

1. Compare Rashi's commentary on Genesis 37.1.

wife. The assumption that the pivot of the narrative is the sin against Uriah is further borne out by 1 Kgs 15.5: 'Because David did what was right in the eyes of the Lord, and did not turn aside from anything that he commanded him all the days of his life, except in the matter of Uriah the Hittite'.

In the narrative concerning Amnon and Tamar the detailed scenic representation deals mainly with what took place before the rape, namely, the planning and the preparations, while the rape itself is recounted tersely. Time also passes quickly when we are told how Amnon was murdered, while it goes slowly in the passages dealing with Absalom's preparations for the murder and David's reaction to it. Similarly, we are informed in a concise way about Absalom's return from Geshur and his seizing of power, while the preparations for these actions—David's persuasion by the woman of Tekoa to permit his son's return and Absalom's efforts to gain general popularity and obtain his father's consent to his journey to Hebron—are conveyed through slow scenes.

The emphases in the passage relating Absalom's death are disclosed in the same way. While time passes rapidly in the account of the battle between the armies of David and Absalom, slow, scenic descriptions are given of David before the battle, of the slaying of Absalom and particularly of the moments before he is killed, and of the conveying of the news of his death to David. Time slows down even more when David's reaction to the news is portrayed.

These findings indicate that these narratives embody a clear tendency to regard the preparations preceding events and the reactions following them as being more important than the events themselves, denoting a special interest in matters pertaining to the human mind, its motives, decisions and attitudes. In other words, the human aspects, whether psychological, spiritual or moral, are granted greater emphasis than factual components.

Narrated time passes fastest in the empty spaces of time when nothing happens. Naturally, it must be assumed that even in these empty sections of time life goes on, but nothing is reported about it, since the daily routine is of no interest or significance as far as the author is concerned. Instead of weaving a continuous and extensive fabric of life in its entirety, the author prefers to select the most important points and omit whatever is trivial or commonplace. As a result of the highly selective nature of biblical narrative, we have little knowledge of the everyday life of people and the way they behaved in their non-heroic moments. On the other hand, the approach which concentrates only on the focal points of the protagonists' lives creates considerable interest and tension, giving the narratives a dimension of intensivity, drama and monumentalism.

While there are time gaps within scenes too, since it is impossible to portray every single moment in a narrative, it is the extensive gaps, namely, those separating passages of scenic representation or summary account from one another which will be discussed here.

There are two kinds of extensive time gaps, those which are bridged and those which are not.

Unbridged time gaps are rare *within* narratives, since passages of summary account generally link scenes, which comprise the bulk of the narratives. Time gaps of this kind are very common *between* the various narratives, however. For example, the narrative concerning Moses (Exodus 2) begins with a section of summary account relating Moses' birth, his concealment by his mother for three months and his being placed in a basket made of bulrushes among the reeds at the river's brink. This is followed by a scenic passage which depicts how Pharaoh's daughter takes the child from the water and gives him to a Hebrew woman to nurse. In this scene Moses is still a baby, while in the ones which follow, recounting the slaying of the Egyptian and Moses' intervention in the dispute between the two Hebrews, he is an adult. The time gap within the narrative is bridged by the information that Moses grew up, conveyed through summary account: 'And the child grew, and she brought him to Pharaoh's daughter, and he became her son... One day, when Moses had grown up ... ' (vv. 10-11).

Further on we are told that Moses fled to the land of Midian because Pharaoh wanted to kill him, and that he dwelt with the priest and married his daughter. A very long period of time elapses between this narrative and the following ones, which deal with the exodus, for God says to Moses: 'for all the men who were seeking your life are dead' (4.19), and Moses himself is eighty years old by then (7.7). This time gap (which exists between different narratives) is not bridged, and neither is the one between the narratives recounting what befalls the Israelites in the wilderness in the first two years after the exodus from Egypt and the narratives dealing with what happens to them in the fortieth year. Not a word is said about the thirty-eight years in which they wandered in the wilderness, and the time gap is not referred to in any way, indicating that these years are of no importance for the author.

Bridged time gaps exist both within a single narrative and between different ones. On occasions they delimit the empty space of time exactly, and on others they are general and undefined.

A certain period of time separates Moses' birth from the point at which he was placed in the basket of bulrushes, and the author defines the period precisely: 'she hid him three months' (Exod. 2.2).

An empty period of time intervenes between Amnon's rape of Tamar and his murder by Absalom in revenge. The narrator skips this period, telling us nothing of what happened then, but connects the two incidents by noting the precise time span: 'After two full years. . . ' (2 Sam. 13.23).

A section of empty time, whose length is noted precisely, elapses between Absalom's flight to Geshur after his murder of Amnon and his later return from Geshur to Jerusalem: 'and he was there three years' (v. 38).

Another period of empty time intervenes between Absalom's return from Geshur and his reconciliation with his father, and this, too, is scrupulously bridged: 'And Absalom dwelt two full years in Jerusalem' (14.28).

Shimei the son of Gera is summoned before king Solomon and warned never to leave Jerusalem. Despite having agreed to this, Shimei leaves the city and pays for his lack of caution with his life. An empty period of time passes between these two facts, and the connection between them is twofold: 'So Shimei dwelt in Jerusalem many days. And it happened at the end of three years. . . ' (1 Kgs 2.38-39).

In all these examples periods of months or even years pass in the twinkling of an eye. Although these periods are not considered important enough to warrant a detailed narrative, the fact that their length is noted exactly indicates that the time factor is considered to be of some importance.

Moses' mother concealed her infant for three months. We can imagine what she went through during that time, and how she worried and feared as to whether she would manage to save her child. The fact that the baby was not discovered during those three months was miraculous, as was his rescue from the water. Thus, the man who was destined to lead his people out of Egypt owed his life to a miracle (miraculous circumstances are often claimed to have attended the birth or infancy of great leaders and founders of nations, cities and religions).

Absalom remained at Geshur for three years. Although no occurrences are mentioned, the fact that this period is noted is undoubtedly meant to indicate that the passage of time affected the protagonists.

The time which passed during those three years affected David by alleviating the pain and sorrow at Amnon's death on the one hand and heightening his longing for Absalom on the other: 'And the spirit[2] of the king longed to go forth to Absalom; for he was comforted about Amnon, seeing he was dead' (2 Sam. 13.39). Joab knew how to use the right moment to send the wise woman of Tekoa to the king, and his good timing doubtless contributed to the woman's success.

Naturally, the three years Absalom remained in Geshur influenced him in a different way. It can be assumed that during those years feelings of anger and hostility began to stir, and that they were directed against his father, on whose account he was obliged to remain in exile. Later on these emotions grew and ripened until they burst out into the open during the revolt.

After Absalom was given permission to return to Jerusalem these feelings of enmity were not allayed but grew stronger when he realized that his father had not been appeased: 'And the king said, "Let him dwell apart in his own house; he is not to come into my presence". So Absalom dwelt apart in his own house, and did not come into the king's presence' (2 Sam. 14.24). This information is reiterated in v. 28: 'And Absalom dwelt two full years in Jerusalem, without coming into the king's presence'. This is a resumptive repetition (see below, p. 215) after the passage recounting his beauty, his long hair and his children. This repetition is not merely a way of connecting passages, however, but also fulfils an expressive role. First of all, in the two verses cited the fact that Absalom was excluded from the king's presence is mentioned not twice, as would be required by the resumptive repetition technique, but three times, indicating that particular emphasis is placed on this detail. In addition, it is obvious that v. 24 pertains to the day on which Absalom returned from Geshur, while v. 28 relates to the period which followed, which

2. According to a Qumran manuscript and the Lucian Version of the Septuagint 'spirit' should be read instead of 'David', as is found in the Massoretic text.

lasted two years. This period of time is stressed ('two *full* years'), implying that it had its effect and was felt to pass slowly. What the effect was is evident from the context. Unlike v. 24, v. 28 tells us that Absalom dwelt in Jerusalem (a redundant piece of information, since this is clear from what has been said in v. 23: 'and he brought Absalom to Jerusalem'); this means that, in contrast to the situation during his sojourn at Geshur, Absalom is now very close to his father, and nevertheless 'he did not come into the king's presence'. Thus, tension is created between the physical proximity to the king and the emotional distance from him. This situation, which involves serious humiliation for the proud-spirited Absalom, continues for two full years, indicating that from a psychological point of view time seems unending. If Absalom was disappointed on his return when, after an absence of three years, he was not permitted to see his father, how much more so was this the case during the extended period when the affront was renewed and experienced afresh every day, making the situation intolerable for him.

The passage between vv. 24 and 28 describing Absalom's beauty and placing particular stress on his hair and his relation to it, establishes a contrast between Absalom's attitude to himself and the king's to him during those two years. Because of Absalom's excessive self-love, which is revealed in this passage, the king's injury to his pride in refusing to see him is particularly painful, making Absalom's mental anguish unbearable. This is proved by his incessant and violent efforts to force Joab to go to the king in order to end this state of affairs. There is undoubtedly a lot of truth in what Absalom orders Joab to say to the king on his behalf: 'Why have I come from Geshur? It would be better for me to be there still. Now therefore let me go into the presence of the king; and if there is guilt in me, let him kill me' (v. 32). What he is saying is that when he was far away he did not feel what he feels now; he cannot bear this tension and wants a clear decision one way or another, either complete forgiveness or the full penalty. As a result of Joab's intervention David decides to be reunited with his son, but time has taken its toll and the past cannot be undone. The feelings of frustration and animosity which Absalom harboured in his heart for two years cannot be expunged, and consequently: 'After this. . .' (15.1) Absalom embarks on the practical preparations for the revolt against his father.

It should be noted that in 14.33, which depicts the reconciliation between David and Absalom, the title 'the king' is mentioned three times in connection with Absalom. This fact, together with the expression, 'and he bowed himself on his face to the ground before the king', does not betoken a warm family atmosphere. It should also be observed that several expressions which appear in this verse recur at the beginning of the next chapter, which relates the preparations for the revolt and in which Absalom plays the role the king fulfils here:

And he summoned Absalom (14.33)	Absalom would summon him (15.2)
And he came to the king (14.33)	Then he might come to me (15.4)
And he bowed himself to him (14.33)	And when he came to bow himself to him (15.5)
And the king kissed (14.33)	And he kissed him (15.5)

It may be concluded from this that the reconciliation was cold and formal, and merely intensified the humiliated Absalom's aspirations to supplant his father the king.

One of Absalom's most obvious traits is his ability to refrain from acting hastily. He does not embark on open revolt until he has made his preparations over a long period of time which is specified precisely by the narrator. Although the Massoretic text which gives the period as being forty years (15.7) seems most improbable, it is evident that Absalom devotes several years (presumably four) to creating the appropriate conditions, and particularly to achieving widespread support among the various tribes, in order to enhance his chances of success. Through careful, painstaking labour he prepares the ground and wins himself popularity among all strata of the nation, being deterred by neither the efforts nor the time required: 'And Absalom used to *rise early* and stand beside the way of the gate. . . . Thus Absalom did to *all* of Israel who came to the king for judgment' (15.2, 6).

The same tendency to refrain from acting in haste is reflected when, after the rape of Tamar, Absalom does not immediately avenge the dishonouring of his sister. He tells her to forget the matter ('Do not take this to heart', 13.20), but does not forget it himself, planning his vengeance carefully. He waits two whole years, and the narrator emphasizes the length of this period: 'After two *full* years' (v. 23). Absalom does not need this period in order to make the necessary preparations but so that the passage of time can cause Amnon (and

David) to cease suspecting that Absalom will take revenge. His calculations are correct and his design succeeds.

It is not inconceivable that Hushai was familiar with and exploited Absalom's tendency to prefer a slow, well-planned effort to hasty action. There is no doubt that Absalom rejected Ahithophel's advice and accepted Hushai's because of the latter's brilliant rhetorical skills, but it seems reasonable to assume that Absalom also preferred Hushai's plan because it involved postponing any immediate and possibly rash act.

As mentioned above, there is a twofold bridging of a time gap in connection with Shimei the son of Gera: 'So Shimei dwelt in Jerusalem many days. And at the end of three years. . . ' (1 Kgs 2.38-39). Solomon had forbidden Shimei to leave Jerusalem, and Shimei had accepted this restriction. The twofold indication of time serves to insinuate that as time went by the authority of the injunction became weaker and the period of Shimei's arrest in Jerusalem—he had formerly lived at Bahurim—seemed very long to him ('many days'), so that as a result he became careless, and when two of his slaves ran away he set out to bring them back. Solomon, who from the outset had apparently desired Shimei's death, made use of the opportunity to have him executed.

In the book of Judges a phrase for bridging time gaps recurs several times: 'And the land had rest forty years' (or 'eighty years') (Judg. 3.11, 30; 5.31; 8.28), marking the periods in which nothing happened. In actual fact, however, this expression intimates that the years of peace and tranquillity did affect the people of Israel, who abandoned the Lord when things went well for them. Only when the years of calm ended and the people of Israel were harassed by one of the neighbouring nations did they return to God and cry to him (see e.g. Judg. 3.11-15).

Such expressions as 'And it came to pass after a time', 'And after this', and 'After these things', also serve to span time. They link different narratives or discrete parts of one narrative, conveying the impression that time has passed. Were it not for these phrases the reader would feel that the incidents recounted consecutively occurred in immediate succession. The implied assumption is that the flow of events continues uninterruptedly, unless some indication is given that this is not the case. The omission of the phrase 'After these things' in Esth. 3.1, for example, would create the impression that king Ahasuerus promoted Haman immediately after Mordecai discovered the plot of Bigthan and Teresh to slay the king. Because this phrase is included, a space of time is created between these two facts. We are unable, however, to determine how long this period lasted because these ways of spanning time are general and do not specify the exact time involved.

Thus, bridgings bring the gaps in the time continuum to the reader's attention. Within these gaps time exists quantitatively but is not shaped qualitatively. Time acts, events occur and people change within the empty spaces too, but all these remain obscure, whereas other periods of time are presented clearly and luminously.

Bridgings are not numerous in biblical narrative. Neither they nor the depictions, interpretations and explanations constitute the main part of the narrative. The mainstay of biblical narrative is, first and foremost, the scenes, followed by the passages of summary account, and it is these two rather than the other components which determine the speed of time. Time gaps, bridgings, summary account, scenic representation and the narrator's interpretation, which involve a successive slowing down of narrated time, may be considered to reflect an ascending order of importance, providing us with a means to determine the relative significance of narrative items. This rank order should, however, be handled with great caution and flexibility, since we are dealing with a work of literature, and no creative writer is totally subject to inexorable laws.

All the narrative elements mentioned above are liable to appear within a conversation too, constituting a narrative within a narrative, as it were. They will determine the internal speed of the conversation in the same way as they do in the narrative as a whole. A conversation within a conversation is slower than summary account within a conversation, and depictions within a conversation are obviously far slower than bridgings or gaps within a conversation.

An example of this can be found in the first, informative part of the speech of the wise woman of Tekoa (2 Sam. 14.5-7). After the king's brief question, 'What is it?' the woman begins by describing her situation: 'I am a widow; my husband is dead. And your handmaid had two sons'. Then she recounts the main event through summary account: 'And they quarrelled with one another in the field; there was no one to part them, and one struck the other and killed him'. She refrains from recounting what happened immediately after the murder (her reaction, the reaction of the son who killed his brother, the funeral, the mourning customs, etc.), and continues with the family's response: 'And now the whole family has risen against your handmaid' (the Hebrew verb is in the past here, instead of the customary 'future' + *waw* conversive, indicating a new beginning after a break in the sequence of narrated events). Then she presents what the family said in direct speech: 'Give up the man who struck his brother, that we may kill him for the life of his brother whom he slew and we will destroy the heir also'. It is clear that the woman does not quote her relatives in a precise form. Not only does she abbreviate and summarize what the family said, but she also attributes to them an interpretation of the outcome of blood vengeance which is more consistent with her view of matters than with theirs, 'and we will destroy the heir also'. The woman concludes this part of her speech by continuing her interpretation of the results of the act of revenge, this time in her own name: 'Thus they would quench my coal which is left, and leave to my husband neither name nor remnant upon the face of the earth'. If we keep in mind the fact that the woman's aim is to convince David to forgive his son Absalom for slaying his brother, it will be clear why she recounts the actual murder through rapid summary account, why she omits her mourning and personal sorrow and why she slows down and lingers on the punishment of the son who killed his brother and the unfortunate outcome of his punishment.

Thus far, matters connected with the duration of time and its varying speeds have been discussed. In addition to calendar time, however, psychological time is also found in narrative. This does not refer to psychological time as experienced by the characters, even though this also exists in biblical narrative (for example, in Gen. 29.20: 'And Jacob served seven years for Rachel, and they seemed to him but a few days because of the love he had for her'); what is meant is the pace of time, the rate at which it proceeds with regard to the reader's subjective feeling.

The pace of time as perceived by the reader is influenced by several factors. Monotony slows it down while interest and suspense speed it up. Most biblical narratives are full of tension, containing numerous unusual events, dramatic incidents, sharp contrasts and fierce clashes. One crisis follows another, the characters become involved in complex situations and the reader eagerly awaits the disentangling of the threads. Everything is extremely dynamic, purposeful and condensed, and the reader's attention is always focused on what is to follow. The narratives concentrate on the principal characters and the main plot, evincing hardly any digressions; their style is direct, simple and uncomplicated. All these elements operate to create a rapid psychological pace.

The pace of the narrative is sometimes held back, however. One of the techniques which have this result is the use of delay, which heightens tension (possibly contrary to expectations) provided it is not too long and does not cause the reader to forget the main topic. For example, there is a delay before David is told of the death of his son, Absalom: an entire passage (2 Sam. 18.19-32) recounts Ahimaaz's request that he be allowed to inform David of the outcome of the battle, Joab's opposition to this and the exchange between them, Joab's command to the Cushite to run to David, Ahimaaz's decision to run too and his overtaking of the Cushite, and David's hopeful vigil between the two gates as he listens anxiously to the watchman's reports concerning the two runners approaching them. All the time the reader is waiting for the crucial moment when David will be told of his son's death. When Ahimaaz is finally standing before the king and giving him his message, the tragic news is still delayed and David receives no answer to his apprehensive question about the fate of his son until the second runner arrives. The effect of this delay—apart from heightening tension—is to emphasize the moment when the tidings do reach David, giving rise to his heart-rending desolation and causing this instant to form the climax of the narrative. (The slowing down of the pace is stressed here in a unique way, for the root form 'run' occurs antithetically no less than twelve times in this short passage.)

The repetition of matters already known to the reader also leads to the slowing down of the pace of the narrative. In biblical narrative the same item is often reported more than once. It has been noted above (p. 116) that information conveyed in the exposition is repeated later on in the course of the plot. In addition, a command, suggestion, prophecy, etc. is often cited at one point, only to be repeated when we are informed of its implementation. Similarly, an event, action or speech is conveyed, and at a later stage one of the characters reports on that same event, action or speech. What is more, these repetitions are often communicated in identical or almost identical terms.

For example, God commands Joshua: 'And when you hear the sound of the trumpet, then all the people shall shout with a great shout; and the wall of the city will fall down flat, and the people shall go up every man straight before him' (Josh. 6.5), and the narrator tells us later on: 'And when the people heard the sound of the trumpet, the people raised a great shout, and the wall fell down flat, so that the people went up into the city, every man straight before him' (v. 20).

What is the purpose of these repetitions? They could easily have been avoided, and in many cases they are in fact circumvented by such formulae as 'And it was so' (Gen. 1.9), 'Noah did this; he did all that God commanded him' (Gen. 6.22), 'and spoke the same words as before' (1 Sam. 17.23), 'Thus and so spoke the maiden from the land of Israel' (2 Kgs 5.4).

The explanation that the object of the repetitions is to slow down the pace is unsatisfactory. Though this does indeed occur, it is only a side effect. Repetitions of course always provide emphasis, but they also fulfil other functions, particularly as regards characterization.

The example cited from the book of Joshua, in which the same phrases are repeated exactly, indicates that everything happens exactly as God commanded, and since Joshua and the people obey Him, even the walls of Jericho do His bidding.

Special attention should be paid to the differences which often exist between the first and second versions, such as addition, omission, expansion, summarization, changed order and substitution (the replacement of one expression by another). In most instances these differences reflect the viewpoint or intention of the speaker, serving to avoid hurting the interlocutor, persuade, impel to action or advance the speaker's interests in some other way.

There are differences, for example, in what the narrator says about Saul's failure to smite Amalek and Saul's own version of this. The narrator informs us: 'But Saul and the people spared Agag, and the best of the sheep and of the oxen and of the fatlings, and the lambs, and all that was good, and would not utterly destroy them; all that was despised and worthless they utterly destroyed' (1 Sam. 15.9); while Saul says to Samuel: 'For the people spared the best of the sheep and of the oxen, to sacrifice to the Lord your God; and the rest we have utterly destroyed' (v. 15).

According to what the narrator says it is clear that Saul and the people thought it a pity to destroy all the good things that had fallen into their hands, and so they destroyed only what was worthless. Saul cannot deny the facts, but justifies the failure to obey Samuel's command by saying that they wanted to sacrifice the best sheep and oxen to God. Saul does not mention in his reply that not only the people but he himself was reluctant to destroy the livestock. He also omits Agag's name, since his excuse based on the intention to offer up the spoils as a sacrifice cannot account for his failure to kill Agag.

Saul's self-exonerating reply does not help him. Samuel does not argue with him about the veracity and accuracy of his statement, but takes it at its face value and asks: 'Why then did you not obey the voice of the Lord? Why did you swoop on the spoil, and do what was evil in the sight of the Lord?' (v. 19). Saul then admits that he has let Agag live, but repeats his contention that the people, (i.e. not himself) took the spoils to sacrifice them to God. Samuel replies that God does not want sacrifices and burnt offerings as much as 'obeying the voice of the Lord'.

There are also differences between the account of Saul's death as recounted by the narrator (1 Samuel 31) and as reported to David (2 Samuel 1). The narrator states that Saul said to his armour-bearer: 'Draw your sword, and thrust me through with it, lest these uncircumcised come and thrust me through and make sport of me' (1 Sam. 31.4). But because the armour-bearer feared to kill the king, Saul took his sword and fell on it. When the armour-bearer saw that Saul was dead he also killed himself by falling on his sword.

According to the version of the young Amalekite who reports to David, Saul turned to him (to the Amalekite, who happened to be on Mount Gilboa) and said: 'Stand beside me and slay me; for anguish has seized me, and yet my life still lingers'. So the Amalekite killed Saul, 'because I was sure that he could not live after he had fallen; and I took the crown which was on his head and the armlet which was on his arm, and I have brought them here to my lord' (2 Sam. 1.9-10).

There can be virtually no doubt that the differences in this case derive from the fact that the Amalekite is not telling the truth. He is lying because he believes that he will be paid well by David if he tells him that he killed his enemy and if in addition he brings him the king's crown and armlet. David's personality is illuminated by the fact that, contrary to the Amalekite's expectations, he is not glad at Saul's death, but is very angry with the young man for having dared to strike the Lord's anointed. The Amalekite is requited for his lie not with a reward but by execution, 'For your own mouth has testified against you, saying "I have slain the Lord's anointed"' (2 Sam. 1.16).

In some instances an event is narrated three or even four times. Adonijah's plot, for example, is recounted four times (1 Kings 1): by the narrator, by Nathan to Bathsheba, by Bathsheba to David and by Nathan to David. Here, too, there are subtle differences between the three reports given by the characters on the one hand and between them and the account conveyed by the narrator on the other.[3]

The narrator tells us first of all who supported Adonijah and who did not, continuing: 'Adonijah sacrificed sheep, oxen and fatlings. . . ' (v. 9) and concluding his account with a list of the people who were and were not invited to participate in the ceremony.

In his conversation with Bathsheba, Nathan abbreviates and summarizes events, giving only the main points: 'You will have heard that Adonijah the son of Haggith has become king. . . ' (v. 11). He does not report all the details the narrator has mentioned, probably because Bathsheba knows them, as is indicated by the phrase 'you will have heard', but he states explicitly that Adonijah has become king, a fact which has not been communicated by the narrator. Thus, despite the omission of details, Nathan goes further in describing Adonijah's move than the narrator.

Bathsheba tells David both that Adonijah is king—like Nathan—and that he has sacrificed sheep, oxen and fatlings in abundance—like the narrator. She even supplements the narrator's description of the sacrifice with the words 'in abundance'.

When Nathan addresses the king he first tells him indirectly that Adonijah is king: 'Have you said, "Adonijah shall reign after me"' (v. 24), then he tells him that Adonijah has sacrificed oxen, fatlings and sheep in abundance—using Bathsheba's phrase—adding details we did not know before: 'And behold, they are eating and drinking before him, and saying, "Long live king Adonijah"' (v. 25).

Thus, no one repeats precisely what was said before, each one adding something to the description of Adonijah's attempt to seize the throne. These reiterations can be termed intensifying repetitions, their object being to strengthen and support the efforts at persuasion in order to incite David to act against Adonijah and ensure that Solomon becomes king. In order to attain this objective it is necessary to overcome resistance, and therefore ever-increasing means of inducement are required. Naturally there is not a great deal

3. N. Leibowitz, *Studies in the Book of Genesis* (Jerusalem, 1972), pp. 250-56.

of resistance from Bathsheba, who is the natural ally in Nathan's attempt to get things under way, and no great efforts are needed to encourage her to cooperate with him. Neither is the resistance on David's part the result of a hostile or opposing stance, but rather of old age and general frailty.

In view of the stated objective, bringing David to intervene actively, it is hardly surprising that both Bathsheba and Nathan refrain from telling the king a fact which has been stated by the narrator, namely, that Adonijah has invited all the royal officials of Judah. Had they noted this, it might have strengthened the old king's tendency to resign himself to a state of affairs against which it would be difficult to fight.

Bathsheba and Nathan also substitute one word so that what they say will be appropriate to their *hearer*. The narrator conveyed events in accordance with Adonijah's viewpoint: 'but he did not invite... Solomon his brother' (v. 10), while Bathsheba and Nathan tell the story to the king in accordance with his viewpoint: 'and your servant Solomon, he has not invited' (vv. 19, 26) (the words 'your servant' serve to stress Solomon's loyalty to the king). For the same reason they also say: 'and he has invited all the king's sons' (vv. 19, 25), whereas the narrator said: 'and he invited all his brothers, the king's sons' (v. 9).

The adaptation of the report to the *speaker* is reflected in the fact that Nathan emphasizes himself (both by mentioning the first person pronoun twice and by placing them at the beginning of the sentence) and his loyalty to the king when he lists those who were not invited: 'But me, I your servant, and Zadok the priest, and Benaiah the son of Jehoiada, and your servant Solomon, he has not invited' (v. 26), while the narrator referred to him as 'Nathan the prophet'.

Despite these reiterations the pace of the narrative is hardly slowed down, primarily because they are brief. Repetitions in the Bible never lead to the leisurely pace of epic.

B. *The Sequence of Time*

Reading a narrative is a process which inevitably takes place in a chronological sequence. The reader takes in one word after another, one sentence after another and one paragraph after another. Does the chronological order of the incidents constituting the plot always conform with the order in which they are read, that is, are events in a narrative always presented in the sequence in which they occur? The answer is of course negative. It is a well-known fact that an author can begin his narrative somewhere in the middle, and later fill in the details about what happened beforehand. This means that the order of narrated time need not necessarily correspond with that of narration time.

What is the relation between the order of narrated time and that of narration time in biblical narratives? And if there is some discrepancy between them, why are facts not put in chronological order?

The biblical narrator generally ensures that there is agreement between the order of narrated time and that of narration time, moulding time within the narrative so that it flows in one direction, from the past to the future.

Moreover, biblical narrators have a special means at their disposal for expressing the sequential order of events, namely, the consecutive *waw* (translated 'and'). This feature organizes the facts of the narrative as a series of successive points in time, connecting them to one another like the links of a chain and making a considerable contribution to creating the sense of continuity and cohesion in biblical narrative. Because it occurs so frequently this *waw* gives biblical narrative its characteristic flavour.

When the narrator does not use the form of the verb with the consecutive *waw* this usually, though not invariably, means that the action referred to does not follow chronologically after the previous one. For example, 'So it went on year by year' (1 Sam. 1.7), where the form of the verb *ya'aseh* indicates that the action is repeated regularly, denoting a custom or habit.

'And the day before Saul came, the Lord had revealed to Samuel' (1 Sam. 9.15). The form of the verb 'revealed' (*gālâ*) testifies that this action preceded (past perfect) what was recounted in the previous verse, namely, that Saul and Samuel were approaching one another. The event related further on, 'When Samuel saw Saul, the Lord told him, "Here is the man. . . "' (v. 17) also occurs beforehand, as can be inferred from the forms of the verbs (*rā'â*, *'ānāhû*; while the action which follows, continuing the narrative sequence from v. 14, comes only in v. 18: 'Then Saul approached Samuel in the gate'.

As the previous example illustrates, the biblical author does not invariably relate events in chronological order, and thereby diverges from the continuous, one-way, forwards flow of time. When does the author do this? Does this happen, for example, when an author wishes to recount different events which occurred simultaneously?

Because of the limitations of language it is not possible to relate several overlapping story-lines at one and the same time, and therefore the author is in a predicament when wanting to present concurrent developments. Does the biblical author solve the problem by going over the same segment of time twice? That is, moving along a certain part of one story-line, turning the clock back and starting out again along the parallel segment of the second story-line, and so on?

The drama of Adonijah's attempt to seize the throne (1 Kings 1) occurs simultaneously at two places: inside Jerusalem, principally at David's palace, and at En Rogel, a little way away. This is, therefore, a narrative with parallel strands, and it is appropriate to scrutinize the way in which it is constructed. After recounting the preparations (vv. 5-8), the narrator describes Adonijah's actions with regard to the sacrifice at En Rogel (vv. 9-10). From here the narrator moves to David's palace and reports on what happens there *after* the news about the sacrifice reached Nathan up to the moment the trumpets are played, the pipes are blown and the people rejoice with great joy at the anointing of king Solomon (vv. 11-40). At this point the narrator interrupts this story-line and returns to Adonijah, but does not fill in the details concerning what has taken place at En Rogel when we were busy following events within the city. The narrator merely allows us to understand that more or less the same situation prevailed at En Rogel as existed when we left it. No significant developments occurred there during this time, Adonijah and his associates simply continued with their sacrifice and reached the end of their feast: 'and they had finished (*killû*) feastings' (v. 41). The verb *killû*, the form of which denotes past perfect, makes it clear that the narrator does not refer to the time they were eating but rather to the stage after they had finished. It can therefore be said that the narrator continues with the Adonijah story-line not from the point of leaving it but from the moment of leaving the parallel one, spanning the time gap within the Adonijah story-line by hinting at the eating of the sacrifice.

The narrator then tells us what happens in the Adonijah story-line from the moment Adonijah and Joab hear the sounds from the city until the hasty dispersal of the guests and Adonijah's flight to the horns of the altar (vv. 41-50). At this point the narrator returns to the parallel strand again, once more without recounting what has happened in the meantime to its main characters. We can assume that during this period Solomon established his position as king at Jerusalem, and this is insinuated by Jonathan's closing words to the guests at En Rogel (vv. 46-48); but the narrator continues with this thread again only from the point of leaving the previous one or, to be more precise, from the moment Solomon hears the news that Adonijah has taken hold of the horns of the altar. From this point the narrator continues with the narrative until the two story-lines finally meet when Adonijah appears before Solomon (vv. 51-53).

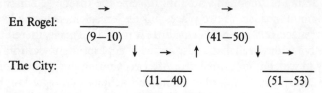

The diagram makes it clear that the author avoids regressing in time to a previous point, simply continuing in a straight chronological line while jumping from one parallel strand to another.

What techniques does the author use for shifting from one strand to another? Are these shifts sudden and abrupt or natural and organic? At the first transfer point there is a connecting link in the form of the prophet Nathan, who is mentioned at the end of the first story-line as well as at the beginning of the second: 'But *Nathan* the prophet or Benaiah or the mighty men or Solomon his brother, he did not invite'. 'Then *Nathan* said to Bathsheba the mother of Solomon, "Have you not heard that Adonijah the son of Haggith has become king and David our lord does not know it?"' (vv. 10-11). From the fact that Nathan is mentioned in v. 11 and we know that he was not invited to the feast at En Rogel, we understand that we have shifted to another place, even though this is not stated explicitly. This conclusion concerning the shift of location is reinforced immediately by the reference to Bathsheba, Solomon's mother, whom we would expect to find at the king's palace rather than amongst Adonijah's guests at En Rogel.

A particularly organic connecting link is found at the point where the noise accompanying the enthronement of Solomon (one story-line) is heard by Adonijah and his associates (the other line). Not only are the sounds mentioned at the end of one story-line and at the beginning of the other, but a natural transition in the proper sense of the word is created here by a physical phenomenon which actually moves from one place to another, and this realistic shift coincides with and justifies the compositional transition: 'Then *they blew the trumpet*; and all the people said, "Long live king Solomon". And all the people went up after him, playing on pipes, and rejoicing with great joy, so that *the earth was split by their noise*. Adonijah and all the guests who were with him *heard it* as they finished feasting. And when Joab *heard* the *sound of the trumpet*, he said, "What does *this uproar* in the city mean?"' (vv. 39-41). There is no need here, of course, to hint that those who heard the noise are in a different place, since this is already known to us.

Adonijah's fear of Solomon and his flight to the altar constitutes the third shift in the narrative. One story-line ends as follows: 'And Adonijah feared Solomon; and he arose, and went, and caught hold of the horns of the altar' (v. 50), and the parallel one begins: 'And it was told Solomon, "Behold, Adonijah fears king Solomon; for, lo, he has laid hold of the horns of the altar"' (v. 51).

The rule is, therefore, that the shifts are based on mentioning the same issue (person, event, action) at the end of one strand and at the beginning of the other.

For the development of the plot in this narrative it is essential that those present at one spot know what is happening at the other. To this end there are go-betweens in the narrative who move from one place to another, taking the necessary information with them. We are not told how Nathan hears about Adonijah's sacrifice. From the way he phrases his statement to Bathsheba we learn that this was not news to her either: 'Then Nathan said to Bathsheba the mother of Solomon, "*You will have heard* that Adonijah the son of Haggith has become king and David our lord does not know it"' (v. 11). It may be that the rumour was already common knowledge, for En Rogel was not far from Jerusalem, and an event such as a sacrifice in which such important people were participating could not remain a secret. Be that as it may, the narrative does not specify anything about this.

Later on in the narrative, however, we find a go-between whose identity is explicitly stated, namely, Jonathan, the son of Abiathar the priest, who goes from the city to Adonijah at En Rogel. Although no mention is made previously of his presence in Solomon's circle at Jerusalem, he has precise details and inside information about what has happened there. This go-between is identified by name, because he is not an insignificant person, his father being one of Adonijah's associates who will later be exiled by Solomon to Anathoth, and thus neither he nor his son and other descendants will be able to serve as priests at Jerusalem.

Jonathan's movement from one place to another is not congruous with the shift from one story-line to another. The shift occurs when the sounds emerging from the city are heard in En Rogel, whereas Jonathan appears on the scene somewhat later and can give details about what happened after the sounds were heard (vv. 46-48).

The go-between who appears at the end of the narrative is anonymous: 'And it was told Solomon. . . ' (v. 51). Here it is of no importance whatsoever who it was who told Solomon what Adonijah had done, just as the identity of the man whom Solomon despatched to bring Adonijah before him is of no significance.

The features which characterize the Adonijah narrative occur in other synchronic narratives too. For example, in the narrative of Absalom's revolt (2 Samuel 15-19), which also contains two parallel story-lines, one concerning David and one concerning Absalom time is not reversed either, and we are given no details concerning what happened in one place while we were observing events in the other. Here, too, we are first told of preparations (both the narrative of Adonijah and that of Absalom refer to chariots, horsemen, fifty runners and the preparation of a group of supporters), and the account of the actual revolt begins with information about a sacrifice in the presence of guests. Before beginning Absalom's story-line separately, the narrator presents the two story-lines while they are still united. Absalom meets David, asks for permission to go and pay his vow and receives the king's blessing; only then does he go to Hebron, and the narrative bifurcates. The two strands converge at the end, when David's army encounters Absalom's in the forest of Ephraim, though David and Absalom themselves never meet again.

At the first point of transition between the two strands there is an anonymous go-between who tells David of the widespread support for Absalom: 'And a messenger came to David, saying, "The hearts of the men of Israel have gone after Absalom"' (15.13), and the story-line centring on David starts at this point. The same item of information also concluded the first section of Absalom's story-line, only it was communicated by the narrator: 'And the conspiracy grew strong, and the people with Absalom kept increasing' (v. 12), thus creating a smooth, natural transition.

From this point on we accompany David as he goes east from Jerusalem to the place at which he decides to stop and rest: 'And the king, and all the people who were with him, arrived weary at the Jordan; and there he refreshed himself' (16.14). The author uses this rest in order to switch to Absalom, who has meanwhile reached Jerusalem together with his adherents. Once again, although we left Absalom at Hebron, the narrator does not tell us about him from that point but from the time he reached Jerusalem, omitting the events which are parallel in time to David's flight from Jerusalem to his resting place.

From this point we continue to follow the developments in Jerusalem until after the scene in which Ahithophel and Hushai give their advice; when Hushai tells the priests what Absalom has been counselled to do, the priests inform the maidservant, and she in turn passes the message on to Jonathan and Ahimaaz, the sons of the priests (17.17).The priests' sons manage to get from En Rogel, near the city, to David, who is in all probability still at the same resting place where we left him. Thus we again reach David's story-line in a natural way, and from this point on we are shown another part of the story-line centring on the king. In accordance with Hushai's recommendation, David hastens to cross the Jordan together with all his followers.

After a minor digression (a ramification of Absalom's story-line) recounting Ahithophel's suicide, the author returns to the main story-line of Absalom, and we are told that he crossed the Jordan too. Thus, the transition from one story-line to another is achieved through the shared feature of the crossing of the Jordan, first by David and then by Absalom.

This part of Absalom's story-line concludes with the information that Israel and Absalom encamped in the land of Gilead, on the other side of the Jordan. The narrator then returns to David's story-line, telling us that the king set up camp at Mahanaim, which was also on the other side of the Jordan. Thus, both sides are near one another, and in a little while the two story-lines will converge during the decisive battle between the two armies.

Before the two meet, however, David's story-line splits into two parts, one concerning David himself, who remains at Mahanaim, and one concerning his army, which sets off to battle. Here, too, time advances in linear progression, and the narrator leaves David at Mahanaim and accompanies the army as it departs. Only after

Absalom has been killed and the two runners, Ahimaaz and the Cushite, have set out to bring the news from the battlefield to David, does the author return to Mahanaim and show us the king sitting between the gates waiting anxiously for information. We can assume that he was sitting there in eager expectancy even before the narrative returned to him, but this is not stated nor even hinted. The two runners serve here as the link between the two secondary story-lines. Shortly afterwards, when Joab returns with the army to Mahanaim, the two secondary lines unite once more and combine to form one entity.

In two places in the narrative of Absalom's revolt the author establishes synchroneity of events in the two separate story-lines. The first instance of synchronization occurs when we are told that Hushai, who has been sent back to Jerusalem by David, reaches the city before Absalom: 'So Hushai, David's friend, came into the city, just as Absalom was about to enter Jerusalem' (15.37). The form of the verb *yābô* indicates that Absalom had not yet entered Jerusalem. This item of information about Absalom appears in the middle of a passage concerning David's story-line, and insinuates that David had forestalled Absalom because the king's representative had reached the city before his adversary entered it. Absalom would assume that Hushai had been in Jerusalem all the time, not imagining that he had been deliberately sent by David.

The second case of synchronization is to be found in 17.24: 'Then David came to Mahanaim. And Absalom crossed the Jordan with all the men of Israel'. This information is transmitted in a passage devoted to Absalom, and makes it clear that by the time Absalom crossed the Jordan David had already reached Mahanaim and therefore had sufficient time to get himself organized.

Synchronization can also be found in other narratives. In the narrative of David and Goliath, for example, the first part gives an account of Israel and the Philistines in the valley of Elah and the second, which is parallel in time, tells about Jesse and David at Bethlehem. The following item suddenly appears in the second part: 'Now Saul, and they, and all the men of Israel, were in the valley of Elah, fighting with the Philistines' (1 Sam. 17.19). This information diverges from the narrative sequence and indicates that the conversation between Jesse and David took place at the same time as Israel was fighting the Philistines.

Synchronization is characteristic of the books of Kings, which record alternately events occurring simultaneously in the kingdoms of Judah and Israel. Items of intelligence such as: 'In the eighteenth year of king Jeroboam the son of Nebat, Abijam began to reign over Judah' (1 Kgs 15.1) are frequent. In these books time is reversed whenever there is a shift from one kingdom to another, but here we are dealing not with one narrative but with a large composition comprising many.[4]

The following conclusions can be drawn about the techniques of constructing synchronic narratives in the Bible: A. Time is not reversed, and even though the narrative splits up into two parallel story-lines time passes by us only once. B. The transitions from one story-line to another are usually smooth and natural. C. The two story-lines are connected by runners, messengers, etc., who transfer information from one place to another (the movement of the go-between is sometimes congruous with the transition between story-lines). D. In certain cases there is synchronization between events in the two story-lines of the plot.

In view of the fact that time is not reversed in synchronic narratives in the Bible, the question arises as to how the sense of simultaneity is engendered in the reader. It appears that a special device, reflection, is used to this end. When we are absorbed in the developments of one story-line, the images of individuals and events from the other one are often evoked, usually being mentioned by characters within the narrative rather than by the narrator. Together with the characters, whose thoughts and feelings are continuously occupied by what is happening in the parallel story-line, we, as readers, are aware of the existence of the other story-line and everything connected with it.

In the narrative of Absalom's revolt, for example, Absalom's name occurs no less than thirteen times within David's story-line, from the moment the revolt begins until the king is informed of his son's death (excluding the frequent repetitions of the name in David's lament). In addition to the explicit mention of Absalom's name, references through such terms as 'son' or 'lad' or through verbs referring to him should, of course, be taken into account.

---

4. Special terms are sometimes used to indicate synchroneity of two different narratives, for instance: 'And it came to pass at that time' (Gen. 38.1); see also S. Talmon, 'The Presentation of Synchroneity and Simultaneity in Biblical Narrative', *Scripta Hierosolymitana* 27 (Jerusalem, 1978), pp. 9-26.

In this context the meeting between David and Shimei the son of Gera is of particular interest. When Shimei curses him, David says: 'Behold, my own son seeks my life; how much more now may this Benjaminite. . . ' (2 Sam. 16.11). The comparison between his son and the Benjaminite, which the king makes in an outburst of emotion, provides telling evidence of the fact that David's mind is continuously preoccupied with thoughts of Absalom. At the moment that Shimei curses and humiliates him mercilessly the king is not concerned solely with the terrible disgrace he is experiencing, but Absalom, who is far away, is as much at the forefront of his thoughts as Shimei, who is shouting at him at close range.

Parallel to Absalom's 'presence' in David's story-line, David is often mentioned in Absalom's, whether by name (four times), through such terms as 'your father' or 'his father' (seven times) or through prepositional and verbal references to him. Moreover, Absaloms story-line contains no reference to anything which is not connected directly with David and the efforts to defeat him.

A particularly potent example of the 'reflection' of the hidden story-line is found in the scene in which Absalom is slain. David is at Mahanaim, but despite his physical absence from the battlefield he is 'present' in the consciousness of the fighters, influencing their actions. The man who saw Absalom caught in the oak tree says: 'Even if I felt in my hand the weight of a thousand pieces of silver, I would not put forth my hand against the king's son; for in our hearing the king commanded you and Abishai and Ittai, "For my sake protect the young man Absalom". On the other hand, if I had dealt treacherously against his life (and there is nothing hidden from the king), then you yourself would have stood aloof' (2 Sam. 18.12-13).

As a result of the latent 'presence' of characters from the parallel story-line, its existence is not forgotten for a moment. Thus, the impression of simultaneity is achieved by psychological means rather than by intervention in the orderly flow of time. If the author had adopted the method of presenting events in one place, going back in time in order to recount what had happened meanwhile in the other place, and so on, the reader, who is fully involved in the incidents he or she is 'witnessing' at that moment, would not feel the simultaneity with the same intensity as is achieved through the technique of the continual reflection of the parallel story-line. It can even be said that the technique of reflection gives substance and significance to the concept of simultaneity over and above mere temporal congruity. The parallel story-lines do not exist independently and develop autonomously but are intertwined, so that the events and actions in one are to a great extent the outcome of those in the other. The development of events in one story-line are determined and affected by those in the parallel one: David's flight from Jerusalem is both a reaction to Absalom's actions and also influences them; there are interrelations between what Adonijah and his adherents do and the steps taken by Solomon's supporters. This state of mutual dependence and influence, of which reflection is only one indication, means that simultaneity is not a question of mere formal co-existence (one alongside the other) but has a qualitative dimension (one together with the other).

Thus, the construction of synchronic narratives in the Bible does not require the reversal of time; there are, however, instances, as has been hinted above, when time is reversed for other reasons.

Flashbacks are sometimes inserted by the narrator when a new character enters the narrative, providing details about background and past. This is not customary, however, and most of the characters are introduced into the narrative without accompanying information concerning their previous vicissitudes.

During the period of the Judges, when the Ammonites were attacking the people of Israel at Gilead, the leaders of Gilead were unable to find anyone to head the battle against the Ammonites and said to one another: 'Who is the man that will begin to fight against the Ammonites? He shall be head over all the inhabitants of Gilead' (Judg. 10.18). At this point Jephthah the Gileadite is mentioned, and in a flashback we are told that he was the son of a harlot, that his father had sons by his legal wife, that they drove Jephthah out of the house so that he should not inherit his father's property together with them, that Jephthah fled to the land of Tob and that worthless fellows collected around him and went raiding with him (11.1-3). Then the narrative returns to the war between the Ammonites and the people of Israel: 'After a time the Ammonites made war against Israel' (v. 4). The elders of Gilead go to Jephthah in order to bring him back from the land of Tob, assuring him with an oath that he will be their head and leader if he agrees to fight the Ammonites (vv. 5-11). Jephthah consents and defeats the Ammonites. What is the purpose of the flashback? It is not essential for the actual narrative about Jephthah's deliverance of Israel from the Ammonites. It does, however, create a sharp contrast between Jephthah's initial rejection and debasement, when he is driven out of his home as the son of a harlot, and the honour done to him later on, when the elders of Gilead beseech him to return and promise to make him their head and leader. The supplication of the elders of Gilead addressed to a man of low position like Jephthah, who is the leader of a band of worthless fellows, reflects the desperate plight of the people of Gilead, and in this way the effect of the deliverance is enhanced.

In 1 Kgs 1.6 we read of Adonijah: 'His father had never at any time displeased him by asking, "Why have you done thus and so?" He was also a very handsome man; and he was born next after Absalom'. This is a characteristic example of the reversal of time; we are taken back from the present, when Adonijah the son of Haggith exalts himself and prepares for himself chariots and horsemen, to the period of his growing up, and thence even further back, to the time of his birth. These items of information, which do not occur in their chronological position but at the beginning of the narrative of Adonijah's attempt to seize his father's place as king, fulfil several functions simultaneously. First of all, the contrast between David's conduct torwards his son and Adonijah's towards his father is emphasized. Secondly, the fact that David allows Adonijah to do whatever he wanted even as a child explains the prince's arrogance. Thirdly, a parallel is hinted at between Adonijah and Absalom ('He was also'), signifying that Adonijah's action was not singular and granting it a cumulative effect, possibly even indicating Adonijah's tendency to imitate the example of his elder brother (compare the matter of the chariots, horsemen and fifty runners). Fourthly, because it is noted that Adonijah was born next in line to Absalom among David's sons, we are given to understand that he considered himself, and not Solomon, to be entitled to the throne. In brief, his entire life, starting from his childhood and including his position within the family as a son and a brother, sheds light on the action Adonijah is about to take. Thus, the glimpses into the past hint at the causes for the developments in the present.

In 1 Kgs 11.14-22, 23-25, we are told of two men who were Solomon's adversaries, Hadad the Edomite and Rezon the son of Eliada. Details from their pasts take us back to the period of David's rule, explaining why they were Solomon's enemies. The second flashback is marked by the form of the verb *bāraḥ* denoting past perfect ('had fled'), while the first is indicated by the phrase 'For when' (*wayhî bihyôt*).

Glimpses into the past often serve to explain the actions or utterances of people or the origin of situations. For example, after Samuel was born Elkanah and all his household went up to sacrifice to the Lord, but Hannah did not accompany them, 'For she said to her husband, "As soon as the child is weaned, I will bring him"' (1 Sam. 1.22). Hannah had obviously said this before the family departed in order to justify her staying at home with the child.

Solomon imposed taxes in order to fund his extensive building projects. One of the places included in his building activities was the city of Gezer, but how had this Canaanite city come into his possession? This is explained by a flashback: 'Pharaoh king of Egypt had gone up and captured Gezer and burnt it with fire, and had slain the Canaanites who dwelt in the city, and had given it as dowry to his daughter, Solomon's wife' (1 Kgs 9.16).

The sailors in the ship in which Jonah was absconding to Tarshish said to him: 'What is this that you have done?' And the narrator adds: 'For the men knew that he was fleeing from the presence of the Lord, because he had told them' (Jon. 1.10). The narrator's comment contains two backward glances, explaining what the sailors said: 'the men knew' precedes their accusatory question chronologically, and 'he had told them' comes even before 'the men knew'.

On occasions the function of the flashback is to recount what has happened meanwhile somewhere else or to someone other than the characters with which the narrative has been dealing (this does not refer to a synchronic narrative but to one with one story-line). For example, in the narrative of Ehud we are told that after Ehud had killed Eglon king of Moab the king's servants came and found the doors of the king's roof chamber locked. They waited until they were utterly at a loss and finally, seeing that the king still did not open the door, they opened it themselves and found their lord dead on the floor. At this point the narrative returns to Ehud, who had meanwhile managed to escape, as the narrator establishes through a backward glance. 'Ehud had escaped while they delayed, and had passed beyond the sculptured stones, and escaped to Seirah' (Judg. 3.26).

David goes with Achish king of Gath and the other Philistines to Aphek to fight Saul king of Israel, but as a result of the pressure of the lords of the Philistines, who do not trust David, he is obliged to leave the Philistine camp. On his return to Ziklag he discovers that during his absence there has been a terrible disaster, which the narrator communicates through a flashback: 'Now when David and his men came to Ziklag on the third day, the Amalekites had made a raid upon the Negeb and upon Ziklag. They had overcome Ziklag, and burned it with fire, and taken captive the women and all who were in it, both small and great; they had killed no one, but carried them off, and went their way' (1 Sam. 30.1-2).

The flashback in 1 Sam. 16.14 appears to serve the function of synchronization: 'And the spirit of the Lord departed from Saul, and an evil spirit from the Lord tormented him'. The forms of both the verbs in this verse (*sārâ, ûbi'atattû*) indicate that what is conveyed here did not happen after the last item mentioned ('And Samuel rose up, and went to Ramah'), but before it. What seems to be implied is that the spirit of the Lord had departed from Saul and that he had been tormented by an evil spirit from the very moment that the spirit of the Lord had come upon David (v. 13). This explanation is supported indirectly by the frequent reiteration of the word 'spirit' in vv. 13-16, 23 (the Hebrew tenses of the four verbs, 'took', 'played', 'refreshed' and 'departed' in v. 23 indicate less a glimpse into the past than the recurrence of these activities whenever the evil spirit from God was upon Saul).

The flashback fulfils a different function when, after stating the fact that Absalom was slain and his body thrown into the pit in the forest, the narrator says: 'Now Absalom in his lifetime had taken and set up for himself the pillar which is in the King's Valley, for he had said, "I have no son to keep my name in remembrance"; he had called the pillar after his own name, and it is called Absalom's monument to this day' (2 Sam. 18.18).[5] The verb 'had said' (*'āmar*) is in the past perfect in relation to 'had taken' (*lākah*) which is also in the past perfect in relation to its context. Absalom's pronouncement precedes the construction of the monument in chronological terms and provides the justification for it. The item of information concerning the erection of the monument is inserted here and not in its chronological place in order to create a sharp contrast between the imposing monument in the Valley of the King and the ignoble pit in the forest, signifying the contrast between Absalom's aspirations, pride and self-love, on the one hand, and the calamitous results to which these aspirations gave rise, on the other. The antithesis is

5. M. Weiss, 'Weiteres über die Bauformen des Erzählens in der Bibel', *Biblica* 46 (1965).

given additional emphasis by the repetition of the same (Hebrew) roots: 'And they *took* Absalom, and threw him into a great pit in the forest, and *set* over him a very great heap of stones'; 'Absalom. . . . had *taken* and *set* up for himself. . . '

Flashbacks introduced by the narrator are comparatively rare in biblical narrative; as to anticipations, the rule is that the narrator avoids altogether informing the reader beforehand what is about to happen. What the future holds is not hidden from the omniscient narrator, but is not usually shared with the reader. There are a few exceptions to this rule, for instance, when the narrator tells us: 'And Samuel did not see Saul again until the day of his death' (1 Sam. 15.35), or when God's intentions are revealed to us, because these can generally be regarded as indication of what will happen in the future. Thus, for example, the narrator tells us about Eli's sons, who would not listen to the voice of their father, 'for it was the will of the Lord to slay them' (1 Sam. 2.25); and the narrator also makes it clear to us that God had ordained to defeat the good counsel of Ahithophel, 'so that the Lord might bring evil upon Absalom' (2 Sam. 17.14).

In the vast majority of cases, however, when the narrator wishes to hint at what is to come this is done as an organic part of the action. One of the participants in the plot who has the capacity to see into the future—whether a prophet, an angel of the Lord or even God himself (either directly or by means of a dream)—informs one of the other participants of events which are about to occur.

The information regarding what is to come serves an important purpose, giving what is tantamount to an interpretation of events in advance and thereby making the reader simultaneously aware of actual developments and their significance. It sheds light on the deeper meaning of what is happening, enabling us concurrently with reading about the events, to transcend them, grasp the causal connections between them and perceive the hidden forces behind them.

Moreover, the revelation of the future also ensures that the various events are not fortuitous but that there is a plan and a purpose. It also enables the characters involved to respond, whether by acceptance, as in the case of Eli the priest (1 Sam. 3.18) or by repentance, as in the case of king Ahab (1 Kgs 21.27). Sometimes a prophecy about the future is transmitted in order to create the possibility of its non-fulfilment; repentance as a result of the prophecy can lead to its being revoked, as happens in the case of the inhabitants of Nineveh (Jon. 3.10).

Flashbacks occurring in the speech of the characters, in contrast to those conveyed by the narrator, should not be regarded as deviations from the normal order of time since they are part of conversations taking place in the present. Nevertheless, backward glances of this kind are immensely important. They do not recount the facts as they actually occurred but rather as the speaker sees them or wishes them to be seen by the interlocutor, thereby making a marked contribution to the characterization of the persons in the narrative. Glimpses into the past within the speech of the characters combine the actual facts with their interpretation, often showing how an individual's present actions are determined by past experiences. Facts from the past 'exist' in the present, operating actively to mould the future, and thus the various times become interrelated and to a certain extent unified.

The flashbacks found in the speech of the characters sometimes repeat matters which have been narrated before and are known to the reader, and sometimes recount events which have not been related previously and are new to the reader.

Longing for the past is a well-known phenomenon; a person complains of present suffering and believes that things were better in the past, remembering the good and repressing the bad. An example of this can be found in the episode of the people of Israel eating the manna in the wilderness. Looking back they speak with longing of Egypt, of the good and varied food they had there when they sat by the fleshpots and ate bread to the full (Exod. 16.3), and do not recollect their suffering and heavy labour: 'And the people of Israel also wept again, and said, "O that we had meat to eat. We remember the fish we ate in Egypt for nothing, the cucumbers, the melons, the leeks, the onions, and the garlic; but now our strength is dried up, and there is nothing at all but this manna to look at"' (Num. 11.4-6).

Absalom twice recalls his sojourn at Geshur, about which nothing was reported in its chronological place. The first time he sums up a long period of three years in a few words, and it is obvious that he is looking back at that period from his present standpoint, which alters his perception of his experiences considerably. He says to Joab: 'Behold, I sent word to you, "Come here, that I may send you to the king, to ask, 'Why have I come from Geshur? It would be better for me to be there still'. Now therefore let me go into the presence of the

king; and if there is guilt in me, let him kill me"' (2 Sam. 14.32). Was
life really so good for him at Geshur, and would it have been better
for him to remain there? What he says in the second flashback,
referring to one particular incident during the three years, contradicts
this contention. In asking his father for permission to go to Hebron in
order to pay his vow, he gives the following reason: 'For your servant
vowed a vow while I dwelt at Geshur in Aram, saying, "If the Lord
will indeed bring me back to Jerusalem, then I will offer worship to
the Lord"' (2 Sam. 15.8). This means that when he was at Geshur he
very much hoped to return to Jerusalem and consequently made his
vow, indicating that his life there was not so pleasant. While
enduring the suffering of the present Absalom forgets the pain of the
past, regarding the former days through rose-tinted spectacles.
Absalom's objective in referring to the 'good' past is to induce Joab to
plead with the king on his behalf. The tenor of what he says is: you
brought me back from Geshur in order to help and benefit me, but in
actual fact you have made my situation worse; now go and set
matters right. It is irrelevant to the author what Absalom 'really' felt
at Geshur ('really' here, of course, in terms of the narrative's internal
world), all that matters is how Absalom perceives his feelings then at
this moment and how he utilizes this view of things for his current
purposes.

It could be claimed that Absalom did not make any vow at Geshur.
The narrator did not tell us about the vow in its place, and it can
therefore be supposed that Absalom invented it to provide an excuse
for his journey to Hebron with a large entourage. If this is so
Absalom is a liar. Even if he did make the vow, as he said he had, he
had not seen fit to pay it during the years that had passed since his
return and conveniently remembered it now in order to deceive his
father as to the reason for his trip to Hebron. As far as the
presentation of Absalom's character is concerned it makes very little
difference, then, whether he really did make the vow or not.

References to the past uttered by characters do not necessarily give
an accurate picture of what happened. Clearly both Absalom's
mutually-contradictory statements regarding the past are influenced
to a considerable extent by his intentions concerning the future, as
regards both the actual evocation of previous experiences and the
way he perceives them.

An interesting glimpse into David's personality is provided by his
final injunctions to his son Solomon (1 Kgs 2.2-9), when he refers to

events which have been narrated before. The things David says in his last testament are of particular significance for understanding his character because they focus on his attitude to people towards whom he adopted a clear stand in the past. Before his death David recalls those individuals and their deeds, determining his final attitude to them.

David speaks about three men, Joab, Barzilai and Shimei the son of Gera, though not in chronological order. It is obvious that Joab's murder of Amasa is associated with that of Abner, but why does David mention Barzilai before Shimei, reversing the order of the events concerning them? If we assume that he remembers them in the order of their importance—from his own subjective viewpoint—it would appear that Joab's actions grieved him more than anything else, and that the kindness of Barzilai and his sons was of greater significance to him than the curses of Shimei the son of Gera.

David justifies his harsh attitude to Joab by mentioning 'how he dealt with the two commanders of the armies of Israel, Abner the son of Ner, and Amasa the son of Jether, whom he murdered, avenging in time of peace blood which had been shed in war' (v. 5). The words 'avenging in time of peace blood which had been shed in war' refer to the fact that Joab did not kill Abner and Amasa in the course of battle but during times of peace, in the guise of friendship, when they suspected nothing. Thus, what causes David particular pain is the treacherous way in which the murders were implemented. If it is because of the acts of deception that David seeks the death of Joab, who had served him devotedly, there is some justification for his vindictiveness. But we cannot ignore his opening words: 'Moreover you know also what Joab the son of Zeruiah did *to me*' (v. 5). This indicates a personal aspect, and almost certainly refers to the fact that Joab hurt David directly by killing Absalom. Another possibility is that David regarded the slaying of the two commanders as a personal injury. If the latter is the case—and the absence of the conjunctive 'and' before 'how he dealt with the two commanders' tends to weight the scales in favour of this interpretation—this may derive from the fact that David bears the guilt for the blood shed by Joab, as is implied by Solomon's reference to the past in sanctioning the murder of Joab: 'And thus take away from me and from my father's house the guilt for the blood which Joab shed without cause' (1 Kgs 2.31-33). The harm to David may also be connected with his desire to keep his hands clean in political matters, as emerges from his conduct towards Saul, or may possibly consist in the public damage resulting from his being accused of hypocrisy. The nation could have suspected David of having had a hand in the murder of Abner and Amasa, who had once been hostile commanders. In this connection it should be noted that the old king's request that Solomon take vengeance upon Joab indicates that his mourning over Abner's death, as described in 2 Sam. 3.28-39, was genuine and was not intended merely to demonstrate to the nation that, 'it had not been the king's will to slay Abner the son of Ner'. Thus, the flashback in David's will sheds light retrospectively on an action whose motives were unclear at the time.

Nothing is reported of David's reaction to Amasa's murder at the time (2 Sam. 20.4-13). All we know is that even though Amasa had headed Absalom's army, David made him the commander of his own army and gave him the difficult mission of summoning Judah within three days. If it had been supposed that David was seeking an excuse to get rid of Amasa by roundabout means, the will shows that, as in the case of Abner, David was not at all pleased by Amasa's death, which served Joab's personal interests and aspirations.

David's instructions regarding the sons of Barzilai endorse the attitude he expressed at the time (2 Sam. 19.33-40). He does not forget the kindness which Barzilai and his sons showed him in his darkest hour, and ensures that his promise to them will be kept after his death.

As regards Shimei the son of Gera, David now makes statements contradicting what he said at the time of the actual events (2 Sam. 16.10-12; 19.22-23). Then David thought that Shimei was cursing him because God had instructed him to do so, and vehemently rejected the offers made by Abishai the son of Zeruiah to kill Shimei (both when he was fleeing Jerusalem and on his return). Now, however, his pronouncements clearly reflect his traumatic experience, and he speaks of the man without a scrap of forgiveness: 'And there is also with you Shimei the son of Gera, the Benjaminite from Bahurim, who cursed me with a grievous curse on the day when I went to Mahanaim' (1 Kgs 2.8). David also remembers that he swore to Shimei not to put him to death, and makes no effort to conceal the fact. In contradiction to that oath, however, he now instructs Solomon to 'bring his grey head down with blood to Sheol' (v. 9). Was David's speech at the time insincere, then, merely deriving from the exigencies of the situation, or was his forgiving attitude genuine but changed with the passage of time? We cannot answer these questions, for even if we are given an occasional glimpse into someone's mind, its inner workings are never made completely transparent to us. In literature, as in real life, there will always be hidden aspects of a person's character, confronting the outside observer with a puzzle, and this is especially so when a personality as complex and many-sided as David's is involved.

The past enters the character's present through memories, the future through expectations and intentions. There are various ways of relating to the future, through expectations, hopes, apprehensions, desires, plans, requests, promises, decisions and orders. The first few items on the list refer to the future in a passive way, while the last few relate to it as something which can be actively moulded and influenced. All these approaches are represented in abundance in biblical narrative. The frequency with which they occur gives biblical narratives a quality of being oriented towards the future and of constantly aspiring to advance without delay. This feature contributes in no small way to the dynamic and dramatic character of biblical narrative.

2. The Shaping of Space

Events are accorded uniqueness by virtue of their position on the coordinates of time and space. These categories also give the narrative a dimension of reality. Unlike legends and fables, in which time and space are not mentioned at all or are not defined in any way (once upon a time, many years ago, in a dark forest, in a distant land), the action of most biblical narratives takes place within a well-defined framework of time and space.

There are, however, appreciable differences between the dimensions of time and space in the narrative. First of all, there is no parallel relationship in the realm of space to that between narration time and narrated time. Space exists within the narrative but the narrative does not exist within space, and therefore the internal space of the narrative is realized not in external space (as is a painting) but in external time. The ways for shaping space in a narrative are also essentially different from those used for time.

A world with extremely wide horizons is spread out before us in biblical narratives. Most of them are not located in one limited place but extend over a variety of regions and sometimes even over many different and distant countries, such as the land of Israel, Egypt, Mesopotamia, Moab, Philistia, etc.

In most cases the narrator takes us to the site of each event, showing or telling us directly what is happening there. Only very rarely do we hear what is happening elsewhere through a messenger. This technique, which is often used in plays, is found a few times in biblical narrative, as, for instance, in the narrative of Jacob's return to his native country and in the narrative of Job. From the messengers Jacob has sent to his brother Esau we hear that Esau has set out to meet Jacob together with four hundred men (Gen. 32.7). Four messengers reach Job's house successively, and from them we learn that the Sabeans have captured Job's oxen and asses, fire has burned his sheep, the Chaldeans have taken his camels and a great wind has blown down the house in which his children were gathered, killing them all (Job 1.14-19). In these narratives the technique of bringing events to our knowledge by means of messengers has been adopted because it is not the actual events which are important but the reactions of the people receiving the information. Jacob takes various steps to cope with the expected attack, thus revealing his fear and guilt feelings; Job accepts his fate, proving his steadfastness in adversity. In some other narratives events are brought to our attention both by the narrator and, in a somewhat different version, by a messenger, as, for instance, the battle of Aphek (1 Sam. 4.20-17). In these cases the differences are significant.

In biblical narratives space is shaped primarily through the movement of characters and the reference to places. Both these features are often used together; the characters go on journeys, during the course of which the names of the places from which they set out and to which they are going or which they pass on the way are mentioned.

When someone discerns the movement of characters we are indirectly given a sense of the existence of space. In 2 Sam. 18.24-27 we read: 'and the watchman went up to the roof of the gate by the wall, and when he lifted up his eyes and looked, he saw a man running alone... and he came apace and drew near. And the watchman saw another man running... and the watchman said, "I think the running of the foremost is like the running of Ahimaaz the son of Zadok"'. The watchman on the roof of the gate sees the two runners, Ahimaaz and the Cushite, indistinctly at first because they are far away, then with ever-increasing clarity as they come nearer, and in this way the sense of space is created.

A similar example is found in 2 Kgs 9.17-20. The watchman standing on the tower in Jezreel sees a company, but cannot yet discern details; then he perceives that the messenger who was sent to the company reached it but did not come back; after that he sees that the second horseman who was sent there reached it but did not return either; finally he sees that the driving is like that of Jehu the son of Nimshi, 'for he drives furiously'. Like the watchman in 2 Samuel 18, this watchman also tells the king from time to time what he can see, but here two horsemen make the connection between the king in Jezreel and Jehu, who is gradually approaching the city. We both accompany these two riders on their way to Jehu and see them from afar through the eyes of the watchman.

In most of the narratives we are informed about the characters' movements in space by the narrator rather than by a watchman or another character. The narrator apprises us of Abraham's journeys from Ur of the Chaldeans to the land of Canaan, throughout the length and breadth of Canaan and from Canaan to Egypt and back. The narrator also informs us that Abraham's servant, and later on Jacob too, goes from the land of Canaan to Mesopotamia and back, Jacob and his sons go down to Egypt, Moses flees from Egypt to Midian and later returns to Egypt, the people of Israel leave Egypt, pass through the wilderness of Sinai and the lands of Edom and Moab until they eventually reach the land of Israel, etc. Thus, the world of the Bible extends before us in all its spaciousness. Even when the people of Israel are dwelling in their own land there is no dearth of information about the movements of characters within the country and to other lands. David escapes to the wilderness of Judah, to the Negeb, and later on to the eastern bank of the Jordan. Elijah wanders from one spot to another within the land of Israel, even going to the mountain of the Lord at Horeb, and Elisha, who is also a great wanderer, goes as far afield as Damascus. It can be asserted with confidence that biblical narratives are dominated by movement. In most narratives the movement of the characters is more or less marginal to the plot, but in some of them movement constitutes a central structural element, serving as the focal point of the plot. This is the case in the narratives of pursuit, such as the one concerning Gideon's chase of Zebah and Zalmunna (Judges 8), those of Saul's pursuit of David (1 Samuel 19–26), and the one of Sheba the son of Bichri, who is hunted by Abishai and Joab (2 Samuel 20). Even in what appears to be a 'static' narrative, like that of the Garden of Eden (Genesis 2–3) movement is highly significant: first to the garden, then to the tree at the centre of the garden, and later on in the opposite direction, from the tree at the centre of the garden to the other trees in the garden, and from there outside the garden.

Places are frequently cited in the Bible, whether cities, villages, rivers, streams, wells, mountains or forests. Within the cities mention is sometimes made of specific houses, such as the royal palace or the dwelling of one particular person. All these contribute to constructing the arena in which events occur and to imparting spatial depth to the narratives.

Whether the reference is to geographical places, such as cities and rivers, or to details within them, such as houses and rooms, these spots are mentioned in the narrative as an integral part of the plot. The characters act, and within the framework of their actions they leave or reach a certain place. The scene of the events moves from one spot to another, thereby granting them their literary existence.

Biblical narratives usually mention only the place characters leave and the one they reach, without dwelling on the territory in between: 'So Abram went, as the Lord had told him; and Lot went with him. Abram was seventy-five years old when he departed from Haran. . . And they set forth to go to the land of Canaan. When they had come to the land of Canaan. . . ' (Gen. 12.4-5). Thus, corresponding to the gaps in time which have been discussed above, gaps in space are also frequent in the Bible.

In some cases, however, the interim stations are mentioned. This is generally done because of the function they fulfil, which may be different in each individual narrative.

It is often difficult to comprehend fully what part is played by the places cited in biblical narrative because the narrator was addressing an audience which was familiar with them. This audience was able to ascribe significance to those spots, which we cannot do today because of the distance in time and our inadequate knowledge of the geographical realities of the biblical period.

In the narrative of Jacob we read: 'Jacob left Beersheba and went toward Haran' (Gen. 28.10), but on the way between these two places another spot is mentioned, Bethel, where Jacob spent the night. Why is reference made to this place rather than any other at which Jacob stopped on his way from the land of Canaan to Mesopotamia?

The narrative draws our attention to that site[6] by using the word
'place' three times at the very beginning: 'And he came to a certain
place, and stayed there that night, because the sun had set. Taking
one of the stones of the *place*, he put it under his head and lay down
in that *place* to sleep' (v. 11). Further on Jacob says: 'Surely the Lord
is in this *place*; and I did not know it' (v. 16). And he adds: 'How
awesome is this *place*. This is none other than the house of God, and
this is the gate of heaven' (v. 17). Finally he called 'the name of that
place Bethel' (v. 19). Emphasis is laid on that spot because God
revealed himself to Jacob there before he left the land of Canaan,
promising him the blessing given to Abraham and Isaac, that God
would guard him wherever he went and bring him back there. As he
leaves for another country Jacob knows that God will be with him
and that he will return in peace to his father's house.

On David's journey from Jerusalem to Mahanaim during his flight
from Absalom several places on the way are mentioned, such as the
brook Kidron, the Mount of Olives, Bahurim and the Jordan. The
narrative of Absalom's revolt is one in which movement fulfils a
crucial structural function, determining the shape of the narrative to
a large extent. There is almost constant movement and the points of
rest are few. The narrative contains two parallel lines of movement,
David's and Absalom's; Absalom traverses the same path that David
took, but belatedly and in one direction only.

When David leaves Jerusalem with all the people they stop at a
place called 'the last house' (2 Sam. 15.17). We do not know where it
stood precisely and what its nature was, and consequently we cannot
ascertain why the narrator notes that David and all the people with
him stood there. The name 'the last house' indicates that the house
was situated far from the centre of the city, probably on the city
limits. Anyone going past the 'last house' left the borders of
Jerusalem and this is where David halted. The mention of this place
would seem to emphasize the fateful and weighty import of the fact
that the king was obliged to leave his city.

This supposition is supported by the information concerning the
next stop on David's journey, the brook Kidron. It is clear from the
context that 'the last house' is situated very near to the brook Kidron.
We are told in detail about the crossing of this brook: 'And all the
country wept aloud as all the people passed by, and the king crossed

6. See above, p. 104.

the brook Kidron, and all the people passed on toward the wilderness. And Abiathar came up, and lo, Zadok came also, with all the Levites, bearing the ark of the covenant of God; and they set down the ark of God, until the people had all passed out of the city' (vv. 23-24). This description is somewhat reminiscent of the crossing of the Jordan, when the people of Israel entered the land of Canaan, as is related in Josh. 3.17: 'And while all Israel were passing over on dry ground, the priests who bore the ark of the covenant of the Lord stood on dry ground in the midst of the Jordan, until all the nation finished passing over the Jordan'. In both places we read that all the people passed by, that the priests who bore the ark stood (set down the ark) until all the people (all the nation) had finished passing, and, in addition, similar expressions are found in both passages. Just as crossing the Jordan in Joshua's time marks the beginning of a new era in the history of the people (entering the land of Canaan), crossing the Kidron marks the end of a chapter in David's life. The king abandons the city to its new monarch, and he himself becomes a fugitive.

The next site mentioned on David's journey is the Mount of Olives: 'And David went up the upward slope of the Mount of Olives, weeping as he went up, barefoot and with his head covered; and all the people who were with him covered their heads, and they went up, weeping as they went up' (2 Sam. 15.30). The first part of David's journey after he crosses the brook Kidron is described movingly: the king is weeping, his head is covered and he is barefoot. This touching account of the king in his humiliation is heightened by the mention of the place, the upward slope of the Mount of Olives, and by the repetition of the phrase 'went up'. The root 'went up' (*'ālâ*) dominates the first part of the verse: 'And David *went up* the *upward* slope of the Mount of Olives, weeping as he *went up*'. This dense repetition of the root focuses our attention on the actual ascent, involving considerable physical exertion for the ageing king, who goes up barefoot instead of mounted, as befits someone of his station. The ascent of the Mount of Olives thus throws into relief the terrible descent in the king's position.

At the beginning of the next chapter we are told that Ziba, the servant of Mephibosheth, brings asses for the king and his household to ride, so that henceforth the king can continue his journey through the wilderness mounted. It is stated specifically that the spot at which David meets Ziba is a little way beyond the summit: 'When

David had passed a little beyond the summit Ziba the servant of
Mephibosheth met him, with a couple of asses saddled' (16.1). The
fact that the precise spot at which the meeting took place is cited
shows that the asses were placed at David's disposal (Ziba says out of
politeness that the asses are for the king's household, but there are
only two asses) only after he had passed the summit, meaning that
David had been obliged to complete the difficult ascent on foot.

The site of the summit itself is also mentioned: 'When David came
to the summit, where God was worshipped, behold, Hushai the
Archite came to meet him with his coat rent and earth upon his head'
(15.32). There is undoubtedly some significance in the fact that the
custom of worshipping God on the summit is noted. It is not stated
that David worshipped there on this occasion, but the contiguity of
the phrases 'where God was worshipped' and 'behold, Hushai the
Archite came to meet him', implies that Hushai's appearance is to be
connected with the finger of God. We are told in the previous verse
that when David learned that Ahithophel had joined Absalom's
conspiracy he beseeched God: 'O Lord, I pray thee, turn the counsel
of Ahithophel into foolishness' (v. 31). Immediately afterwards, when
David reaches the summit, 'where God was worshipped', Hushai,
through whom God will turn Ahithophel's counsel into foolishness,
appears.

The next stop on David's journey east is Bahurim, the residence of
Shimei the son of Gera, of Saul's family, who goes out to curse and
abuse the king: 'When king David came to Bahurim, there came out
a man of the family of the house of Saul, whose name was Shimei,
the son of Gera; and as he came he cursed continually' (16.5).
Bahurim is mentioned twice more as the place where Shimei the son
of Gera lived: 'And Shimei the son of Gera, the Benjaminite from
Bahurim, made haste to come down with the men of Judah to meet
king David' (2 Sam. 19.16); 'And there is also with you Shimei the
son of Gera, the Benjaminite from Bahurim, who cursed me with a
grievous curse on the day when I went to Mahanaim' (1 Kgs 2.8). It
would seem that the reference to Bahurim as the place where Shimei
lived in all these passages serves to stress what is hinted in the terms,
'the Benjaminite' and 'a man of the family of the house of Saul'.
Bahurim is situated in the territory of Benjamin, Saul's tribe, and
Shimei's hostile attitude to David derives from the fact that he
belongs to the tribe of Benjamin and the family of the house of Saul.
Thus it is implied that the tribe of Benjamin harbours feelings of

resentment against the rule of David's house, and both David and Solomon are required to be on their guard and act with caution in this respect.

Bahurim is mentioned once more in the narrative of Absalom's revolt, in connection with the transmission of information from Jerusalem, which is momentarily Absalom's stronghold, to David, who is in the wilderness. Jonathan and Ahimaaz are waiting at En Rogel, which is at the spot where the brook Kidron meets the valley of Ben Hinnom. They make their way from there to David, to tell him about the counsels given by Ahithophel and Hushai, but because a lad saw them and told Absalom, the latter's servants are sent to pursue and seize them: 'But a lad saw them, and told Absalom; so both of them went away quickly, and came to the house of a man at Bahurim, who had a well in his courtyard; and they went down into it. And the woman took and spread a covering over the well's mouth, and scattered grain upon it; and nothing was known of it' (2 Sam. 17.18-19).

The fact that Jonathan and Ahimaaz hide at Bahurim of all places is not without significance. We cannot help remembering Shimei the son of Gera, who lived at Bahurim and had cursed David only shortly beforehand. The attitude of the anonymous man, in whose courtyard the two messengers hide, and of his wife, who does everything possible in order to conceal them from their pursuers, is in sharp contrast with Shimei's. This proves that in that Benjaminite town David has loyal supporters who are prepared to help his servants even when David's position as ruler is precarious. The behaviour of these anonymous residents of Bahurim reflects back on Shimei's actions, just as his underscores theirs. With regard to the structure of the narrative the two events which occur at Bahurim hint at a turning-point in the plot. Shimei's curses reflect David's decline, while the rescue of Jonathan and Ahimaaz at the same spot signifies David's resurgence. The reversal in the direction of the plot starts with the rejection of Ahithophel's counsel and the acceptance of Hushai's, and the scene in which the two men proffer their advice is the axis upon which the narrative revolves. The encounter with Shimei occurs before this decisive event, while the rescue of Jonathan and Ahimaaz takes place right after it. Shimei's action is the last item related in David's story-line before the narrator transfers us to Absalom's camp at Jerusalem while the events connected with Jonathan and Ahimaaz are the first recounted when we return to David's story-line. Thus, the two events which occur at Bahurim are contrasted with one another.

After David has passed Bahurim he and all the people with him reach the wilderness, and no places of settlement or any defined sites are mentioned. The narrator notes: 'And the king, and all the people who were with him, arrived weary; and there he refreshed himself' (16.14). This makes it clear that the exhausting journey through the wilderness continued (and herein lies the contribution to creating the sense of space) until an unnamed place was reached where they could rest. The context indicates that the spot was near the Jordan, for when Jonathan and Ahimaaz pass Hushai's message on to David the king is beside the water, and upon hearing it he hastens to cross the Jordan. Why did he not go across it as soon as he reached it? It would seem that he did not wish to pass over the river unnecessarily, since apart from the physical effort involved, crossing the Jordan signified separation, disruption and a radical change of situation, in a similar way as moving across the Kidron did. The crossing of the Jordan, which is related in 17.22, means for David that he has left his own country and entered an area which is associated with the house of Saul and the Ammonites.

The city to which David escapes, Mahanaim, previously served as the capital of Ish-bosheth, Saul's son, who ruled Israel from there after his father's death (when David ruled only over Judah from Hebron). Upon David's arrival there three men come out to meet him, and the narrator gives not only their names but also their places of origin (v. 27). We are told that the first, Shobi the son of Nahash, is from Rabbah of the Ammonites. He is most likely the brother of Hanun the son of Nahash the king of the Ammonites, who insulted David's messengers when they came to comfort him on the death of his father, and who was later defeated by Joab and David in the war which resulted from this 'diplomatic incident' (2 Samuel 10). The second, Machir the son of Ammiel from Lo-debar, is known to us because Mephibosheth, the son of Jonathan, the son of Saul, stayed with him before being invited to come to Jerusalem and eat at David's table as one of the king's sons (9.4-5). The third, Barzilai the Gileadite from Rogelim is apparently related to Saul by marriage (on the assumption that Adriel the son of Barzilai the Meholathite, who is mentioned in 1 Sam. 18.19, and in 2 Sam. 21.8, and who married Merab, Saul's daughter, is the son of this same Barzilai; this is a reasonable assumption because the town of Mehola, or Abel Mehola,

Adriel's place of origin, was almost certainly on the east bank of the Jordan, in the land of Gilead).[7]

It is surprising that these people, who are affiliated to the royal houses of Saul and the Ammonites, welcome David warmly and extend him valuable aid. The list of the food and chattels they bring David (17.28-29), which includes no less than thirteen items, emphasizes and substantiates their friendly attitude. It could be claimed that they had become David's clients and were consequently obliged to help him, but the fact that men of their high standing did actually extend their aid, and on their own initiative, proves that they believed in David and his rule and were prepared to support him. Thus, in this matter, too, David's ascent within the narrative is evident. Contrary to expectations, David has loyal allies not only in Bahurim but also east of the Jordan. At Bahurim the aid was oblique and concealed, whereas at Mahanaim it is direct and overt. It is, therefore, with good reason that the narrator specifies the names and origins of the three dignitaries from the land east of the Jordan.

The forest of Ephraim is also mentioned in the narrative of Absalom's revolt, being the place where the crucial battle between the armies of David and Absalom takes place (18.6). The site is noted here to explain the defeat of the larger army—Hushai had after all advised Absalom to gather an army which was as extensive as the sand upon the shore—by the smaller one belonging to David, and to attribute it to the conditions of the terrain. The quantitative difference between the two armies is implied at the beginning of v. 7: 'And the people of Israel were defeated there by the servants of David', namely, people against servants, the many against the loyal and devoted few, quantity against quality. The topographical conditions of the forest annul the advantage of numbers, even turning it into a disadvantage. The narrator tells us: 'and the slaughter there was great on that day, twenty thousand men' (v. 7), adding in explanation of this 'great slaughter': 'The battle spread over the face of all the country; and the forest devoured more people that day than the sword' (v. 8). 'Devoured more people' refers to Absalom's army, which was designated 'people', and not to the servants of David.

7. N. Glueck, 'Three Israelite Towns in the Jordan Valley—Zarethan, Succoth, Zaphon', *BASOR* 90 (1943); *idem*, 'Some Ancient Towns in the Plains of Moab', *BASOR* 91 (1943).

The narrator resorts to metaphor in relating that the forest caused the deaths of many of the people: 'And the forest devoured more people that day than the sword'. The use of a metaphor in a prose text which gives a matter of fact account of a battle is a device designed to attract attention. We would expect to find metaphors in poetic and rhetorical texts rather than in a dry military report. The metaphor of the devouring sword is fairly frequent in the Bible and should be regarded as a dead or fossilized metaphor. This is not the case with the devouring forest, however, which has no parallel in the Bible. This metaphor may have been influenced by the common metaphor attributing the capacity to devour to the sword, but in turn influences it; placing the metaphor of the devouring sword after that of the devouring forest serves to revive the former. Because the metaphor of the devouring forest has gained our attention we also pay heed to that of the devouring sword, which may evoke David's cynical statement on a previous occasion: 'Do not let this matter trouble you, for the sword devours now one and now another' (11.25). This was said in reference to the death of Uriah, and the metaphor of the devouring sword, which appears in both passages, hints at the connection between what David did to Uriah and what happened in the forest of Ephraim. In both cases the death of one individual among all those who fell in battle had particular significance for David, overshadowing everything else. Uriah's death causes David to forget his anger at the great number of casualties in the unsuccessful battle at Rabbah of the Ammonites, and Absalom's death completely adumbrates the victory of David's servants, turning the joy of victory into mourning. In both cases the importance of the person's death for David is accentuated by the fact that the way the news of his death is transmitted to David, and his reaction to it, is related at length and in detail (11.18-25; 18.19-19.8). In both cases David gives Joab explicit instructions concerning the man involved, to bring about the death of the one (Uriah), and to prevent the death of the other (Absalom). In this way the narrator insinuates that the death of Absalom is David's punishment for having caused Uriah's, as can also be learned from Nathan's speech, in which the word 'sword' occurs three times in this connection (12.9-10).

Thus, places in the narratives are not merely geographical facts, but are to be regarded as literary elements in which fundamental significance is embodied.

It should, however, be emphasized that places in biblical narratives are not fashioned in a plastic, concrete way. In this connection, a distinction should be made between mentioning sites and describing them. Places in the Bible are merely cited, during the course of the action, and are not depicted clearly and vividly. No images are put before us neither of scenery, cities, villages, nor of buildings or the interiors of rooms. We are not shown Jacob's (long) journey from Beersheba to Haran; we are not given a picture of the city of Jerusalem and its streets and houses; nor are we helped to envisage the forest of Ephraim or any other natural spot. The places exist as a background to the events, as the arena within which the plot unfolds, but we are not given a graphic description of their appearance. In contrast to time, which is entirely abstract and cannot be sensed directly, space is concrete and can be perceived by the senses; consequently, space will not be felt to be real in a work of literature unless it is described explicitly. This does not mean that the description must be a detailed one. Space can certainly be realized in a narrative through a stylized sketch which illuminates only what is most characteristic. In biblical narrative, however, the physical environment is not described at all, neither in detail nor in general outline (apart from one exception in Esth. 1.6, where the court of the garden of the king's palace is described in all its sumptuous glory; this description is not an end in itself, but serves to emphasize the marvel that a simple Jewish girl is elevated to the position of wife to the wealthy and magnificent king).

The fact that, unlike time, space remains vague and undefined in biblical narrative cannot be dismissed by claiming that literature is a temporal, not a spatial, art (in contrast to painting and sculpture). After all, the ability of a work of literature to draw pictures of places and scenes with the help of words, thereby achieving a high degree of verisimilitude, is well known.

The absence of depictions in biblical narrative is connected with the tension which exists in a work of literature between the categories of time and space. This tension, which does not exist in non-literary reality, derives from the fact that a work of literature can create space only by means of a sequence of consecutive words. As a result of this, narration time continues when a more or less detailed description of places or scenes is given, while narrated time comes to a standstill (see above, p. 146). By stopping narrated time a static element is introduced, and this is incompatible with the dynamic and vigorous nature of biblical narrative. The biblical narrative is wholly devoted to creating a sense of time which flows continually and rapidly, and this is inevitably achieved at the expense of the shaping of space. Because space is fundamentally static and unchanging it is an alien element in biblical narrative, based as it is primarily on presenting fluctuations and developments, which are a function of time. The lack of descriptions of places is naturally connected with the absence of detailed descriptions of people's appearances, their clothes, implements, etc. All these would hold up narrated time and interrupt the pace at which the narrative was progressing. Biblical narrative has no desire to linger and enjoy the view, it hurries forward in order to keep up with the rapid development of events.

Accordingly, the Bible does not provide us with a description of the sanctuary which served the people of Israel in the wilderness, or of the Temple which Solomon built. We do have a very detailed account of the *making* of the sanctuary (Exodus 35–40) and the *construction* of the Temple (1 Kings 6–7), because in this way the flow of narrated time is not hampered and the narrative continues its progress uninterruptedly.

Biblical narratives bring the bustle of life before us and are imbued with movement and activity. Because they are dramatic, they have recourse primarily to the dimension of time in order to facilitate the development of the plot, and space is only of secondary importance for them.

Chapter 5

STYLE

In every narrative it is possible to discern three strata: 1. the stratum of language—the words and sentences of which the narrative is composed; 2. the stratum of what is represented by those words, namely the 'world' described in the narrative: the characters, events and settings; 3. the stratum of meanings, that is the concepts, views and values embodied in the narrative, which are expressed principally through the speech and actions of the characters, their fate and the general course of events.

Each of the last two strata is based on and determined by the one before it. The first stratum is the most basic one, the words constituting the raw material of which the narrative is made. The second stratum devolves from the first, and is the one which draws most of the reader's attention, comprising the story of the narrative, the characters, their traits and adventures. The third stratum devolves from the second and is the most abstract one; interpretation is needed to extricate the ideas and meanings, which are not usually expressed directly and overtly.

The present chapter deals with the first stratum, that of language. On this level, the narrative presents itself as an ordered system of linguistic units, a continuum of carefully organized structures. In contrast to silent movies or pantomime, which consist of non-verbal elements, and unlike talking movies or plays, which consist of both verbal and non-verbal elements, the chain of events in a narrative is expressed solely through linguistic symbols. The world described in the narrative is created purely by the power of words, and its entire existence rests upon language. Since the way language is used determines the nature of the world of the narrative, including that of the characters populating it, and since it is upon the linguistic design that all the meanings embodied in the narrative are dependent, it is necessary to examine the way in which the writers have used their medium and how they have exploited the various linguistic possibilities in each case. In other words, we must investigate the style of the narrative.

There are a variety of definitions and views of the nature of style. The semantic definition, which regards style as inseparable from meaning, is the one which will be adopted here. Apart from the principal, explicit meaning of words and sentences there are the finer, secondary and connotative ones. The study of stylistic details reveals these nuances of meaning, which may be compared to the overtones in music which, while not carrying the melody itself, determine the timbre of the sounds and therefore influence the character of the piece to a considerable extent. Style has expressive value, it enriches or emphasizes the main meaning reflected in the sentences, while at the same time, because of the emotional charge often transmitted through it, determining the reader's attitude to what is happening. Expressive force exists in all linguistic utterances, in similes, metaphors, etc. (which should not be regarded merely as embellishments), as well as in sounds and rhythm, vocabulary, grammatical forms, syntactical structures and types of sentences. All these aspects of language may be stylistically important.

Every linguistic feature, however accepted and trite, should, therefore, be regarded as a stylistic phenomenon. There is no such thing as a sentence without style, whether it be exalted or simple, clear or vague, rhetorical or mundane. If a sentence were to be modified slightly, for example by using a synonym, by changing a grammatical form or by altering the order of words, the style (and with it the precise meaning) would immediately be affected.

Special importance, however, on the stylistic-meaning level, should be attached to unusual and infrequent words and structures (stylistic 'devices'). Whether it be a rare word, an unaccustomed collocation, exceptional word-order, non-literal usage or the repetition of a linguistic element, every deviance from accepted linguistic norms attracts the reader's attention and provides emphasis. When reading, therefore, we should be aware of every linguistic element, giving special consideration to unusual expressions and structures.

It could, nevertheless, be claimed that the close examination of the details of linguistic utterances is justified only in the case of poetry and not in analyzing narrative. The language of poetry is usually 'condensed' and concentrated, while in narrative words are 'transparent' and fulfil a referential function, namely, they do not attract attention to themselves, merely serving a denotative function and constituting the means for the construction of characters, events, the background, etc. According to this view, stylistic devices are not appropriate in narrative, and a high-flown rhetorical style detracts from, rather than adds to, the narrative, diverting attention from the essential points.

Although it is true that language does not have the same impact in narrative as in poetry, the linguistic design of a narrative is by no means unimportant. While the language of a narrative is not usually as 'condensed' as the language of poetry, neither is it as 'transparent' as the language of science, for example. Narrative does not use only the basic meanings of words, as science does, but employs their subsidiary meanings too. The language of narrative is distinguished not only from that of science, but also from that of daily speech because, unlike the latter, it is carefully moulded.

In short narratives in particular, like those of the Bible, we find a terse style of expression, which is necessitated by the limited extent of the piece. The author of a short story is obliged to be sparing, to write in an extremely compact way and to place as heavy a burden as possible on the words used. Consequently, it is appropriate to pay attention to even the minutest details of biblical narratives and to their linguistic features.

This, however, gives rise to a problem. We do not know all the subsidiary meanings of the words and linguistic structures that appear in biblical narratives, and we will never have a complete picture of all the nuances and shades of meaning which enriched the language of the Bible for its contemporary readers. Moreover, since we are unaware of the full extent and precise nature of the Hebrew language in biblical times (the Bible itself contains a very limited part of the language used at the time) it is impossible to assess accurately the rarity or deviance of any given word or linguistic phenomenon.

These problems cannot be resolved completely. All we can do is to consider any particular stylistic phenomenon not with reference to the language of the biblical period in general but to the limited context in which it appears, taking as our norm the narrative within which it occurs, or biblical narratives in general, or even biblical literature as a whole. We will also have to utilize what can be learned from the Bible itself as regards subsidiary meanings, the emotional charge and the implications of the words and linguistic structures. This is not very much, and most of the fine shades of meaning will necessarily remain obscure. Since there is no way we can overcome this obstacle, however, and our knowledge of the language of the biblical period, in all its details and niceties, will always remain limited, we have no choice but to be content with the little we can wrest from the Bible.

The best approach to a discussion of style is by undertaking a stylistic analysis of an entire narrative unit. Only in this way can the stylistic phenomena be seen within their context (the same stylistic device can fulfil various functions in different contexts), the interaction between them observed and their special significances discerned. Analyses of this kind of some narrative units will be presented below. First, however, we will review separately several stylistic phenomena which occur repeatedly in biblical narrative.

1. *Stylistic Devices*

A. *Sound and Rhythm*

On the level of words it is necessary to distinguish between their sound and their meaning. In poetry the sounds of words fulfil a far more important role than in prose, but in prose, too, and in narrative in particular, sound patterns which are worthy of attention sometimes occur. Their importance in biblical literature is particularly great because it is believed that a great deal of this literature was originally oral and was intended for the ear rather than the eye. Even after it was written down it was still customary to read it out aloud.

In order to discuss the sound stratum of words it is helpful to distinguish between: a. the sound in itself, and b. the repetition of sounds.

a. *The Sound in Itself*

There are two facets to the contention that the sound in itself has expressive value: either the sound of a word imitates a natural sound (onomatopoeia) or it reflects an atmosphere, feeling or idea (sound-symbolism). The former is very rare and the latter is very subjective. If someone feels that there is a connection between a certain sound and a specific meaning, between the sounds *m*, *r* and *sh* and a forest or water, for example,[1] this link may well be associative rather than

---

1. 'The repeated *m*, *r* and *sh* sounds suggest a forest or a body of water, with the waves lapping the surface in the darkness'. L. Finkelstein, 'The Hebrew Text of the Bible; a Study of its Cadence Symbols', L. Bryson *et al.* (eds.), *Symbols and Society; Fourteenth Symposium of the Conference on Science, Philosophy and Religion* (New York, 1955), p. 418.

intrinsic; if this is so it cannot simply be assumed that other people, including those who lived during biblical times, felt or feel the same. It seems more likely that anyone who senses a connection of this kind is merely attaching qualities and meanings to the sounds of words which are really embedded in the semantic rather than the sound stratum.

Furthermore, the attribution of certain meanings to specific sounds requires precise knowledge of their pronunciation, and we do not have reliable information about the exact articulation of Hebrew in biblical times. We cannot assume that the written text in our possession today, with its vocalization and accents, provides a faithful picture of the Hebrew language as it sounded more than 1500 years before the period of the Massoretes and vocalizers of Tiberias, who determined the form of the text as it stands today. It is impossible to enter into a detailed discussion of this problem here; let it suffice to state briefly that the various systems of vocalizaton (the Tiberian, the Palestinian, the Babylonian and the mixed), the ancient transcriptions (in Origen's Hexapla, in the Septuagint and in other ancient translations) and the spelling of the manuscripts found in the Judean desert often reflect different traditions of pronunciation, which often varied considerably from one another. Which of these traditions is closest to the pronunciation used during biblical times? We cannot answer that question. The comparative study of Semitic languages can provide very little assistance in solving this problem. Furthermore, even during biblical times there was no uniformity in pronunciation, neither as regards time (changes apparently occurred) nor as regards place (there were regional-tribal differences). In the light of all this it seems preferable not to attempt explaining the meanings of sounds in the Bible.

b. *The Repetition of Sounds*
There are various types of repetitions of sounds, such as paronomasia (the repetition of words close but not identical in sound), alliteration (the repetition of a consonant at the beginning of words), assonance (the repetition of a vowel) and rhyme (the repetition of sounds at the ends of words). These are objective features which can be discerned even if the exact pronunciation of the sounds is not known. The mere fact that a certain sound is repeated is sufficient. When the sound which is repeated is a consonant we are on particularly firm ground and can draw conclusions about the significance of the feature.

Sounds frequently recur in different words so as to link them together and connect their meanings. The similarity between the sounds of the words hints at the similarity between the things those words signify or, sometimes, at the contrast between them. Thus, the relations between the sounds create or draw attention to the relations (whether parallel or opposing) between the meanings.

Here are a few examples:

Paronomasia

> *w^e'ādām 'ayin la'abod 'et hā'adāmâ. w^e'ēd ya'aleh min hā'āreṣ w^{e}hišqâ 'et kol p^{e}nê hā'adāmâ. wayyîṣer YHWH 'elohîm et hā'ādām 'āpār min hā'adāmâ.*

and there was no man to till the ground; but a mist went up from the earth and watered the whole face of the ground—then the Lord God formed man of dust from the ground (Gen. 2.5-7).

> *wayyihyû š^{e}nêhem 'arûmmîm hā'ādām w^e'ištô w^{e}lo' yitbošāšû. w^{e}hannāḥāš hāyâ 'ārûm mikkol ḥayyat haśśādeh.*

And the man and his wife were both naked, and were not ashamed. Now the serpent was more subtle than any other wild creature that the Lord God had made (Gen. 2.25; 3.1).

> *wayyo'mer hakî qārā' š^{e}mô ya'aqob wayya'q^{e}bēnî zeh pa'amayim 'et b^{e}korātî lākāḥ w^{e}hinnēh 'attâ lākaḥ birkātî.*

Esau said, 'Is he not rightly named Jacob? For he has supplanted me these two times. He took away my birthright; and behold, now he has taken away my blessing' (Gen. 27.36).

The aetiological explanations of proper names are also based on paronomasia:

> *w^e'aḥarê kēn yāṣā' 'āḥîw w^{e}yādô 'oḥezet ba'aqēb 'ēśāw wayyiqrā' š^{e}mô ya'aqob.*

Afterward his brother came forth, and his hand had taken hold of Esau's heel; so his name was called Jacob (Gen. 25.26).

> *wayyo'mer 'ēśāw 'el ya'aqob hal'îṭēnî nā' min hā'ādom hā'ādom hazzeh kî 'āyēp 'ānokî 'al kēn qārā' š^{e}mô 'edôm.*

And Esau said to Jacob, 'Let me eat of that red pottage, for I am famished!' Therefore his name was called Edom (Gen. 25.30).

Alliteration

bᵉrē'šît bārā' 'elohîm. . .

In the beginning God created . . . (Gen. 1.1).

ûštēy pārôt 'ālôt ašer lo' 'ālâ 'alêhem 'ol.

And two milch cows upon which there has never come a yoke (1 Sam. 6.7).

lᵉ'aṭ lî lanna'ar lᵉ'abšālôm.

Deal gently for my sake with the young man Absalom (2 Sam. 18.5).

ûmalkat šᵉbā' šōma'at 'et šēma' šᵉlomō lᵉšēm YHWH.

Now when the queen of Sheba heard of the fame of Solomon to the name of the Lord (1 Kgs 10.1).

Assonance

wᵉhā'āreṣ hāyᵉtâ tohû wâbohû.

The earth was without form and void (Gen. 1.2).

'ēyn qôl 'anôt gᵉbûrâ wᵉ'ēyn qôl 'anôt ḥalûšâ.

It is not the sound of shouting for victory, or the sound of the cry of defeat (Exod. 32.18).

Rhyme

lûlē' ḥaraštem bᵉ'eglātî lo' mᵉṣā'tem ḥîdātî.

If you had not ploughed with my heifer
you would not have found out my riddle (Judg. 14.18).

wayyibqa' 'elohîm 'et hammaktēš 'ašer ballehî—wayyēṣᵉ'û mimmennû mayim wayyēšt watāšāb rûḥô wayyeḥî.

And God split open the hollow place that is at Lehi, and there came water from it; and when he drank, his spirit returned, and he revived (Judg. 15.19).

The Rhythm

The rhythm is produced by organizing the length, emphasis or pitch of the sounds. There is a close connection between rhythm and intonation. Unlike poetry, where the rhythm is schematic and regular (metre), the rhythm of prose is irregular. Although in artistic prose there is a tendency towards some degree of equilibrium as regards the emphases, lengths or pitches of the syllables, prose does not have the fixed pattern of stressed and unstressed or long and short syllables that is found in poetry.

Because of the irregular rhythm of prose, literary critics have not yet succeeded in describing it systematically or defining its types. In discussing biblical prose an additional difficulty is presented by the fact that we do not know precisely and with certainty what was the length, pitch and stress of the syllables as they were pronounced in biblical times (the stress may have been on the penultimate syllable), and it is therefore impossible to make any definite and well-founded statement about rhythm in biblical narrative.

In contrast to analyzing prose rhythm on the basis of syllables, it is both feasible and useful to examine it on the basis of sentences. The examination of sentence length in biblical narrative is feasible because it does not require precise knowledge of pronunciation; and it is useful because an abundance of long or short sentences determines the character of the style and also because sentence length has expressive value. A series of long sentences can express tranquillity, for example, while a string of short ones might reflect unease, haste or tension, among other things. (We should beware of laying down hard and fast rules on this point, and the function of sentence length should be examined separately in each instance.)

Apart from length, attention should be paid to another feature of sentences, one which pertains to their syntactical structure, namely, what A.L. Strauss has called the dynamic or static nature of sentences: 'Considerable dynamism is achieved by placing subordinate clauses before the main clause; for we are eager to know the "main" subject-matter of the main clause, while the subordinate clause(s) delay(s) this information, thus creating a certain tension and expectancy. A sentence built on tension of this kind will be called "dynamic". A sentence whose main subject-matter is made known to us immediately (the main clause preceding the subordinate one), is devoid of tension and will be called "static" (coordinate clauses are a series of main clauses)'.

The distinction between dynamic and static sentences is also possible in non-compound sentences: 'A sentence which begins with the predicate, with adverbial adjuncts of place and time, makes the reader "tense" about its subject. A sentence which starts with the subject, making us immediately aware of what it is about, is quieter in character. We must conclude then that the rhythm of prose is evident in sentence structure'.[2]

Here are a few examples:

> Now Abraham was old, well advanced in years; and the Lord had blessed Abraham in all things (Gen. 24.1).

This is a static, balanced sentence expressing peace and tranquillity.

> O Lord, the God of my master Abraham, if now thou wilt prosper the way which I go, behold, I am standing by the spring of water; let the young woman who comes out to draw, to whom I shall say, 'Pray give me a little water from your jar to drink', and who will say to me, 'Drink, and I will draw for your camels also', let her be the woman whom the Lord has appointed for my master's son' (vv. 42-44).

Here we have a compound and dynamic sentence expressing tension and suspense.

> Then he took his staff in his hand and chose five smooth stones from the brook, and put them in his shepherd's bag or wallet: his sling was in his hand and he drew near to the Philistine (1 Sam. 17.40).

This is a long sentence with a slow, calm rhythm.

> Then David ran and stood over the Philistine, and took his sword and drew it out of its sheath, and killed him (v. 51).

In this case we have short clauses with a rapid, urgent rhythm.

> And he instructed the messenger, 'When you have finished telling all the news about the fighting to the king, then, if the king's anger rises, and if he says to you, "Why did you go so near the city to fight? Did you not know that they would shoot from the wall? Who killed Abimelech the son of Jerubbesheth? Did not a woman cast an upper millstone upon him from the wall, so that he died at Thebez? Why did you go so near the wall?" then you shall say, "Your

2. A.L. Strauss, *Bedarkei Hasifrut* (Jerusalem, 1959), pp. 46-47 (Heb.). *Cf. also N. Frye, 'Verse and Poetry', A. Preminger (ed.), *Princeton Encyclopaedia of Poetry and Poetics* (Princeton, 1974), p. 885: 'When the sentence structure takes the lead and all patterns of repetition [recurrent rhythm] are subordinated to it and become irregular, we have prose'.

servant Uriah the Hittite is dead also"' (2 Sam. 11.19-21).

This is a compound and dynamic sentence whose structure places additional emphasis on the last few words.

> Then David arose from the earth, and washed, and anointed himself, and changed his clothes; and he went into the house of the Lord, and worshipped; he then went to his own house; he asked, they set food before him and he ate (12.20).

This is a string of short, simple clauses expressing considerable activity and restlessness.

> When the turn came for Esther the daughter of Abihail the uncle of Mordecai, who had adopted her as his own daughter, to go in to the king, she asked for nothing except what Hegai the king's eunuch, who had charge of the women, advised (Esth. 2.15).

Here we have a dynamic sentence, arousing expectancy and anticipation.

> The king loved Esther more than all the women, and she found grace and favour in his sight more than all the virgins; so he set the royal crown on her head, and made her queen instead of Vashti (v. 17).

These are static, measured and serene clauses with a stable rhythm which conveys solemnity (also because of the parallelism of the versets!).

B. *The Meaning of the Word*

It is customary to distinguish between the principal and secondary meanings of a word or sentence. In literature the secondary, accompanying and connotative meanings are at least as important as the main one. For instance, in the sentence: 'The woman whom thou gavest to be with me, she gave me of the fruit of the tree, and I ate' (Gen. 3.12), what is stated on the principal level of meaning is merely that the woman gave Adam fruit from the tree, that he ate, and that the woman who gave him the fruit was the one whom the Lord had given to be with him. But what is suggested by Adam in this sentence is that Adam ate *because* the woman gave him of the fruit of the tree and that the guilt is therefore the woman's first and foremost. In addition, there is an implied accusation against God himself, since He gave the woman to be with Adam. Had God not *given* the woman

to be with Adam she would not have *given* him of the fruit of the tree,
and he would not have eaten.

The primary meaning of the Hebrew word *pere'* is wild ass. One of
the characteristics of this animal is that, unlike the ordinary ass, it
cannot be tamed and domesticated, but leads a free life in the
wilderness (cf. Job 39.5-8). This characteristic is among the
connotations of the word and it is this which operates in Gen. 16.12.
The angel who meets Hagar, Sarai's slave-girl, in the desert promises
her that she will give birth to a son, Ishmael, who will be *pere' 'ādām*
(a wild ass of a man). This is usually taken to mean 'a wild man', but
the angel, whose object was to comfort and encourage Hagar, clearly
meant something different, namely, that the son would be a free
man, independent like the nomadic tribes of the desert, not a slave
like his mother.

As the last example shows, connotative meaning is the main
ingredient in metaphor and similar non-literal language. The
exploitation of the non-literal meanings of words often occurs in
literature and is also a feature of colloquial speech, though in the
latter we are usually no longer aware of the literal meanings, for
expressions have become stale and worn-out with use. This has
happened with such phrases as 'the head of the bed' (Gen. 47.31) and
'the house of Israel' (Exod. 16.31). Fossilized expressions can be
revived by hinting at their original meaning—as is sometimes done in
literature—thus restoring their full stylistic value to them. Thus, in
Judg. 9.36, the expression 'mountain tops' ('heads' in Hebrew)
contrasts with 'the centre of the land' ('navel' in Hebrew) in the
following verse, and the term 'head' or 'heads' (in the sense of a
group or company of soldiers) often occurs in this context. In 2
Samuel 7 the word 'house' is used both in the sense of a dynasty
(nine times) and a building (six times): David wishes to build a house
for the Lord, and the Lord promises to make him a house.

When a word is not employed in its literal meaning there are three
possibilities: a. that there is contiguity between the literal and the
non-literal meaning; b. that there is similarity between the literal and
the non-literal meaning; c. that there is opposition between the literal
and the non-literal meaning.

a. *Contiguity*
Metonymy: The word is used in a non-literal sense, there being
contiguity or direct continuity between its literal and non-literal

Narrative Art in the Bible

meanings, namely, the things denoted by the word in its two meanings belong to allied or adjoining spheres. Because of the close and constant tie between the two spheres, an item from one sphere can represent something from the other (as in the phrase 'the house of Israel'). There are different kinds of metonymy, paralleling the types of connection between the literal and non-literal meanings. A few examples from the Bible are given below.

The outer framework represents the inner content: 'Now *the earth* was corrupt in God's sight, and *the earth* was filled with violence' (Gen. 6.11); 'While *the city* of Susa shouted and rejoiced' (Esth. 8.15). The reference is to the inhabitants of the earth and of the city.

The source represents its product: 'Cursed is the ground because of you; in toil you shall eat *it* all the days of your life' (Gen. 3.17). It is not the earth but its produce which will be eaten.

The means stands for the end: 'Now the whole earth had one *tongue*' (Gen. 11.1), one language; 'and sacrifice to the Lord our God, lest he fall upon us with pestilence or with the *sword*' (Exod. 5.3), with pestilence or with war; 'because *their hand* also is with David' (2 Sam. 22.17), their help is with David.

The action replaces the result: 'Isaac loved Esau because he ate of his game' (literally 'because *the hunt* was in his mouth') (Gen. 25.28). The reference is to the animals he hunted.

An external, accompanying feature represents the thing itself: '*In the sweat of your face* you shall eat bread' (Gen. 3.19), by hard work; 'also *lifted up his hand* against the king' (1 Kgs 11.26), rebelled and mutinied.

Synecdoche: As with metonymy, there is contiguity between the literal and non-literal meaning, but the relation between the two meanings is one between the part and the whole.

'So when the woman saw that *the tree* was good for food. . . ' (Gen. 3.6), the fruit of the tree was good for food; 'In the sweat of your face you shall eat *bread*' (Gen. 3.19), food in general; 'For all *flesh* had corrupted their way upon the earth' (Gen. 6.12), every man, or every living thing, had corrupted their way; 'a land flowing with *milk and honey*' (Exod. 3.8, and elsewhere), a land of plenty; 'Our cattle also must go with us; not a *hoof* shall be left behind' (10.26), not a single beast shall remain.

b. *Similarity*

Metaphor: The word is used in a non-literal sense, there being similarity but no direct continuity between its literal and non-literal meanings, and the things which the word indicates in its literal and non-literal meanings belong to completely different and separate spheres. In many cases one sphere is abstract or spiritual while the other is concrete.

Metaphors refer to a certain detail belonging to one sphere by means of an item from another, for example, to a phenomenon from the human world through one from the world of plants, animals or inanimate objects or vice versa (as in the phrase 'the head of the bed'). Metaphors reveal a common basis or analogy between phenomena from divergent spheres, despite the differences between them.

The value of metaphors is that they are able to carry and transfer considerable emotional charge or illuminate something in a new (and sometimes surprising) way, often achieving a concrete representation or a vivid image. That is why metaphors are often used in poetry. They also feature in prose, however, particularly in the speech of individual characters. Here are a few examples:

> The *voice* of your brother's blood *is crying* to me from the ground (Gen. 4.10).

> And the earth opened its *mouth and swallowed* them up (Num. 16.30).

> After whom do you pursue? After a *dead dog*! After a *flea*! (1 Sam. 24.14)

> The life of my lord shall be *bound in the bundle* of the living (25.29).

> And the lives of your enemies he *shall sling out from the hollow of a sling* (25.29).

> You shall be *shepherd* of my people Israel (2 Sam. 5.2).

Simile: Similes differ from metaphors in that they do not have two meanings, one literal and one non-literal, but resemble them in that they also raise common elements or analogies between phenomena from divergent spheres. Like metaphors, similes clarify the subject discussed or reveal new aspects of them through connotations which function alongside the principal meaning. The prepositions 'like' and 'as' are typical of similes. There are open similes, which do not note the point of similarity between the two aspects compared, and there are closed ones, which do so explicitly. Like metaphors, similes are frequently found in poetry, though they also occur in prose.

Biblical similes are often supplemented by the stylistic device of exaggeration; in these cases they fulfil the additional function of intensification and reinforcement.

> I will indeed bless you, and I will multiply your descendants *as the stars of heaven and as the sand which is on the seashore* (Gen. 22.17).

> Behold, Miriam was leprous, *as white as snow* (Num. 12.10).

> And we seemed to ourselves *like grasshoppers* (13.33).

> Now Asahel was as swift of foot *as a wild gazelle* (2 Sam. 2.18).

> And the king made silver *as common as stone* in Jerusalem, and he made cedar as plentiful *as the sycamore of the Shephelah* (1 Kgs 10.27).

> A little cloud *like a man's hand* is rising out of the sea (18.44).

> The people of Israel encamped before them *like two little flocks of goats* (20.27).

When the simile is expanded and grows into a story, it becomes a parable, such as the parable of Jotham (Judg. 9.8-15) or the parable of the poor man's ewe lamb (2 Sam. 12.1-4).

c. *Opposition*

Irony: There is a contrastive relation between the literal and the intended meanings of the words (this refers to verbal, not dramatic, irony, see p. 125). A special kind of irony results from pretending naïveté, and affecting not to understand the true situation.

> But Michal the daughter of Saul came out to meet David, and said, 'How the king of Israel honoured himself today, uncovering himself today before the eyes of his servants' maids, as one of the vulgar fellows shamelessly uncovers himself!' (2 Sam. 6.20).

Michal meant that David had debased himself.

> And at noon Elijah mocked them, saying, 'Cry aloud, for he is a god; either he is musing, or he has gone aside, or he is on a journey, or perhaps he is asleep and must be awakened' (1 Kgs 18.27).

Elijah pretends to believe that by calling out loud, the prophets of Baal may arouse their god to act.

> And when he had come to the king, the king said to him, 'Micaiah, shall we go to Ramoth-Gilead to battle, or shall we forbear?' And he answered him, 'Go up and triumph; the Lord will give it into the hand of the king' (2 Sam. 22.15).

Micaiah means the opposite of what he says, and this is apparently obvious from his tone, because the king responds immediately by demanding that he speak only the truth.

Rhetorical question: A question which is not asked for the sake of achieving an answer, since the answer is well known to the speaker. The purpose of the question is to persuade the audience by implying that the answer is self-evident or known to everybody and therefore not to be doubted or discussed.

> And Jacob became angry with Rachel and said: 'Am I in stead of God, who has withheld from you fruit of the womb?' (Gen. 30.2).

> 'But now he is dead, why should I fast? Can I bring him back again?' (2 Sam. 12.23).

The use of rhetorical questions is very frequent in biblical prose. For instance, in 2 Samuel 19 more than twenty cases are to be found.

C. *The Repetition of Words*
The repetition of words (or roots) is a stylistic feature often found in biblical narrative. There are various kinds of repetition, in accordance with its position in the text or the functions it fulfils.

Duplication
The same word appears twice successively (generally to express a strong emotion), for example:

> But the angel of the Lord called to him from heaven, and said, '*Abraham, Abraham!*' (Gen. 22.11).

> Let me eat some of that *red, red* stuff (25.30).

> *O my son Absalom, my son, my son Absalom!* Would I had died instead of you, *O Absalom, my son, my son!* (2 Sam. 18.33).

And he said to his father, 'Oh, *my head, my head!*' (2 Kgs 4.19).

Sometimes one word separates the two that are repeated, for example:

> *Answer me*, O Lord, *answer me* (1 Kgs 18.37).

In some cases the word which is repeated is at the beginning of several consecutive sentences or clauses, while in others it is at the end (usually for emphasis).

At the beginning (anaphora):

> Until I come and take you away to *a land* like your own land, *a land* of grain and wine, *a land* of bread and vineyards, *a land* of olive trees and honey (2 Kgs 18.32).

At the end (epiphora):

> To you be *peace*, to your house be *peace*, and to all that you have be *peace* (1 Sam. 25.6).

Key Words

A word or root is repeated meaningfully within a text or series of texts.[3] Not every word or root which is repeated within a text or sequence of texts can be considered a key word. In this connection attention should be paid to three aspects: 1. how frequently the word is used in the Bible; 2. how frequently the word is used within the text or series of texts; 3. how near the repeated words are as regards their position in the text. The greater the frequency of the word in the Bible, the more densely should it occur (more often or with greater proximity); and the rarer it is, the less intensively need it occur (less often and at a greater distance).

In the story of Cain and Abel (Gen. 4.1-16) the word 'brother' which is not rare in the Bible, appears seven times, six of them being in four verses (vv. 8-11), that is, very densely.

In contrast, the collocation 'go forth' (*lek l°kā*), which is very rare in the Bible, occurs once at the beginning of the narratives about Abraham: 'Go forth from your country and your kindred and your father's house' (Gen. 12.1), and once, ten chapters later, at the end of them: 'and go forth to the land of Moriah' (22.2); apart from this, it occurs only twice more, and in the feminine form (Song 2.10, 13).

---

3. M. Buber & F. Rosenzweig, *Die Schrift und ihre Verdeutschung* (Berlin, 1936), p. 211.

According to Buber, the key word establishes a relationship between separate stages of the narrative, conveying the essential point directly. It reveals the meaning and the implicit message of the narrative, without adversely affecting its pure artistic form in any way. In other words, the meaning is not expressed by any supplement to the actual story, through exposition of the ideas or views, but becomes apparent from the story itself, through the repetition of the key words.

Through the key word '*brother*' in the story of Cain and Abel it is intimated that the most shocking aspect of the incident is that not just murder but fratricide has been committed. All men are brothers according to the Bible, however, being the descendants of the same couple, as indicated by the verse: 'Of *every man's brother* I will require the life of man' (Gen. 9.5). Consequently, every murder is fratricide in this sense.

The phrase '*go forth*' serves as a bridge between two narratives about Abraham. The first tells about the demand at the beginning of his history that he detach himself from his land, his home and his father's house and go to the unknown country, at God's command, 'the land which I will show you'. The second, at the end of his history, describes the most difficult demand of all, that he go to the land of Moriah and sacrifice his only, beloved son on one of the mountains 'which I will tell you'. Abraham's entire life in the land of Canaan is bounded by these two experiences, and it is the way he comports himself which clearly expresses his religious stature, making him an example for all those who follow him.

Sometimes the key word recurs in a slightly altered form, and then the significance lies in these changes. This is the case, for example, in Exod. 32.1-14, where the word 'people' is repeated as 'this people', 'your people', 'his people'.[4] At first the narrator reports *the people's* sin regarding the golden calf. Then God's words to Moses are recorded: 'Go down; for *your people* whom you brought up out of the land of Egypt have acted corruptly' (v. 7), indicating that the people belongs to Moses and that God disowns it. Denial and reservation are also expressed in the continuation of God's speech: 'I have seen *this people*, and behold, it is a stiff-necked *people*' (v. 9). Moses on the other hand replies: 'O Lord, why does thy wrath burn hot against *thy*

4. M. Buber & F. Rosenzweig, *Die Schrift und ihre Verdeutschung* (Berlin, 1936), pp. 262-64.

people, whom thou hast brought forth out of the land of Egypt' (v. 11), suggesting that the people is God's, whom He, not Moses, has brought out of Egypt. The same implication underlies Moses' next phrase: 'and repent of this evil against *thy people*' (v. 12). God finally accedes to Moses' request: 'And the Lord repented of the evil which he thought to do to *his people*' (v. 14); in other words, the Lord acknowledges the people as his once again.

The key word may also recur with a change in its meaning. Thus, in the first two chapters of the book of Job the verb *bārēk* occurs six times with two opposing meanings, to bless and to curse.[5] At the beginning we read that Job would offer sacrifices at the end of his sons' feasts, for 'It may be that my sons have sinned and *cursed* God in their hearts' (1.5); this proves what a God-fearing man Job was, for his sons' sin was only hypothetical and in their thoughts. This is followed by the passage in which Satan speaks to God about Job: 'Thou hast *blessed* the work of his hands, and his possessions have increased in the land. But put forth thy hand now, and touch all that he has, and he will *curse* they to thy face' (1.10, 11), namely, if you cease blessing him, he will 'bless' (i.e. curse) you, and not merely in his thoughts but openly. This is an ironic turn of phrase worthy of Satan's cynical approach. After four great disasters have befallen Job in rapid succession, he says: '*Blessed*' be the name of the Lord (1.21), that is to say, Job really does bless God, but in the opposite sense to what Satan had intended. The repetition of the same verb with the opposite meaning underlines the contrast betwen Satan and Job in the clearest possible way. On the second occasion when Satan speaks to God he says: 'But put forth thy hand now, and touch his bone and his flesh, and he will *curse* thee to thy face' (2.5), and this time he is aided (though for very different reasons) by Job's wife, who says to her husband, in her desire to help him in his suffering: '*Curse* God and die' (2.9). But 'in all this Job did not sin with his lips' (2.10), and he does not curse God. In the final chapter (at the end of the narrative) the verb *bārēk* appears a seventh time: 'And the Lord *blessed* the latter days of Job more than his beginning' (42.12), to inform us that Job's former situation was restored and even improved.

On occasions it is not a single word which is repeated but an entire

5. M. Weiss, *The Story of Job's Beginning* (Jerusalem, 1983), p. 81.

phrase or sentence within a narrative or a series of narratives, constituting a (linguistic) motif. Repetition of this kind may be verbatim or may evince slight changes, and both the actual repetition and the modifications are important in reflecting the similarity or difference between situations, in describing characters, in emphasizing a topic or a concept, etc.

So they went both of them together (Gen. 22.6, 8).

Then I shall become weak, and be like any other man (Judg. 16.7, 11, 17).

In those days there was no king in Israel; every man did what was right in his own eyes (17.6; 18.1; 19.1; 21.25).

Arise, go to Nineveh, that great city, and cry against it (Jon. 1.2; 3.2).

In all this Job did not sin (with his lips) (Job 1.22; 2.10).

(What is your petition? It shall be given you.) And what is your request? (even to the half of my kingdom) (Esth. 5.3, 6; 7.2; 9.12).

Resumption

Several words recur after the interposition of other words or sentences, in order to create continuity with the principal trend of thought. At the end of the parable of Jotham we read: 'Now therefore, if you acted in good faith and honour when you made Abimelech king...' (Judg. 9.16). The narrator continues by listing Jerubbaal's merits and the deeds of the citizens of Shechem and a few verses later repeats the beginning of the verse: 'If you then have acted in good faith and honour...' (v. 19), and only then concludes the sentence. The repetition links the subordinate clause ('if') with the main one ('rejoice') after the deviation from the principal line of argument.

God says to Samuel: 'Hearken to the voice of the people...' (1 Sam. 8.7), and after a few words of explanation about the fact that by asking for a king the people have rejected God, not Samuel, He returns to the main line of thought and says once more: 'Now then, hearken to their voice...' (v. 9).

In the narrative about Absalom after he had been permitted to return from Geshur to Jerusalem we read: 'And the king said, "Let him dwell apart in his own house; he is not to come into my presence". So Absalom dwelt apart in his own house, and did not come into the king's presence' (2 Sam. 14.24). The following verses give a description of Absalom's beauty, thus interrupting the account of events; the narrator resumes the thread of the story in v. 28, where we read: 'So Absalom dwelt two full years in Jerusalem, without coming into the king's presence'.

There is an example of a double resumption in Exod. 6.26-30 (compare with vv. 10-13), after a break in the story-line caused by the list of names of Jacob's descendants.

Envelope

The same group of words appears in precisely the same form or with slight changes at the beginning and end of a passage, that is, both the beginning and the end of the passage are identical or virtually so. The framework serves primarily to provide emphasis.

> What was it that he told you? do not hide it from me... May God do so to you and more also, if you hide anything from me of all that he told you (1 Sam. 3.17).

> Let not the king sin against his servant David.... why then will you sin against innocent blood by killing David without cause? (19.4-5)

> Why did you go so near the city to fight?.... Why did you go so near the wall? (2 Sam. 11.20-21)

> But let us fight against them in the plain, and surely we shall be stronger than they... then we will fight against them in the plain, and surely we shall be stronger than they (1 Kgs 20.23-25).

D. *Word Order*

The Accumulation of Nouns and Verbs

Several verbs or nouns (sometimes adjectives) follow one another without any interposition or with hardly any interposition between them by other parts of speech. If the nouns or verbs are more or less synonymous the accumulation creates an effect of emphasis; if they are not, it expresses a special significance, which should be determined in each instance by the content and the context. Here are a few examples:

> and he ate and drank and rose and went and Esau despised his birthright (Gen. 25.34).

This depicts Esau as a man of action who does not spend time in contemplation.

> But the descendants of Israel were fruitful and increased and multiplied and grew exceedingly strong (Exod. 1.7).

This gives a graphic picture of the way Israel became numerous.

> and he went and fled and escaped (1 Sam. 19.12).

This emphasizes the speed of David's actions.

> And they mourned and wept and fasted until evening for Saul and for Jonathan his son and for the people of the Lord and for the house of Israel (2 Sam. 1.12).

This stresses the depth of their pain through the conglomeration of verbs, and the extent of the tragedy through the concentration of nouns.

> And that man was blameless and upright, fearing God, and turning away from evil (Job 1.1).

This underlines Job's exceptional righteousness.

The nouns are sometimes ranged in a certain order, from weak to strong (gradation), conveying a particularly strong impression of emphasis. For example:

> Go forth from your country and from your kindred and from your father's house... (Gen. 12.1).

> Take your son, your only one, whom you love, Isaac... (22.2).

Sometimes the nouns are organized so as to stress opposition (which occasionally expresses all-inclusiveness):

> While the earth remains, seedtime and harvest, cold and heat, summer and winter, day and night, shall not cease (Gen. 8.22).

> Then they utterly destroyed all in the city, both men and women, young and old... (Josh. 6.21).

> Nothing was missing, whether small or great, sons or daughters... (1 Sam. 30.19).

Inversion

The customary order of words in sentences in biblical narrative is like that in Gen. 4.4, for example: 'And the Lord had regard for Abel and his offering'. If the following verse reads: 'But for Cain and his offering he had no regard', this constitutes an inversion of the usual order. Inversion generally emphasizes the beginning of the sentence, but sometimes, as in this case, expresses contrast.

Contrast is conveyed by inverting the customary order in the following sentence too: 'that you will not take a wife for my son from the daughters of the Canaanites, among whom I dwell, but to my country and my kindred you will go' (Gen. 24.3-4) instead of: you will go to my country and my kindred.

Divine intervention determining the course of events is emphasized by the word order of the verse: 'From the Lord the thing comes' (24.50) instead of: The thing comes from the Lord.

The extent of suffering is stressed by the order in the verse: 'My affliction and the labour of my hands God saw' (31.42) instead of: God saw my affliction and the labour of my hands.

2. *The Style of Narrative Units*

There are two ways of analyzing the style of a narrative unit. One approach focuses on analyzing and describing *one* or *a few* stylistic phenomena which are seminal to the narrative and leave their mark upon it. The other concentrates on analyzing and discussing in as systematic and exhaustive a way as possible the *whole* complex of stylistic phenomena in the narrative (while it is impossible to deal with each and every one, it is feasible to attempt a comprehensive investigation).

A. *The Narrative of Adonijah (1 Kings 1)*
The former approach to stylistic analysis will be illustrated first. This method requires us to read the unit several times in order to absorb it fully, until a particular word, form or stylistic feature, which is tightly bound up with the entire unit, strikes the eye. If we read the narrative of Adonijah in this way we will soon find that there is one line which is prominent for several reasons. The verse is: 'Solomon your son shall be king after me, and he shall sit upon my throne'. This passage contains parallelism which, as is well-known, is characteristic of biblical poetry but not of prose, and therefore stands out against its environment and attracts the reader's attention. The same parallelism, moreover, which appears for the first time in 1 Kgs 1.13 recurs in v.17, and with slight changes in vv. 24, 30 and 35. This frequent repetition also arouses attention since it deviates from

customary usage. Further examination of the parallelism reveals that it also contains metonymy: the predicate in the second verset, 'shall sit upon my throne', is a (fairly common) metonymous expression, whose significance is clarified here in advance by the parallel predicate in the first part, 'shall be king'. The subject in the second verset is emphasized by the pronoun, 'he', which in Hebrew is redundant both grammatically and as regards the addition of information; the addition of the pronoun serves to emphasize that Solomon and no one else will rule after David.

Each of the two versets also occurs separately, though not without undergoing a certain transformation. Immediately after the parallelism appears for the first time, and as its direct continuation, we find the words: 'Why then is Adonijah king?' It is easy to recognize these words as the first part, 'Solomon your son shall be king after me', despite the changes which have been made in it, such as the change of tense (or of the aspect of the verb), the recasting as a question and the conversion of the subject from Solomon to Adonijah. This way of placing a sentence in slightly modified form directly adjacent to the previous, similar one, namely, repetition with alteration in juxta-position, serves to stress opposition. The opposition here is between the oath which David swore to Bathsheba and the actual situation which has arisen; and the question which is put to the king, 'Why then. . . ', hints that he is held responsible for this opposition. Thus, there is here an implied accusation against David, although it is not said that he has made Adonijah king. Naturally, the sting lies in Bathsheba's pretending that Adonijah has become king as a result of the king's command.

This is what is implied in the words Nathan tells Bathsheba to say. Bathsheba, however, phrases the sentence somewhat differently when she comes before David. The parallelism, 'Solomon your son shall be king after me, and he shall sit upon my throne', is repeated exactly as it occurred before, but Bathsheba appends a supplement to it in the form of a modification of the first verset, departing from Nathan's version. Instead of the question, 'Why then is Adonijah king?' Bathsheba says: 'And now, behold, Adonijah is king'. This form also stresses the opposition between the oath and reality (the words 'and now', provide additional emphasis of the opposition), but in addition Bathsheba's words build up the contrast between the protasis of v. 18, 'And now, behold, Adonijah is king', and its apodosis, 'And you, my lord the king, do not know it', namely, between the actual situation and the king's information (the opposition between the protasis of v. 18 and its apodosis is stressed by phonological similarity: 'And *now* (*'attâ*), behold *Adonijah is king* (*'Adoniyyâ mālāk*); and *you* (*'attâ*), *my lord the king* (*'adonî hammelek*) do not know it'). What Nathan says is likely to arouse the king to act and spur him to intervene actively by making him aware of the opposition which has arisen, supposedly at his responsibility, between his oath and the actual situation. Bathsheba's version, on the other hand, should have the effect of inciting him by specifically mentioning the fact that the king's information does not accord with the true state of affairs: this lack of information should be deeply wounding to the king's self-respect. In other words, the way the *prophet* puts things hints at the moral impediment embodied in the failure to fulfil the oath and David's responsibility for this, while the *woman's* words are directed at David's feelings as a man and a king. Although it was Nathan who had informed Bathsheba that the king was in ignorance of all this, it is she who decides to mention it explicitly to him. On the other hand, nothing in what Bathsheba says hints at David's guilt, for this, even if only implied, could cause the king to grow angry with whoever accuses him, that is, Bathsheba, and to refuse to accede to her request as a result. If the king's anger is to be aroused, then care should be taken to direct it towards the right channel, namely, Adonijah, who acted without his father's knowledge. That is the intent behind the detailed account of Adonijah's sacrifice in the presence of all his guests.

When he comes before the king, Nathan also begins by repeating the parallelism, though with a change of syntactical subject: 'Adonijah shall be king after me, and he shall sit upon my throne' (v. 24). Another modification is that the parallelism is placed within the framework of a question: 'Have you said. . ?' (in the Hebrew the emphasis being on 'you'). Nathan's tactics can be characterized as feigned ignorance. He asks, in supposed bewilderment, whether this has been ordered by the king, and if so why he was not informed of it. The use of questions in his speech accords with the statement he has previously told Bathsheba to make, in which he has also embedded a supposedly innocent question. The question there, however, ('Why then is Adonijah king?') takes it for granted that David is the ruler who controls everything; this assumption has an ironic sting which is intended to arouse David to act as a king should and take the reins of power into his hands. Nathan's questions on the other hand indicate doubt whether what has happened was at the king's order ('Have *you* said. . . ? Has this thing been brought about by my lord the king?'). His misgivings are phrased carefully, but in such a way as to induce David to admit that this thing was not in fact ordered by him, an admission which need not necessarily be expressed explicitly but rather through a practical decision as to who is to inherit his throne.

Nathan does not mention the oath, since this was a private matter between David and Bathsheba, as is stated in vv. 13, 17 and 30. But he uses the language of the oath, namely, the parallelism, replacing Solomon's name with Adonijah's. This substitution again results in an opposition, this time between the way the parallelism is phrased here by Nathan and the way it appeared on the two previous occasions. This opposition resembles that between the entire parallelism and the first verset as it occurred twice by itself, as regards both wording and function. The promise that Solomon shall rule is contrasted by Nathan with the fact that Adonijah is ruling. But now the issue has widened. The modification appears not only in the first verset of the parallelism, but is also carried over to the second one. The substitution of Adonijah's name for Solomon's inevitably alters the referential function of the pronoun 'he', in the second verset; thus the entire parallelism as pronounced by Nathan hints *twice* at the fact that Adonijah is king, and the result is emphasis of the contrast. It can, therefore, be stated that the repetitions and modifications of the first verset, whether occurring independently or as part of the entire parallelism, serve each time to convey and underline the opposition.

The second part of the parallelism also occurs independently, both in Bathsheba's words to David and in Nathan's, and the change which it undergoes is identical in both cases: instead of 'and he shall sit upon my throne', as in the entire parallelism, we find: 'who should sit on the throne of my lord the king after him?' (20, 27). The principal change is the replacement of the pronoun 'he' by the interrogative 'who', indicating the uncertainty and ambiguity created as a result of the contradiction between the oath and reality; David is now being asked to make a decision and resolve this contradiction. The separate appearance of the second verset causes a weakening of its metonymic meaning, which, as mentioned above, is defined in the entire parallelism by the predicate 'shall be king', in the first part; the literal sense of sitting on a throne is beginning to emerge here.

In his reply, David refers to the parallelism twice. The first time (v. 30) he repeats it in exactly the same form as Bathsheba used: 'Solomon your son shall be king after me, and he shall sit upon my throne in my stead'. (He adds only the phrase, 'in my stead'.) This is an unequivocal affirmation of the oath, as cited by her. The addition of the phrase, 'in my stead', can be understood in the light of David's decision to implement the oath forthwith. Nathan and Bathsheba used only the phrase 'after me', referring to the period after the king's death, while David himself thinks it appropriate to place Solomon on his throne immediately and during his lifetime, and consequently uses the phrase, 'in my stead'. Unlike 'after me', 'in my stead' does not refer to time, and therefore includes both David's lifetime and the period after his death. The first time David uses the parallelism he merely *adds* 'in my stead' to 'after me' (v. 30), while the second time (v. 35) the new phrase *replaces* the old one, indicating that on the first occasion the idea (of making Solomon king forthwith) was just being formed, while on the second it had already become a firm decision in the king's mind.

The cardinal modification in the second use of the parallelism by David (v. 35) is the reversal of its versets: 'and he shall sit upon my throne and he shall be king in my stead'. By changing the customary and familiar order and placing the matter of sitting upon the throne at the beginning of the parallelism its literal, non-metonymic meaning is emphasized. In this way it is hinted that only by actually sitting on the royal throne, not by making a declaration or even by being anointed, can the ruler's position be assured in actual fact. The same literal meaning is also evident the last two times the phrase occurs, both of them at the end of the report of Solomon's anointing given by Jonathan the son of Abiathar to Adonijah and his guests at En Rogel: 'Solomon sits upon the royal throne' (v. 46); 'And the king also said, "Blessed be the Lord, the God of Israel, who has granted one of my offspring to sit on the throne on this day, my own eyes seeing it"' (v. 48). It is obvious, therefore, that the actual sitting on the throne is regarded as the decisive phase and the culminating point of the process of becoming king. It was Adonijah who started the proceedings of having himself made king, but when David heard of this he made haste to place Solomon on his throne, making him the victor. By making literal use of an expression which was originally metonymic, the crucial point of the narrative is conveyed.

Attention should be paid to the fact that there was no physical impediment to prevent Solomon from sitting on the royal throne, for although David was still alive the throne was vacant. The text is at pains to hint at this by noting that David was bed-ridden: 'And the king bowed himself upon the bed' (v. 47, and also vv. 1-2, 15).

In conclusion, we have isolated a particular stylistic feature and followed its vicissitudes in an attempt to assess its functions. The feature we have chosen is not accidental, being central to the narrative, highly conspicuous, and continuing to appear throughout it. The various forms and mutations of this feature reflect important events which occur within the narrative, such as the attempts to arouse David to action on Solomon's behalf and the 'competition' between Adonijah and Solomon, during the first stages of which Adonijah was in the lead while at the later and decisive stage—that of sitting on the royal throne—Solomon gained the upper hand over his opponent.

By focusing our attention on one particular, prominent and deviant stylistic feature we were obliged to ignore the more common linguistic elements which are in fact the principal components of a work of literature.

For this reason a stylistic analysis of a narrative unit will be presented here using the alternative method, involving a comprehensive and systematic study of the whole complex of stylistic aspects, with the intention of clarifying the functions of both customary and unique features. The text used for this analysis is the speech made by Hushai the Archite, David's friend, to Absalom.

B. *Hushai's Speech (2 Sam. 17.7-13)*

By virtue of this speech Hushai succeeded in having Ahithophel's advice rejected, not because of *what* he said, because his plan was less advantageous to Absalom than Ahithophel's, but because of the *way* he said it. For this reason it is appropriate to examine the details of Hushai's speech, ascertain the accompanying meanings as far as is possible, including the associations and emotional charge with which his words are imbued. This will show us that Hushai's plan is the opposite of Ahithophel's not only in its general outline but also in its minute details and the way it is presented.

The mission with which Hushai was charged—to argue against Ahithophel's advice—was extremely difficult for two reasons.

First of all, Ahithophel was regarded as an authority; everybody treated his advice 'as if one consulted the oracle of God' (16.23), while Hushai's advice, though valued by Absalom—as is indicated by the fact that he was asked to give his opinion—was far less esteemed than Ahithophel's. It seems reasonable to assume that, as David's friend, Hushai remained somewhat suspect in Absalom's eyes. At first Absalom did not involve Hushai in the consultation at all, and the idea of asking his advice occurred to him only as an afterthought, as is indicated by the word, 'also', in 17.5: 'Then Absalom said, "Call Hushai the Archite *also*, and let us hear what he has to say *also*"'.

Secondly, the advice Hushai had to counter was not only extremely good, but had also been acknowledged as such by Absalom and all the elders of Israel (v. 4). In consequence, Hushai had to use very sophisticated tactics in order to induce his audience to change its mind, to dismiss the good plan as bad and accept the bad plan as good.

> Then Hushai said to Absalom, 'This time the counsel which Ahithophel has given is not good' (v. 7).

Hushai's first words are intended to overcome the first difficulty. He begins by rejecting Ahithophel's advice, but is careful not to make a general statement that Ahithophel's advice is not good, adding the words, 'this time': 'This time the counsel which Ahithophel has given is not good'. In this way he kills two birds with one stone. On the one hand, he says indirectly that Ahithophel's advice is usually good, indicating that he joins in the general admiration accorded to Ahithophel. On the other hand, right at the beginning of his speech he introduces an unexpected element against the background of the unmitigated approval customarily granted to Ahithophel's counsel. His implied agreement with the general view prepares his audience to hear him willingly, since people are not usually inclined to listen to opinions which are diametrically opposed to their own. Hushai hints that there is a common basis between himself and his audience upon which it is possible to build, while at the same time, through the element of surprise in his words, he arouses curiosity and suspense. By striking a balance between these two psychologically potent elements, Hushai considerably increases his chances of gaining his audience's favourable attention, and certainly acts most circumspectly and effectively against the general opinion in Ahithophel's favour. This general opinion, Hushai hints, is usually justified, but this does not preclude the necessity of examining the advice on its merits.

Because of the element of surprise in his words, Hushai waits a

while to see how his audience reacts, as can be learned from the
seemingly superfluous repetition of the words 'Hushai said' (7, 8). It
would appear that the audience is stunned into silence, for the
narrator does not report its reaction. After a brief pause Hushai
begins the main part of his speech, in which he attempts to contend
with the second difficulty confronting him.

The speech is patently built of two parts. The first part (vv. 8-10) is
devoted to exposing the weak points in Ahithophel's advice (which in
actual fact are its strong points, but Hushai is interested in
presenting them as weaknesses), while the second part (vv. 11-13),
which begins with the words, 'But my counsel is', elucidates the
alternative plan, which is supposedly better.

The first part is further sub-divided into two sections: Hushai first
shows why Ahithophel's plan has no chance of succeeding; then he
explains that not only will this plan not achieve the desired end but,
on the contrary, will cause damage and bring disaster on Absalom
himself.

> Hushai said moreover, 'You know your father and his men, that
> they are mighty men, and that they are enraged, like a bear robbed
> of her cubs in the field. Besides, your father is a man of war; he will
> not spend the night with the people' (v. 8).

At the beginning of Hushai's speech the stress on the pronoun
'you' (in the Hebrew text) is prominent: '*You* know'. Previously
Absalom had emphasized this pronoun in addressing Hushai: 'Thus
has Ahithophel spoken; shall we do as he advises? If not, *you* speak'
(v. 6). Absalom's last two words convey an impolite and blunt
command (in Hebrew), indicating that he wishes to act the ruler
giving orders to his subjects. At the same time they reflect Absalom's
desire that Hushai be the one to give his opinion, since as David's
friend he was well-acquainted with him and his habits. Hushai
replies by hinting, through emphasizing the word 'you', that in this
respect there is no need to rely on him, Hushai, since Absalom
himself is also well-acquainted with David. In other words, what
Hushai is about to say is well-known to Absalom; naturally a son
knows his father, as is indicated by the repeated designation 'your
father' (twice in this verse and once in v. 10). Ahithophel, on the
other hand, did not use the designation 'your father' (in the advice
which Hushai is attempting to undermine, although in Ahithophel's
previous advice, suggesting that Absalom go in to his father's

concubines, he did use the term 'your father' since it was necessary to stress the fact that incest was involved. This is also the term used by the narrator at that point: 'And Absalom went in to his father's concubines'). Ahithophel used the name David once (v. 1), the designation 'the king' once (v. 2) and the periphrasis 'the man whom you seek' once (v. 3). This shows that Ahithophel did not take particular care to phrase his speech in such a way as to accord with his listener's point of view, while Hushai, who had greater psychological insight, used the term 'your father', in order to make his speech conform to Absalom's point of view. In addition, had Hushai used the name David, it could have reminded his listener of the close relationship between Hushai and David, which Hushai was interested in obscuring; while the use of the designation 'the king' could have aroused suspicion that Hushai was still loyal to David.

Ahithophel called David's adherents 'the people who are with him' (v. 2), while Hushai calls them 'his men'. By this he hints that those who went with David are not just 'people' (or a mass), but 'men' and that it is no mere chance that they are with him, for they are *his* men, close to him and devoted to him. The implication is that they will fight for him with all their might, and that it will not be as easy to bring them over to Absalom's side as Ahithophel had suggested: 'And I will bring all the people back to you' (v. 3).

Hushai refers to the attributes of David and his men in a subordinate clause, while he mentions David and his men as a direct object: 'You know your father and his men, that they are mighty men, and that they are enraged'. He could have formulated the sentence in this way: 'You know that your father and his men are mighty men and that they are enraged'. Both these syntactical forms are found in the Bible. For example: 'And God saw the light, that it was good' (Gen. 1.4), or 'The Lord saw that the wickedness of man was great in the earth' (6.5).

The first kind of syntactical structure indicates that the subject apprehends the object (sees it, knows it) in its entirety, and from this total conception arrives at its essence, while the second structure implies that the subject apprehends one from among the object's various qualities, probably the one which is most important at that moment. Thus, in the first case the quality which is mentioned will be the central and essential one of that object, while in the second it will be the one to which the subject pays attention. Thus, we can compare, 'The sons of God saw the daughters of men that they were fair' (Gen. 6.2) with, 'And when the woman saw that the tree was good for food' (3.6). The first example suggests that the sons of God saw the daughters of men, and realized their characteristic quality, while the second implies that the woman discerned one particular property (and in the continuation of the verse two others: 'and that it was pleasant to the eyes, and a tree to be desired to make one wise') from among the various aspects of the tree. The first kind of syntactical structure fulfils diverse functions in the Bible, and Hushai uses it here as a means of persuasion. As is the case with a rhetorical question, the persuasive power of the syntactical structure used by Hushai derives from its implied assumption. When a rhetorical question is used the underlying assumption is that there is only one possible answer, which is undoubtedly right and is universally known. In the case of the syntactical structure under discussion the implicit assumption is that knowing the object necessarily entails recognition of the fact that the quality mentioned reflects the essence of the object and is more typical of it than anything else. Thus, Hushai's words are formulated in such a way as to imply that Absalom's knowledge of his father and his men necessarily involves awareness of the fact that they are mighty men and that they are enraged, and that these are not merely two of their many qualities but their essential ones, the focal points of their personalities.

In this context Hushai repeats the word *hēmâ* (translated 'they are'). This repetition emphasizes 'mighty' and 'enraged' by separating these two characteristics, thus giving each one of them independent weight and status. If he had said: 'That they are mighty men and enraged', neither characteristic would have stood out separately.

This does not mean that there is no connection between these characteristics and that they do not function in concert; on the contrary, what makes David and his men such dangerous adversaries is that they are not only mighty men and not only enraged, but simultaneously both mighty men and enraged. Each quality on its own is enough to create serious problems, and all the more so when the two of them are combined.

Hushai places additional emphasis on these characteristics by using the simile 'like a bear robbed of her cubs in the field', depicting them in a vividly impressive way, thereby arousing fear and apprehension in his audience. The word 'bear' in the image illustrates and reinforces the quality of 'mighty men', while 'robbed of her cubs', emphasizes 'enraged'.

Thus, Hushai stresses David's qualities in a variety of ways. His objective in doing so is to create a counterweight to the basic assumption on which Ahithophel's plan was founded. Ahithophel based his plan on a supposition concerning David's condition, namely, that he was 'weary and discouraged' (v. 2). Because of this, Ahithophel claimed, he would be able to throw David into panic and cause the people who were with him to flee, enabling him to strike down the king alone (v. 2). Hushai is unable to refute Ahithophel's basic assumption, since it is extremely reasonable (cf. 2 Sam. 16.14: 'And the king, and all the people who were with him arrived *weary*; and there he refreshed himself'). That is why Hushai counters the argument concerning David's condition with one about his character, since a person's behaviour is determined by his characteristics no less than by his condition.

Ahithophel's plan of campaign was, then, to surprise David and the people who were with him by a sudden attack at night. Hushai rebuts this by saying: 'Your father is a man of war; he will not spend the night with the people'. This means that since David is experienced in warfare it will be impossible to surprise him with a night-attack, for he will envisage a possibility of that kind and will be prepared for it:

> Behold, even now he has hidden himself in one of the pits, or in some other place (v. 9).

Hushai depicts a vivid picture ('behold') of David's actions at that very moment ('even now'), while Absalom is still engaged in consultations. It will be out of the question to throw David into a panic, to make the people flee and then to strike the king alone, because it will simply be impossible to find him! The impracticality of finding David is emphasized by the two vague and undefined adverbial adjuncts of place: 'in one of the pits, or in some other place'. There was no need whatsoever for an adjunct of place to express the thought, as it would have been sufficient to say: 'Even now he has hidden himself', and there was certainly no need for two of them. By using them, however, Hushai makes it very obvious that there are so many potential hiding-places that there is no possibility of finding the king.

After hinting that there is no chance of Ahithophel's plan achieving the desired end, Hushai goes on to describe the dangers it involves. Mighty and enraged men who are experienced in warfare and hiding in unknown places are liable to strike the first blow from their secret positions:

And when some of the people fall at the first attack, whoever hears it will say, 'There has been a slaughter among the people who follow Absalom' (v. 9).

This refers not only to the direct danger of some of Absalom's men being killed as a result of the action of David's men, who have become the attackers rather than the attacked, nor merely to the far-reaching conclusions that someone who hears of this might draw, but hints at the creation of a rumour. The words, 'whoever hears it will say' (*wešāmaʿ haššomēaʿ weʾāmar*), have connotations in Hebrew of rumours (*šemûʿâ*) and spreading them. As is the way with rumours, the disaster assumes gigantic proportions, and the killing of the first few victims rapidly becomes 'a slaughter' (as is the case with the rumour in 2 Sam. 13.30, where the killing of Amnon alone becomes the slaying of all the king's sons). The results are obvious: if there were to be a slaughter 'among the people who follow Absalom' (Hushai takes care not to call them 'Absalom's men', but 'the people who follow Absalom', hinting that it is a rabble which follows him), the people who support him now could turn their backs on him. In other words, Absalom cannot allow himself to risk the danger involved in a swift and sudden attack of the kind which Ahithophel recommended, since even a partial and initial failure could cause Absalom to lose everything. Hushai again depicts the rumour which could turn partial failure into a total disaster for Absalom in a vivid way, this time putting it in direct speech. Absalom, as it were, hears the actual rumour with his own ears, and Hushai can assume that this will serve to increase Absalom's apprehensions.

Then even if he be a valiant man, whose heart is like the heart of a lion, it will utterly melt with fear (v. 10).

Biblical commentators have interpreted the pronoun 'he' in this sentence as referring to either Ahithophel, David or the anonymous 'whoever hears it' mentioned just before. The first possibility is unreasonable, for Ahithophel has not been mentioned at all in this context. The second possibility has the advantage of combining the lion simile with the bear simile, together depicting David as someone who inspires fear and awe, but has the disadvantage of making it necessary to read 'will utterly melt' as a question, without there being any indication (such as the interrogative particle) that the sentence should be read in this way (reading a sentence as a question involves reversing its meaning, and so particular caution is required in adopting this procedure). Consequently, the third possibility seems preferable, particularly since 'all Israel' is mentioned immediately afterwards. 'Whoever hears it' is some unknown person from among 'all Israel'; even if he is a valiant man his heart will 'utterly melt with fear', and all the more so if he is not valiant.

This sentence contains a wealth of literary devices: two metaphors ('heart' and 'melt'), a simile ('like the heart of a lion'), repetition of the verbal root (*himmēs yimmās*—'will utterly melt') and opposition ('the heart of a lion'—'will utterly melt'). Using all these devices in concert Hushai creates an extremely vivid picture of fear, which cannot fail to impress his audience and exert a strong influence on it. Hushai continues with a sentence specifying the cause.

> For all Israel knows that your father is a mighty man, and that those who are with him are valiant men (v. 10).

This sentence serves to reinforce the element of fear. The association of the information about the valour of David and his men with the rumour about the 'slaughter' among the people who follow Absalom, is sure to create terror among Absalom's supporters, leading to his downfall. Contrary to what Ahithophel said about throwing David into a panic, it is Absalom's followers who will be gripped by confusion.

At this point, at the end of the first part of his speech, which is devoted to undermining Ahithophel's plan, Hushai repeats several details which he has mentioned at the beginning. This repetition emphasizes these details, driving the point home to his audience, while at the same time setting a clear boundary to this part of the speech and summarizing it before proceeding to the second part.

'For all Israel knows' reiterates 'You know', and thus Hushai stresses once again that what he says is not based solely on his own personal knowledge. Whereas at the beginning, however, Hushai says that Absalom knows, he now expands the scope of his claim by saying that all Israel knows. And if *everyone* knows, then it must be correct and beyond all doubt!

'That your father is a mighty man, and that those who are with him are valiant men' echoes 'your father and his men, that they are mighty men, and that they are enraged'. Hushai once again places special emphasis on the characteristics of David and his men but this time by means of the word order: in the Hebrew text the attributes (*gibbôr, bᵉnê ḥayil*) are placed at the beginning of the clauses (a mighty man is your father; valiant men are those who are with him). Whereas Hushai repeats the attribute 'mighty' exactly, he replaces 'enraged' by 'valiant men'. The term 'valiant men' refers back to 'valiant man' at the beginning of the same sentence. If he alluded there to an anonymous person from among Absalom's supporters, Hushai is hinting here that not only among Absalom's men is there a valiant man, but that David's followers are of the same ilk. Hushai takes care to use the singular ('a valiant man') when speaking of Absalom's men and the plural ('valiant men') when referring to David's. By doing so he insinuates that whereas among Absalom's supporters there may be one or a few men who are valiant, all or most of David's are. In the first case the valiant man is mentioned in a concessive clause ('even if he be a valiant man'), while in the second in an absolute statement ('those who are with him are valiant men'). This indicates that it is only a possibility that there is a valiant man among Absalom's followers, while it is a certainty that David's men are valiant. This also constitutes an indirect answer to Ahithophel's suggestion, 'Let me choose twelve thousand men' (v. 1): If chosen men from Absalom's camp go out to fight ('Let me choose'), they will find themselves facing valiant men, not just ordinary people.

The first part of Hushai's speech contains a great many phrases which are also found in the narratives about David's earlier years:

That they are mighty men	These are the names of the mighty men whom David had (2 Sam. 23.8)
And that they are enraged	And every one who was in distress, and every one who was in debt, and every one who was enraged gathered to him; and he became captain over them (1 Sam. 22.2).
Like a bear robbed of her cubs in the field	Your servant has killed both lions and bears (17.36)
Your father is a man of war	Behold, I have seen a son of Jesse the Bethlehemite, who is skilful in playing, a man of valour, a man of war (16.18)

| Even now he has hidden himself | See therefore, and take note of all the hiding places where he hides (23.23) |

Hushai may be referring associatively to the heroic period, when David showed quite clearly that he had both courage and initiative and was able to prevail in difficult and highly dangerous situations. Absalom's men would therefore have to contend with a formidable opponent, who was their superior by far. Ahithophel's plan—according to Hushai—did not take this fact sufficiently into account. It was based on a mistaken assumption, had no chance of succeeding and would lead to disaster.

After undermining the basis of Ahithophel's plan, Hushai takes the next step and presents his own scheme to Absalom. At this stage, however, he is confronted by a problem he has himself created. He has praised the warlike qualities of David and his men, describing them so convincingly that it seems impossible to overcome them. How can Hushai formulate a plan which will make it feasible to gain the upper hand over them nonetheless?

Hushai's solution to the problem is based on the assumption that quantity can overcome quality. A huge army—not the small body of select men proposed by Ahithophel—would be able to defeat David and his men. Mustering and organizing a large army takes time, and this is precisely Hushai's intention, to gain time for David, who has been forced to flee in haste.

Hushai displays the power of numbers to his audience in various ways. The similes in this part of the speech serve this purpose too: 'as the sand by the sea for multitude', 'as the dew falls on the ground'. These similes differ from those which were employed in the first part: 'like a bear robbed of her cubs in the field', and 'like the heart of a lion'. The images in the first part of the speech are taken from the world of beasts, illustrating quality and designed to engender fear in the audience, whilst those in the second part are taken from the world of inanimate nature, illustrating quantity and designed to create confidence in the audience. In each case the kind of image is suited to its end.

The expression 'all Israel', which occurs twice, and the idiom 'from Dan to Beersheba' also serve to create an impression of quantity and multitude, as is the case with the plural 'we' recurring in 'we shall come upon him', 'we shall rest upon him', 'we shall drag it', and the duplication (in Hebrew) of the root *hē'āsop yē'āsēp* ('be surely gathered to you'). All these devices operate together, reinforcing one another. As a result the audience will be deeply impressed, and may even become intoxicated with the power and glory of this tremendous body of fighting men.

> But my counsel is that all Israel be surely gathered to you, from Dan to Beersheba, as the sand by the sea for multitude, and that your presence go to battle (v. 11).

In contrast to Ahithophel, who made himself too prominent, using the first person singular in every verb—'I will set out', 'Let me choose', 'I will come upon him', 'I will strike down', 'I will bring back',—Hushai does not mention himself at all in the actual implementation of the plan, placing Absalom at the centre. The focus on Absalom began at the outset, when Hushai referred to him at the beginning of his speech as the initial subject, with emphasis, '*You* know'. Similarly, instead of saying, 'that all Israel be gathered', Hushai says, 'that all Israel be gathered *to you*'. But the effort to give prominence to Absalom reaches its culmination in the solemn pronouncement, 'and that your presence (literally, your face) go to battle'. The same expression, namely, the same synecdoche combined with the same verb, appears in reference to God in Exod. 33.14, 15: 'My presence will go with you', 'If thy presence will not go with me'. This means that Absalom himself in all his glory will head this enormous army and lead it into battle. Hushai plays on Absalom's desires and aspirations, directing his words towards the delusions of grandeur and excessive self-love of the ambitious prince.

Hushai's psychological percipience is also reflected in the fact that he introduces widely-used phrases into his speech. Although, as has been stated above, our knowledge of the language of the biblical period is limited, and we are therefore unable to determine with certainty how original Hushai's language was, we do know that some of the expressions he used are not uncommon in the Bible. The term 'from Dan to Beersheba' occurs seven times in the Bible, five of them in the books of Samuel, once in Judges and once in Kings; the same expression occurs twice in a reversed form, 'from Beersheba to Dan', in Chronicles. The simile 'as the sand by the sea' is found often in the Bible, occurring (with slight changes) in Genesis, in each of the Early Prophets, in the Later Prophets, and in the Hagiographa (in most cases this image illustrates a very large number, as it does in

Hushai's speech, but in Prov. 27.3 and Job 6.3 it depicts weight). The metaphor of a melting heart is also used often, occurring ten times in the books of Deuteronomy, Joshua, Samuel, Isaiah, Ezekiel and Nahum. The simile 'like a bear robbed of her cubs' is found in Joshua and Proverbs. And phrases similar to 'and of him and all the men with him not one will be left' appear in Exodus, Judges, Samuel and Psalms. If a certain expression occurs in several books belonging to different types of biblical literature, this indicates with a reasonable degree of certainty that it was a widely used term. By using well-known expressions Hushai creates the impression that what he says is based on widely-known and acknowledged facts. A claim based on something which has long been known to its hearer and accepted by him as a true and undisputed fact, is able to convince him more readily; he will nod his head in agreement and fail to realize that the subject really deserves more thought. This accounts for the considerable persuasive power of commonly used sayings and idioms. Hushai makes use of this power in citing familiar phrases, metaphors and images.

> So we shall come upon him in some place where he is to be found, and we shall rest upon him as the dew falls on the ground; and of him and all the men with him not one will be left (v. 12).

In the first part of his speech, when he was trying to undermine Ahithophel's advice, Hushai claimed that it would be impossible to find David, that 'he has hidden himself in one of the pits, or in some other place'. Now, however, when his object is to demonstrate that according to his plan it will be possible to overcome David, he has to hint that it is possible to find him. In speaking of David's hiding place, Hushai again makes use of the term 'some place', as he did in the first part of his speech. To all intents and purposes there has been no change and Hushai does not contradict what he said previously. The omission of 'in one of the pits', however, and the addition of 'where he is to be found' imply that 'some place' is no longer something undefined, one of a great many places, but is the place, wherever it may be, where David is to be found. The phrase 'where he is to be *found*' implies that it is possible to *find* him; David is no longer referred to as 'hiding', but as 'found'.[6]

6. S. Laniado, *Kli Yakar—Commentary on the Early Prophets* (Venice, 1603) (Hebrew).

And when they come to that place, all Israel shall rest upon him 'as the dew falls on the ground'. The connotation of the verb 'rest' is clarified by such places as Exod. 10.14, where we read: 'And the locusts came up over all the land of Egypt, and rested on the whole country of Egypt', and Isa. 7.19, where it is said of the fly and the bee: 'And they will all come and rest on the steep ravines, and on the clefts of the rocks, and on all the thornbushes, and on all the pastures', namely, will light upon and cover everything with their masses. This sense of the term is reinforced by the comparison 'as the dew falls on the ground'. Because this is an open comparison, namely, the point of correspondence between the compared objects is not noted (in contrast to the simile 'as the sand by the sea *for multitude*') it can be understood not only as an illustration of vast numbers but also as intimating that the action will extend to and include everyone, and that no one will be able to oppose it.

The outcome of this large-scale campaign can only be that 'of him and all the men with him not one will be left', or in other words, total destruction. This is again opposed to Ahithophel's advice, 'I will strike down the king only, and I will bring all the people back to you. . . . and all the people will be at peace'. At this point Hushai takes care to use the term 'and all the men with him', and not 'his men', as in the first part of his speech, because now he is not interested in indicating how close and devoted they are to David.

> Moreover, if he be gotten into a city, then shall all Israel bring ropes to that city, and we will draw it into the river, until there be not one small stone found there (v. 13).

In the second part of his speech Hushai refers to David as a passive object: 'we shall come upon him', 'we shall rest upon him', 'and of him. . . . not one will be left', while in the first part David appeared as an active subject, for obvious reasons. This trend is particularly clear in the clause 'if he be gotten into a city' (w^e'im 'el 'îr yē'āsēp), where Hushai was obliged to speak of an action taken by David but nevertheless makes it a passive phrase. The verb 'be gotten' (yē'āsēp) echoes 'be surely gathered' (hē'āsop yē'āsēp) in v. 11, though the meaning is different; before it meant the gathering together of all Israel whereas here it refers to retreat (cf. Jer. 47.6). By this repetition Hushai is hinting at a causal relation: if all Israel is gathered (yē'āsēp) this will lead to David's retreat (yē'āsēp).

In actual fact it is just at this point that the obvious weakness of

Hushai's advice is apparent. Whereas Ahithophel wanted to set out immediately and pursue David without delay, Hushai aspires to postpone the action and gain time for David (it should be noted that he disguises his real objective very well). Ahithophel's intention to press forward and chase David forthwith is reflected in the fact that the sentences or clauses in which he expresses his ideas are short, simple and paratactic, creating a rapid rhythm. Hushai's desire to delay the action and hold back the advance, on the other hand, is reflected in the fact that his sentences are long, complex and hypotactic, creating a certain cumbersomeness as well as a slow rhythm. Thus, 'Let me choose twelve thousand men, and I will set out and pursue David tonight', as against 'If he be gotten into a city, then shall all Israel bring ropes to that city, and we will draw it into the river, until there be not one small stone found there'.

Absalom and his advisors cannot, however, be unaware of the possibility that David may make use of the delay in order to establish himself in one of the fortified cities. David himself recognized a similar danger at the time of Sheba the son of Bichri's revolt, and consequently ordered Abishai to pursue him immediately, 'lest he get himself fortified cities' (2 Sam. 20.6). Hushai of course is not interested in calling attention to this matter and therefore speaks of a city as such, avoiding the adjective 'fortified' (unlike David when he gave the command mentioned previously).

Be that as it may, Hushai is aware of the fact that it can be argued against him that the delay in implementing his plan may lead to a long and difficult siege of the city in which David may fortify himself. Hushai replies to this potential argument—the formulation '*If* he be gotten into a city' indicates that this is in fact its nature—by saying that even in this case there will be no need for siege or protracted battles, since: 'Then shall all Israel bring ropes to that city, and we will draw it into the river, until there be not one small stone found there'. Thus, because of their vast numbers all Israel can drag that city with ropes from its high position into the depths of the river, to the last particle. The speech, which is coloured throughout by a plethora of images and figurative language reaches its apogee in this respect at its close. In order to conceal the weakness of his plan, Hushai appeals to his audience's emotions, using fantastic descriptions in order to inflame its imagination. Excitement suppresses rational consideration. Hushai's use of exaggeration, which has featured earlier in his speech ('as the sand by the sea for multitude', 'as the dew falls on the ground', 'and of him and all the men with him not one will be left') reaches a pinnacle here: 'until there be not one small stone found there'. Hushai no longer refers to David. There is no need. The 'to be found' of the previous sentence ('where he is to be found') now becomes 'not found' ('until there be not one small stone found') encompassing everything and everyone, including David. The failure to mention David here at the end signifies his non-existence. Victory will therefore be complete, and all this without even so much as mentioning the possibility of any fighting. 'That your presence go to battle' was Hushai's advice, but there will be no need to fight, neither if David is 'in some place where he is to be found', for then they will simply rest upon him, nor if 'he be gotten into a city', for then they will just drag the entire city into the river. Absalom will gain victory and glory without making any effort or taking any risk.

To sum up, Hushai's speech is full to overflowing with rhetorical devices and appeals to his audience's emotions, and that is why Absalom and all the *men* of Israel are convinced by it (while Ahithophel's advice pleased Absalom and all the *elders* of Israel).[7] Ahithophel's advice was better in actual fact, but Hushai's presentation was superior, as regards both psychology and rhetoric, and so he prevailed in the contest.

7. 2 Sam. 17.4, 14. Cf. Levi ben Gershon (Gersonides), *ad loc.*

Chapter 6

THE NARRATIVE OF AMNON AND TAMAR

This chapter contains an analysis of an entire narrative according to the various features discussed separately in the preceding chapters. The narrative selected for an overall analysis of this kind is that of Amnon and Tamar, because from a literary point of view it is typical of biblical narrative in general. Though it is unique, as is every narrative, the method applied here will be appropriate for most other biblical narratives.

The analysis will be undertaken in two stages: first, the literary design of the narrative sequence will be examined step by step, paying particular attention to stylistic details: after that, several literary characteristics of the narrative as a whole will be discussed.

Before dealing with the details of the literary design of the narrative of Amnon and Tamar (2 Sam. 13.1-22), however, it is necessary to consider a problem whose clarification is essential for understanding the narrative: whether Amnon was permitted to marry Tamar, who was his half-sister on his father's side. From the narrative itself it appears that he was permitted to marry her, for when he asks her to lie with him she says: 'Now therefore, I pray you, speak to the king; for he will not withhold me from you' (v. 13). The laws of the Bible, however, expressly forbid marriage between a stepbrother and sister (Lev. 18.9; 20.17; Deut. 27.22). The Rabbis and, following them, the traditional Jewish exegetes resolved the discrepancy between Tamar's statement and biblical law through midrashic interpretation.[1] Modern scholars have claimed that at that

1. Tamar's mother, Maacah the daughter of the king of Geshur, had been captured in war. David had lain with her before she had been converted and therefore, Tamar, who had been conceived then, was permitted to marry Amnon by Jewish Law (*b. Sanhedrin* 21a; *Yebamot* 23a).

time marriage between a step-brother and sister was still permitted
(this view is based on the custom among neighbouring nations,
particularly Egypt, as well as on Gen. 20.12, where we read that
Sarah, Abraham's wife, was the daughter of his father but not of his
mother). A minority of scholars believe that Amnon was not
permitted to marry Tamar, in accordance with biblical law, and that
she said: 'I pray you, speak to the king; for he will not withhold me
from you' only in order to hold Amnon at bay and gain time. This
assumption is not acceptable, however, because even if Tamar said
these things just to gain time they must have had some basis in fact
in order to have carried conviction. It could be claimed that had
Amnon been able to marry Tamar, all he had to do was ask his father
for her from the outset instead of resorting to stratagems, but this can
be answered by contending that Amnon did not wish to marry her
but merely to satisfy his lust. Thus it may be concluded that Tamar
was not forbidden to Amnon and consequently, his crime was not
incest but rape, which is reprehensible at all times, but particularly
so when it involves a brother and sister.

> Now after this Absalom, David's son, had a beautiful sister, whose
> name was Tamar, and Amnon, David's son, loved her. And Amnon
> was so tormented that he made himself ill because of his sister
> Tamar; for she was a virgin, and it seemed impossible to Amnon to
> do anything to her (vv. 1-2).

The narrative begins with an exposition in which the characters
are introduced. We are told four things about the protagonists: their
names (Absalom, Tamar, Amnon), their family relations (David's
son, sister, and again David's son), Tamar's external appearance
(beautiful) and Amnon's feelings about Tamar (he loved her). All
these four features are crucially important for the narrative. The
names are needed, of course, so that it will be possible to identify the
characters in the narrative. The family ties between the individuals
are important because they constitute the basis of the imbroglio on
which the narrative stands. Tamar's beauty is, undoubtedly, the
reason for Amnon's love for her, which in turn provides the motive
for all that follows. Thus, everything in the exposition is essential for
understanding the narrative.

The structure of the first verse should be given some attention.
The same information about the characters could have been
conveyed by constructing the verse differently, for example: Now

Amnon, David's son, loved Tamar, Absalom's sister, who was very beautiful. Although virtually the same information is conveyed here as in the biblical verse, there are fine differences which are significant. The biblical verse is built in such a way that, in addition to communicating information about the characters, it also hints at what is to come.

Absalom, David's son, is mentioned at the beginning of the verse; this is surprising, because he plays only a minor role and at the conclusion of this narrative only, and it would have been sufficient to have introduced him then, stating his relation to Tamar. In any case, it is remarkable that he—rather than one of the principal characters, Amnon or Tamar—is given a prominent position at the beginning of the first verse. It would seem that he is cited here because of the central role he is to fulfil in the later developments following Amnon's rape of Tamar. This means that even though the narrative of Amnon and Tamar is to be regarded as a separate and complete literary unit, the opening verse indicates that it serves as a prologue or first stage in the chain of narratives which follow it.

Absalom, David's son, opens the verse and Amnon, David's son, closes it, while Tamar is in the middle, between the two brothers. This structure reflects the situation which is to arise in the future, when these two sons of David will confront one another and Tamar will be the cause of dissension and disharmony between them. There is nothing in the verse to indicate that the friction between the two brothers is the result of a conflict of political interests between them, namely, rivalry over the succession, since David is not referred to as the king, and there is no direct or indirect hint of matters pertaining to the kingdom. The tension between Absalom and Amnon is based on familiar ties: Tamar is the axis, and her two brothers are at the two opposing poles.

In contrast to Absalom and Amnon, each of whom is defined as David's son, Tamar is called Absalom's sister and not David's daughter. This should be regarded as intimating that she and Absalom have the same mother (cf. vv. 4, 20, 22), even though further on in the narrative she is also called Amnon's sister by both the characters (David, Amnon, Absalom and Tamar herself) and the narrator. The reference to her as Absalom's sister is appropriate to what happens later when Absalom rather than David acts on her behalf and avenges her humiliation.

The connection between Absalom and Tamar is further indicated by the fact that in the Hebrew text they are mentioned in linked clauses of the same kind, namely, nominal clauses, while Amnon is mentioned in a verbal clause.

A nominal clause, by its very nature, usually expresses a situation, while a verbal clause tends to communicate an action, a process or an event. The first part of the first verse does indeed denote a situation, which existed before the plot began and which does not change throughout it (the close relationship between Absalom and Tamar), while the second part refers to a process which takes place on the internal-emotional level, preceding and giving rise to the external events of the plot and changing during the course of the narrative (Amnon's love for Tamar, which turns into hatred).

Because of the crucial importance of love in this narrative the narrator is not content with the direct statement made in the first verse concerning Amnon's feelings ('he loved her'), but uses other means of emphasizing this love and indicating its intensity. In v. 2 the narrator again penetrates right into Amnon's inner self ('Amnon was so tormented'), informing us that this love tortured Amnon to such an extent 'that he made himself ill'. The actual plot begins with the conversation between Jonadab and Amnon, which also serves to illustrate Amnon's ardour; the agonies of love make Amnon look 'haggard', and in reply to Jonadab's question as to the reason for his appearance Amnon says that he loves Tamar, the sister of his brother Absalom (v. 4). In this way the narrator's assertions are supplemented by the testimony of the party concerned. These items of direct evidence are complemented by the indirect proof of Amnon's appearance. Thus, Amnon's love is given unusual prominence at the beginning of the narrative, and the reader cannot help but pay attention to it. What is the precise nature of this love, however, remains as yet unclear.

The word 'love' has positive connotations, in literature in general and in the Bible in particular. It is often used in the Bible to denote spiritual affinity, an elevated and pure emotion, and it certainly does not refer just to physical lust. The love of God is often mentioned in the Bible, God serving as either subject or object. Mention is also made of love which is in fact deep friendship, as was the love between David and Jonathan. There is also, of course, the love between a man and a woman, but even in this case the reference is not only to mere physical attraction but often also to a deep emotion, as in the case of Jacob's love for Rachel, when not only did the seven years he worked for her seem 'but a few days because of the love he had for her' (Gen. 29.20), but even many years later, when Jacob was a very old man, the memory of his beloved wife and the traumatic experience of her death had not faded: 'For when I came from Paddan, Rachel to my sorrow died in the land of Canaan on the way, when there was still some distance to go to Ephrath. . .' (Gen. 48.7).

Thus, in being informed of Amnon's fierce love for Tamar, the reader has no reason to assume that this is a passing carnal desire. In reading of Amnon's suffering because of his love the reader might even feel a certain sympathy and compassion for him. At the beginning of the narrative Amnon is not presented in a negative light and he does not arouse feelings of disapproval or disgust; quite the contrary. The reversal in the reader's attitude occurs gradually, until finally only intense contempt and loathing are felt. It should be noted that the gradual change in the reader's attitude to Amnon is achieved despite the fact that the narrative is short.

The reader may first have doubts about Amnon's personality when reading in v. 2: 'And Amnon was so tormented that he made himself ill because of his sister Tamar; for she was a virgin'. Both the medieval Jewish commentators and the modern exegetes tend to regard the subordinate clause, 'for she was a virgin' as the explanation for what follows, in the sense that because she was a virgin she did not leave the house freely (or according to others: she was well guarded), and consequently 'it seemed impossible to Amnon to do anything to her'. If this were the case, however, we would expect this causative clause to follow rather than precede the main clause, to which it is subordinate: 'and it seemed impossible to Amnon to do anything to her for she was a virgin'.[2] Thus, it seems more likely that the fact that she is a virgin is noted in order to explain what comes before, i.e., the fact that she is a virgin causes Amnon to be so tormented that he makes himself ill.[3]

In this context it should be noted that the fact that Tamar was a virgin is mentioned in this narrative both at this point and when we

---

2. Transposing the disjunctive accent *'atnāḥ* from the word *hî'* (she) to *'aḥotô* (his sister), as most of the modern scholars have proposed, does not' solve the problem.

3. Cf. David Kimhi (Radak): 'For she was a virgin, therefore he desired her even more'; while Caspi writes that 'this reason serves to explain both what precedes and what follows'.

are informed that she rent her long robe, which the narrator tells us
was worn by the virgin daughters of the king (v. 18). Thus, it is stated
explicitly that Tamar was a virgin at the beginning of the narrative
and that she was one no longer by its end. Amnon loves her intensely
when she is a virgin, but rejects her as soon as she ceases to be one.
From this it may be concluded that the explanation 'for she was a
virgin' at the beginning of the narrative serves to indicate the nature
and basis of Amnon's love.

Doubts about Amnon's character are also liable to be aroused by
what we read in the second part of v. 2: 'and it seemed impossible to
Amnon to do anything to her'.[4] The text does not make it clear what
it is exactly that seems to Amnon to be impossible to do to Tamar.
The word 'anything' (m^e'$\hat{u}m\hat{a}$) is so wide and general in its meaning
that almost any content can be attributed to it. Only later on in the
narrative does it become apparent what Amnon wanted to do to
Tamar. At this stage the narrator avoids stating explicitly what
Amnon's intentions are, and consequently his character does not
stand out as being clearly and unequivocally negative. Had the
narrator wanted to show Amnon in a distinctly negative light right
at the outset of the narrative less vague terms would have been
used.

The second part of v. 2 serves nevertheless to illuminate Amnon's
moral character, though retroactively. When Amnon later rapes
Tamar the word 'anything' is filled with content, and we then
understand that Amnon did not act on a momentary impulse. Thus,
it cannot be claimed that the rape was not planned and that during
the meeting between Amnon and Tamar, which was originally
intended to serve an innocent purpose, Amnon's desires suddenly
overcame him. There is no doubt that Amnon intended to do
something to Tamar, namely, to lie with her, but this is not yet clear
at this point.

In the first part of v. 2, 'And Amnon was so tormented that he
made himself ill because of his sister Tamar; for she was a virgin', the
word 'sister' is redundant in terms of the information it conveys.
From v. 1, where we read that Tamar is Absalom's sister and that
both Absalom and Amnon are David's sons, it is clear that Tamar is
Amnon's sister by his father. Why, then, is the fact that she is his
sister mentioned again in v. 2?

4. *yippālē'* = impossible, cf. Gen. 18.14; Jer. 32.17, 27; *yippālē' b^e'eyney*
= it seemed impossible, cf. Zech. 8.6.

Abarbanel claims that the word 'sister' here explains why Amnon is so tormented that he makes himself ill: 'How can he desire his sister?' But this interpretation runs into difficulties. First of all, it is based on the assumption that Amnon was not permitted to marry Tamar, which was accepted by Abarbanel but, as noted above, not by most scholars, whether traditional or critical. Secondly, if the reason for Amnon's torment was the fact that Tamar was his sister, we could expect a structure of the following kind: 'And Amnon was so tormented that he made himself ill because of Tamar, for she was his sister', but the version before us explicitly gives as the reason the fact that Tamar was a virgin.

The term 'sister' in reference to Tamar, whether with regard to Amnon or Absalom, occurs eight times in this narrative. In addition, the word 'brother' in reference to either Amnon or Absalom, occurs nine times (this does not include the word 'brother' in v. 3, which refers to the relationship between David and Shimeah). This means that these terms serve to present the actions of the characters in the light of the family relationships between them, thereby expressing an implicit judgment: either these actions are appropriate to these family relationships or they are not. Absalom acts in accordance with what is expected of him as Tamar's brother, while Amnon's behaviour is diametrically opposed to what one would assume from a brother towards his sister (and as a result gives rise to Absalom's hostility towards Amnon, which does not befit brothers).

> But Amnon had a friend, whose name was Jonadab, the son of Shimeah, David's brother; and Jonadab was a very wise man. And he said to him, 'Why are you so haggard, O son of the king, every morning? Will you not tell me?' Amnon said to him, 'I love Tamar, my brother Absalom's sister'. Jonadab said to him, 'Lie down on your bed, and pretend to be ill; and when your father comes to see you, say to him, "Pray, let my sister Tamar come and sustain me with food, and prepare the sustenance in my sight, that I may see it, and eat from her hand"' (vv. 3-5).

Verse 3 serves as a link between the exposition and the first item in the chain of events. Like v. 1, it introduces one of the characters in the narrative, and here, too, this character is presented in nominal clauses. Furthermore, just as Tamar was introduced there as Absalom's sister, Jonadab is presented here as Amnon's friend.

A question arises as to the literary function of Jonadab the son of Shimeah. If we assume that in a short story, which is condensed and sticks to essentials, there are no secondary characters who are unnecessary and do not contribute to the main issue, it is not at all clear why Jonadab is introduced. Naturally, it cannot be claimed that he is mentioned for the sake of historical accuracy, since, as is well known, even the writing of history involves the careful selection of material from a vast quantity of facts and details. There is no need to point out that the authors of biblical narratives keep details down to a minimum. Why, then, did the author see fit to bring Jonadab into this narrative?

It is true that Jonadab devises the plan to bring Tamar to Amnon's house, but is there any significance in the fact that the stratagem whereby the rape is made possible is conceived by someone else and not by Amnon? The rape itself is the main point, after all, and there can be no doubt that the responsibility for it rests solely with Amnon, even if someone else helped him by making suggestions. Anyone who decides to accept and implement advice cannot place the blame on the person who gave it but must take the responsibility for his actions.

If Jonadab's presence in the narrative is not due to literary imperfection (which is also possible, of course), the explanation might be that this narrative, as will be indicated later, does not convey external events only but also gives the psychological causes which led to them; thus, the author wishes to make it clear what caused Amnon to do what he did, mentioning Jonadab's advice as one of the main factors. Jonadab's counsel does not diminish Amnon's guilt and responsibility one whit, but it contributes to explaining—albeit partially—how it came about that Amnon committed the rape. Jonadab's personality also illuminates Amnon's: Amnon needs Jonadab's advice because he himself is incapable of working out a plan which would extricate him from his emotional plight. In other words, Amnon does not have Jonadab's acumen.

The appearance of Jonadab and the advice he gives confronts us with other problems. Jonadab is introduced in v. 3 as Amnon's friend, the son of Shimeah and a very wise man. Because he is the son of David's brother (Shimeah, David's brother, is known to us from 1 Sam. 16.9 as Shammah) he is cousin to Amnon, Tamar and Absalom. It seems surprising, therefore, that Jonadab puts a proposal to Amnon which can do serious harm to his kinswoman, Tamar. It may be that, as Amnon's friend, Jonadab's loyalty to Amnon takes precedence over his consideration for his cousin Tamar, and in order to bring Amnon out of his depression he is prepared to sacrifice her. Be that as it may, the advice he gives, which helps one person at the expense of another, and a cousin at that, casts a dark shadow over Jonadab's morals.

In view of Jonadab's low moral standards it is surprising that the narrator defines him as a very wise man, since in the Bible the term 'wisdom' is customarily used in a positive sense, which derives generally—though not invariably—from its moral (and religious) value. In the Wisdom Literature it is even identified with the fear of God and the departure from evil (Job 28.28). How, then, can the narrator characterize as wise someone who is credited with planning a contemptible act against his cousin Tamar?

It has been claimed that the phrase, 'and Jonadab was a very wise man' is meant ironically,[5] but this argument is not acceptable because Jonadab does in fact appear to be very wise. His sagacity is displayed, amongst other things, by his ability to turn a disadvantage into an advantage. His scheme exploits Amnon's haggardness and sick appearance, and he advises him to lie on his bed and pretend to be ill. He even utilizes the main obstacle in Amnon's path—the king himself! Instead of attempting to bypass the king and achieve the objective without his knowledge and behind his back, Jonadab makes the king (an active) partner, thereby obviating any objections Tamar or anyone else might raise to her visiting her brother's house.

Jonadab's shrewdness is also indicated by the fact that although he shows Amnon how to trick Tamar into coming to his house, he does not tell him what to do afterwards. Jonadab's advice will merely bring Tamar to her brother's house (which in itself is not objectionable); what happens afterwards is not included in his counsel and he cannot therefore be held accountable.

Jonadab also evinces his wisdom on his second appearance in the (extended) narrative. Of all those present at the king's palace he is the only one who does not believe the rumour that Absalom has killed all the king's sons. He is sure that Amnon alone has died because unlike the other courtiers, and even David himself, he realizes that 'by the command of Absalom this has been determined from the day he forced his sister Tamar' (13.32).

It is not only because of Jonadab's astuteness that the narrator's

---

5. R.N. Whybray, *The Succession Narrative—A Study of II Sam. 9–20 and 1 Kings 1-2* (London, 1968), p. 85.

definition of him as a very wise man should not be regarded as ironic, however. Interpreting a statement as ironic has the effect of inverting its meaning completely, and therefore this should be done only with the greatest circumspection. Thus, irony should not be assumed unless there are clear indications that the narrator meant the reverse of what was said. In the present instance there are no such indications.

The Rabbis and many traditional exegetes as well as some modern ones[6] have solved this problem by saying that Jonadab was clever in evil-doing. Thus, even though wisdom in itself is positive, Jonadab uses it for ignoble purposes.

The statement that Jonadab was a very wise man does not appear to involve any evaluation of him, on the moral level. The term 'wise' is apparently used here in a neutral sense; Jonadab is not someone who is wise in the sense of the book of Proverbs where wisdom implies righteousness, but rather as the clever adviser who utilizes his abilities to serve his friend in advancing his aspirations, regardless of their ethical nature. The narrative's moral stance is reflected not in the characterization of Jonadab but in the fact that even the wise friend cannot avert the consequences of the base act, and the villain receives his punishment.

But how did Jonadab not foresee that the rape would have serious consequences for Amnon? Surely, a deed of this kind could not pass without a reaction from the father or brother of the victim, and how could the wise Jonadab have failed to realize this?

It cannot be claimed that Jonadab meant to do Amnon harm—as he did to Tamar—since he was introduced to us explicitly as Amnon's friend. It is, however, possible to assume that even though he was Amnon's friend he was not sincere and did not act as a friend ought, just as Amnon did not act as a brother ought, in the vein of: 'Let every one beware of his friend, and put no trust in any brother' (Jer. 9.4). This assumption is borne out by Jonadab's statement at the end of the chapter, which is not in harmony with the friendship between him and Amnon. Jonadab says there: 'For by the command of Absalom this has been determined from the day he forced his sister Tamar' (v. 32). The term 'forced' (*'annotô*) has grave and accusatory undertones, which we would not expect to hear from

6. *B. Sanhedrin* 21a; Rashi; Kimhi; Gersonides; Abarbanel; H.P. Smith, *The Books of Samuel* (International Critical Commentary; Edinburgh, 1899).

a friend, who would probably use euphemistic, or at least neutral, terms. Jonadab also says (v. 33): 'Now therefore let not my lord the king so take it to heart as to suppose that all the king's sons are dead; for Amnon alone is dead'. This gives the impression that Amnon's death is not a particularly serious matter, and it is even more surprising that this dismissive tone is adopted by the friend of the murdered man, especially since he uses the phrase, 'for Amnon alone is dead' twice (vv. 32, 33), as if he considers Amnon's death to be a matter of trifling importance. It is difficult to understand these expressions even if their intention is to comfort the king.

It is conceivable, then, that Jonadab is not loyal to his friend Amnon, and this seems reasonable in view of his immoral character. Another possibility is that the word 'friend' refers to an official position in this instance, as in 'the king's friend' (1 Kgs 4.5), or denotes a companion rather than an intimate associate. In either case, Jonadab's advice is not that of a friend.

There is another possible explanation for Jonadab's advice, and that is that it was not his intention that Amnon should rape Tamar. All he tells Amnon is to pretend to be ill and ask his father to send Tamar to him to prepare him food and feed him with her hand. Jonadab does not say either explicitly or implicitly how Amnon should behave and what he should do once Tamar is in his house. We, as readers, draw conclusions about Jonadab's intentions from what actually happens afterwards, and suppose that what took place between Amnon and Tamar is in accordance with Jonadab's plan. But this assumption could well be mistaken. Tamar's humiliating expulsion from Amnon's house after the rape is certainly not part of Jonadab's plan, for the narrator explains it as being due to the fact that Amnon's great love for Tamar suddenly turned into deep hatred. If Tamar's banishment does not conform to Jonadab's plan, it is possible that the actual rape was not envisaged by him either. Jonadab may not have intended Amnon to use force but rather to try to persuade Tamar (and in actual fact the brutal rape is preceded by an attempt on Amnon's part to convince Tamar to lie with him of her own free will, and only after he has not managed to win her over by words does Amnon use his greater strength and force her). Jonadab may not have had even this in mind, simply contriving an innocent assignation at which Amnon could enjoy the proximity of his beloved.

If this is the case, then what Amnon did was at his own prompting. It cannot, however, be asserted that what happened was the result of his being suddenly overcome with desire during the meeting between him and Tamar, for, as explained above, v. 2 hints that Amnon had impure intentions of 'doing something to her'. We are not told, however, that he revealed these intentions to Jonadab (he told him only that he loved his sister Tamar), and it is consequently possible that the idea of rape did not occur to Jonadab.

According to this interpretation there is nothing in Jonadab's advice to harm his cousin Tamar or to bring about serious consequences for his friend Amnon in the form of punishment or revenge. Moreover this obviates the discrepancy between the fact that Jonadab was 'wise', a term which bears a positive, even ethical, connotation in the Bible, and the immoral advice he gives Amnon, as the accepted interpretation has it. Similarly, the fact that Jonadab is not punished for his part in this disgraceful deed, neither by man nor by God, does not present any problem. And finally, this interpretation accounts for Jonadab's pronouncement at the end of the chapter, which is not what one would expect to hear from a friend. Jonadab really was a loyal and devoted friend to Amnon, but his attitude changed as a result of the rape, after which he kept aloof from him and ceased being his true friend.

Thus, this view can resolve all the problems connected with Jonadab and his counsel. If there are still any doubts, they are due to the fact that this interpretation is based on the assumption that Jonadab's advice contains no more than what appears on the surface. As in real life, in literature in general and biblical narratives in particular, intentions may exist, however, which are not stated explicitly. (In the narrative of Bathsheba, for example, we are not told why David urges Uriah to go down to his house, yet there is no doubt in our minds what the king's purpose is.)

As soon as Jonadab is introduced he takes an active part in events. A natural connection is established between the verse in which he is presented and the one in which his actions are recounted; the fact that he is Amnon's friend and a very wise man (v. 3) is immediately reflected in the question he puts to Amnon: 'Why are you so haggard, O son of the king, every morning?' (v. 4). This indicates his perceptiveness as well as his concern for Amnon's situation.

Jonadab's question, which starts the external action, leads directly to the central subject of the narrative. The dialogue between Jonadab and Amnon, which develops as a result of the question, brings the planning of the deed before us through scenic representation; we hear what is said by the participants themselves rather than through the narrator's report. We are given the opportunity to witness a secret consultation which undoubtedly takes place *tête-à-tête*.

Jonadab's question illustrates what the narrator has told us previously about Amnon, that he was so tormented that he made himself ill; Amnon's mental suffering is so great that it is apparent in his external appearance. This is a powerful reflection of Amnon's state of distress.

The question is addressed expressly to Amnon through the phrase, 'O son of the king', which occurs neither at the beginning nor at the end of the question but adjacent to the word 'haggard'. The proximity of the title 'son of the king' to the word 'haggard' emphasizes the contrast between the usual state of a prince, who lacks for nothing and whose appearance is good, and Amnon's present condition and haggard looks. In this way Amnon's mental agony is given added weight.

The phrase 'every morning' is distinguished in the Hebrew by the repetition of the word 'morning' (*babboqer babboqer*). This reiteration, which is not uncommon in the Bible (occurring another dozen times), expresses the meaning, 'every morning' in an emphatic way. Here it hints at two things simultaneously. The first is that Amnon's haggard looks are not a matter of a day or two but have been apparent for quite a while, indicating that Amnon's affliction has continued for some time and his love for Tamar is no mere passing fancy. The second is that because of his mental anguish Amnon has been unable to sleep, and that is why he looks ill particularly in the morning.[7]

Jonadab continues by saying: 'Will you not tell me?' in order to urge Amnon to answer his question; this indicates that Amnon does not seem to be willing to unburden himself immediately. Although Jonadab has noticed that something has been troubling Amnon for some time, his friend has not yet confided in him. Through the word 'me' Jonadab hints at the close relationship between himself and Amnon, intimating that even if Amnon does not wish to reveal his thoughts to others he will not conceal them from him (Jonadab). Jonadab does not, however, give prominence to himself by putting

7. Kimhi.

the pronoun *lî* ('me') before the verb instead of after it (*halô' lî taggîd* rather than *halô' taggîd lî*).

In Amnon's reply the direct object, Tamar, is placed in the Hebrew at the beginning of the sentence (*'et Tāmār 'aḥôt 'Abšālom 'āḥî 'anî 'ohēb*). This sentence structure places the emphasis on the cause of Amnon's condition and also reflects the fact that Tamar is uppermost in his mind. By adding 'my brother Absalom's sister', Amnon hints at the complex family relationships and problems this love involves.

Jonadab's immediate reaction to Amnon's confession is to present a detailed plan of action, telling Amnon what to say when his father comes to see him (giving rise to speech within speech). These words are repeated by Amnon himself when he speaks to his father, as well as by David when he addresses Tamar (and also by the narrator, in reporting the fulfilment of the request).

> So Amnon lay down, and pretended to be ill; and when the king came to see him, Amnon said to the king, 'Pray let my sister Tamar come and make a couple of cakes in my sight, that I may be sustained from her hand'. Then David sent home to Tamar, saying, 'Pray go to your brother Amnon's house, and prepare the sustenance for him (vv. 6-7).

When repetitions such as these occur in a narrative the points in common as well as the differences between the various versions should be examined in an attempt to grasp their significance.

Jonadab	Amnon	David
Pray let my sister Tamar come and sustain me with food, and prepare the sustenance in my sight, that I may see it, and eat from her hand.	Pray let my sister Tamar come and make a couple of cakes in my sight, that I may be sustained from her hand.	Pray go to your brother Amnon's house and prepare the sustenance for him.

The main point, namely, that Tamar should go to Amnon's house, appears at the beginning and is expressed in identical terms (apart from differences arising from the change of the interlocutors) by all three speakers. All three of them mention the family relationship explicitly (my sister, your brother) less as a means of identification than as an indication that it is fitting that Tamar should help her brother recover and that the proprieties will be observed if the virgin Tamar visits his house.

As far as the differences are concerned, it emerges that the request grows shorter with each speaker. Jonadab's statement is wordy and contains several clauses, constituting a long and complex sentence. This construction suits the content of what he says, reflecting the complicated and detailed plan which dictates each move in the chain of actions necessary for its success. At first glance the order in which Amnon is supposed to say things appears strange and illogical, for 'sustain me with food' precedes 'and prepare the sustenance in my sight', while in reality the order should be the reverse. A closer look at the sentence Jonadab tells Amnon to say, however, reveals that it does not convey a series of actions which follow one another in consecutive order, but rather—as the Hebrew tenses show—two requests: the first, 'Pray let my sister Tamar come', and the second, 'and sustain me with food'. The second request appears to constitute the object of the first: let Tamar come in order to sustain me with food. In actual fact, however, the relationship is the reverse, the true aim being contained in the first request, 'let Tamar come', while the second request serves as its motivation. In order to obscure the genuine objective Jonadab focuses attention on the second request, 'and sustain me with food', by elaborating on it: 'and prepare the sustenance in my sight, that I may see it, and eat from her hand'. The two verbs, 'prepare' (*we'aśetâ*) and 'eat' (*we'ākaltî*), which in Hebrew are in the past + *waw* and depict an action, depend and elaborate on the verb 'sustain' (*wetabrēnî*), which is in the future simple and expresses a request. The second of these two actions, 'and eat from her hand', is more important because it involves physical proximity. Once again, Jonadab camouflages the real purpose by diverting attention to the less important action, adding the subordinate clause 'that I may see it'. This subordinate clause (the Hebrew verb is in the future) explains and expands on what has been hinted before in the phrase 'in my sight': 'and prepare the sustenance in my *sight*, that I may *see* it'. The phrase 'in my sight' is intended to prevent Tamar preparing the food at her house and sending it to Amnon's house with a servant, just as 'from her hand' is designed to prevent a situation arising in which someone else feeds the patient.

Thus, the structure of the sentence is as follows:

Pray let my sister Tamar come   -   and sustain me with food
_____

and prepare the sustenance in my sight   -   and eat from her hand
_____

that I may see it

The really important points are given at the beginning and end of
the sentence: Tamar's coming to visit Amnon, and her feeding him
from her hand. The details and amplifications create the impression,
however, that the main object is that Amnon should see how Tamar
prepares the food so that his appetite will be stimulated, he will eat
and recover. This impression is reinforced by the use of the root *brh*
(sustain), which Jonadab employs twice: 'and sustain me' and
'sustenance'. The noun occurs only in this narrative (in Ezek. 34.20
it has a different meaning), and the verb appears twice in the Bible,
in the narrative of Abner's burial, when David refuses to eat bread or
anything else till the sun goes down (2 Sam. 3.35), and in the episode
of the sick child, when David does not agree to eat food with the
elders of his house (12.17). These contexts indicate that the reference
is to eating intended to revive someone who is grieving or mourning.
By reiterating this root Jonadab stresses that the object of Tamar's
coming is to revive and sustain the patient, and obviously if that is
the aim the request cannot be declined.

What Amnon says is phrased more simply than Jonadab has
suggested. Amnon's speech contains three main clauses, which
contain only requests (as indicated by the fact that all three verbs in
Hebrew are in the future), without the details and reasons that
Jonadab has proposed. Amnon's phrasing is less sophisticated than
Jonadab's; the main point is no longer delicately camouflaged and
the three requests are of equal importance: 'let my sister Tamar
come... and make... that I may be sustained'.

Instead of 'that I may eat from her hand', which is Jonadab's
phrase, Amnon says, 'that I may be sustained from her hand', hinting
that by eating from Tamar's hand he can be revived. Furthermore,
while Jonadab speaks of food in general, Amnon specifies what he
wants to eat: cakes.

It can be said that Jonadab chooses his words according to the
hearer's point of view, so as to obscure the true aim and make it
impossible for the request to be refused, while Amnon's phrasing
reflects the speaker's point of view. Some of Jonadab's subtleties have
disappeared and the aspects which are of importance to Amnon are
more evident.

David's instruction to Tamar, that she should go to the house of
her brother Amnon and prepare food for him, is short and to the
point. The verbs are in the imperative, and as a father (and king) he
is in a position to command without needing to explain and justify

himself. Nevertheless, it should be noted that David uses the polite word 'pray', putting the matter to Tamar as a request rather than a command. David speaks of 'sustenance' in general without specifying, since as far as he is concerned it is immaterial what food Tamar prepares for Amnon provided it is 'sustenance', food which will strengthen and revive the patient. Conspicuous by its absence is the detail which is mentioned by both Jonadab and Amnon, namely that Tamar should feed Amnon. David omits this detail, which involves undue physical proximity, for the same reason that he says to Tamar 'go to your brother Amnon's *house*', and not 'go to your brother Amnon'. (The fact that everyone lived in a separate house is also intimated by the narrator when saying: 'Then David sent home to Tamar'.) David refers only to the actions to be performed, namely that Tamar go to Amnon's house and make him food, and refrains from mentioning the personal aspects of preparing the food in his sight and feeding him. This shows that what is the main point for Jonadab and Amnon does not even enter David's mind. His phrasing reflects a simple and naïve grasp of the matter.

After we have heard the request three times—as put by Jonadab, Amnon and David, each time in a slightly different version—we are informed of it a fourth time by the narrator, who reports on its implementation. These repetitions (which could, naturally, have been avoided) slow up the pace of the action and thereby heighten the tension. The slowing down of time and the enhancement of suspense is also achieved by the detailed account of Tamar's preparation of the food, which enumerates every particular:

> So Tamar went to her brother Amnon's house, where he was lying down. And she took dough, and kneaded it, and made cakes in his sight, and baked the cakes. And she took the pan and emptied it out before him, but he refused to eat. And Amnon said, 'Let every one leave my presence'. So every one left his presence (vv. 8-9).

When Tamar reaches Amnon's house she finds him lying down (the participle, *šokēb*, points to an existing situation). Amnon did not lie down only for his father's visit, but continues with his play-acting. In this way he prevents Tamar from entertaining any suspicions; on the contrary, her desire to help and sustain her brother will be increased. The fact that Amnon is in bed also prepares the way for the rape.

From what the narrator tells us, 'So Tamar went to her brother

Amnon's house', we learn that, in accordance with David's instructions, Tamar feels that she goes to Amnon's house, not to Amnon. She goes to perform a task. The purpose of her going is to *do* something for Amnon, not necessarily to *see* Amnon himself (of David who went to visit Amnon on his sickbed it was said, 'and when the king came to *see* him'). She goes to undertake that duty because Amnon is her brother, and as such she is obliged to help him and there is no fear that the proprieties will not be observed. The narrator does not only convey objective facts but simultaneously reflects (by implication) Tamar's feelings and thoughts; this applies to the use of both the word 'house' and 'her brother'.

The fact that Tamar's object is merely to fulfil a practical duty also emerges from the absence of any conversation between her and Amnon, for immediately upon reaching his house she sets to work. We are confronted with a succession of verbs in short clauses, creating a rapid pace: 'And she took . . . kneaded . . . made . . . baked . . . took . . . emptied'. All this indicates that Tamar is absorbed in her work (and Amnon, who is lying in idleness, can feast his eyes on her meanwhile). One action follows another, Tamar works quickly and does not busy herself with anything else. It should be noted, however, that the narrator presents events to us relatively slowly (again, thereby heightening the tension): details are recorded to such an extent that instead of 'and she kneaded the dough' we find, 'And she took dough and kneaded it', and instead of 'and she emptied the pan out before him' we read, 'And she took the pan and emptied it out before him'.

In view of the fact that all Tamar's labours are in vain because Amnon has no interest in the food she has made and has no intention of eating it, there is more than a little irony in the narrator's long and detailed account of the various stages of its preparation. There is a hint of this irony in the words 'she had made' in v. 10. These words are quite redundant in terms of the information they convey, since it is already a well-known fact that Tamar has made the cakes, but the narrator mentions it again at the precise moment that she brings the fruits of her labours to Amnon's chamber. For a moment it seems that her toil has been useful, but it rapidly transpires that this is not so and that Amnon does not want her cakes.

The words, 'and emptied it out before him' indicate that Tamar did not intend to feed Amnon. She was not aware of Amnon's request that she do so either, for David had not passed it on to her. These words end the series of verbs of which Tamar is the subject, and are followed by a succession of verbs of which Amnon is the subject. This marks the transition from Tamar's activity to Amnon's, which is accomplished in a natural way, for the subject of 'emptied' is still Tamar, whereas the pronoun 'him' refers to Amnon. Amnon's first action is still of a fairly passive nature, since he refuses to do something (to eat), and only afterwards does he become more active, until he is finally extremely vigorous.

Amnon's unwillingness to eat is reported briefly, 'but he refused to eat' without any detailed explanation, and by the narrator rather than by Amnon himself. The reader is not given any reason for this refusal. Tamar might attribute it to Amnon's illness, but this cannot be done by the reader, who knows that Amnon is only shamming. Jonadab's advice does not provide the reader with any explanation either, for it makes no mention of any refusal to eat. It is, therefore, unforeseen and inexplicable, engendering tension and expectancy in the reader.

The next step in the narrative is not concerned with eating but with the fact that every one is sent out of Amnon's presence. Thus, tension is intensified, for still no explanation is given for Amnon's refusal to eat, and the narrative seems to switch to another tack. The narrator slows down the pace again (therefore further increasing suspense) by a virtually verbatim repetition: first giving Amnon's command, 'Let every one leave my presence', and then recording its implementation: 'So every one left his presence'. Amnon's command indicates that either something unusual is about to happen or something secret is to be said, and whatever it is must be kept from the general public. The reader cannot yet know what is about to happen or be said, since Jonadab's advice contains nothing that hints at it, and consequently the tension and expectancy is heightened even more.

> Then Amnon said to Tamar, 'Bring the sustenance into the chamber, that I may be sustained from your hand'. And Tamar took the cakes she had made, and brought them into the chamber to Amnon her brother. But when she brought them near him to eat, he took hold of her, and said to her, 'Come, lie with me, my sister' (vv. 10-11).

After everyone has left, Amnon asks Tamar to bring the sustenance into the chamber so that he can eat from her hand. Was it necessary to send everyone out for this, the reader wonders, or is there another reason? There is no answer to this question either in Jonadab's advice, which does not say anything about what happens at this stage. At any rate, the narrative has again returned to the issue of eating.

Amnon uses the root *brh* (sustain) twice in addressing Tamar, thereby intimating that for his recovery it is necessary that Tamar bring the food into the (inner) chamber where he is lying and feed him there with her own hands. This is intended to convince Tamar to accede to his request.

For a moment it seems that the mystery of Amnon's refusal to eat is solved. It probably sprang from the fact that Tamar did not intend to feed him, merely placing the food in front of him. This, at any rate, is what Tamar might understand as the reason for his refusal. Only now has Amnon informed her that he wishes her to feed him. Consequently, she goes into his bedroom and has no apprehensions about feeding him there, because, after all, he is her brother: 'and brought them into the chamber to Amnon her brother'.

Until this point a clear and regular pattern can be discerned in the narrative, consisting of an utterance (proposal, request, command) and its implementation, the latter being reported in almost identical terms to the proposal, request or command.

> Jonadab said to him, 'Lie down on your bed, and pretend to be ill; and when your father comes to see you, say to him . . .'
> So Amnon lay down and pretended to be ill; and when the king came to see him, Amnon said to the king. . .
>
> 'Pray let my sister Tamar come . . . and prepare the sustenance in my sight',
> Then David sent home to Tamar, saying, 'Pray go to your brother Amnon's house, and prepare the sustenance for him'.
> So Tamar went to her brother Amnon's house, etc.
>
> And Amnon said, 'Let every one leave my presence'.
> So every one left his presence.
>
> Then Amnon said to Tamar, 'Bring the sustenance into the chamber, that I may be sustained from your hand'.
> And Tamar . . . brought them into the chamber to Amnon her brother. . .

Accordingly, we would expect the continuation to be, 'and he was sustained from her hand'.

But the continuation is not as we have anticipated. The regular pattern is broken at this point, conforming with the unexpected development in the plot. Everything has led up to the act of Amnon being fed by Tamar, what Jonadab tells Amnon to say ('and eat from her hand'), what Amnon actually says to the king ('that I may be sustained from her hand') and what Amnon says to Tamar ('that I may be sustained from your hand'), but he never in fact eats from her hand. A detailed account is given of Tamar's preparation of the food, we are told that she brought it into Amnon's chamber and even that she brought it near him to eat, but it is not stated that he ate. Tamar does what she is supposed to do and has already extended her hand to feed him, but Amnon does not do what is expected of him. Amnon extends his hand too, though not to hold the food that is being offered him but in order to hold Tamar herself (he grips her to prevent her escaping when she realizes what he wants). It should be noted that all this is depicted in a slow and detailed way through vivid scenic representation. We hear the exchange between the two protagonists and see their moves with our own eyes.

From what Amnon says to Tamar, 'Come, lie with me, my sister', we gather that Amnon first tries to persuade her to submit voluntarily (although he is holding her in case she does not agree). He speaks to her gently, in a tone designed to win her heart. It would have been enough for him to say 'Lie with me', as Potiphar's wife said to Joseph (Gen. 39.7, 12), but Amnon requests rather than commands. The words 'Come' and 'my sister' serve the sole purpose of persuasion. The use of the phrase 'my sister' is not surprising for, as has been shown above, Amnon was permitted to marry Tamar even though she was his sister, and the term is used here to express affection and close affinity (as 'my sister' in Song 4.9, where there is no family relationship).

The four words Amnon addresses to Tamar in order to convince her to lie with him (*bô'î šikbî 'immî 'aḥôtî*) all end with the *î* sound. This is by no means inevitable, for Amnon could have phrased his request differently (for example, *bô'î nā' 'aḥôtî wᵉ'eškᵉbâ immāk*, 'Come, I pray you, my sister, and let me lie with you'). The repetition of a sound should not be regarded as a purely phonological feature but as having expressive value. Rhyme establishes, reveals or emphasizes the connection between the meanings of words. In the present case, the *î* sound refers to Tamar in the first two words (second person feminine) and to Amnon in the second two (first person), establishing a close connection between Tamar and Amnon, which Amnon desires and attempts to realize. The first and the last words serve the purpose of persuasion, while the nucleus of the sentence, as regards both its meaning and its position, consists of the words 'lie with me' (*šikbî 'immî*), where the *î* sound referring to Tamar is contiguous with the one referring to Amnon. Thus, the sounds of the words coincide with and reinforce their semantic aspects.

If we compare what Amnon says to Tamar here to what he says to her in v. 15, after he has raped her and his love has turned to hatred, we will find that there too the words he uses end with the same sound *qûmî lēkî* ('Get up, go'). Thus, all the words which Amnon addresses to Tamar during the course of the narrative, six in number, end with the *î* sound. Despite the similarity in sound, however, the second phrase does not resemble the first (similarities in sound sometimes point up opposition in meaning). There is a precise contrast in the content of 'Come, lie down' in v. 11 and 'Get up, go' in v. 15. These four verbs create a logical continuum of events: Come—lie down—get up—go, the first verb contrasting with the last, and the second with the third. Thus, the four verbs are arranged in chiastic order, which also reflects and emphasizes opposition. While there are four words (in Hebrew) in the first utterance, there are only two in the second. The words of address or persuasion are missing, and this gives Amnon's second utterance the tenor of a short and brutal command (this is felt clearly if we compare his phrase, 'Get up, go' with what the lover says to his beloved in Song 2.10 and 13, which is distinguished by its gentle tone even though the same verbs are used, 'Get up, my love, my fair one, and go away'). The two *î* sounds in Amnon's second utterance refer to Tamar alone (second person feminine); the sound referring to Amnon (first person) has disappeared, indicating that there is no longer any connection between them.

> She answered him, 'Do not, my brother, do not force me; for such a thing is not done in Israel; do not do this wanton folly. As for me, where could I lead my shame? And as for you, you would be as one of the wanton fools in Israel. Now therefore, I pray you, speak to the king; for he will not withhold me from you' (vv. 12-13).

Tamar's reply is conspicuous for its length, indicating her valiant effort to thwart Amnon's intentions. This length also holds back the advancement of the plot to some extent, delaying the awful moment of the rape, and this also heightens the tension.

Tamar's reply comprises three parts: (1) an appeal to Amnon to refrain from harming her; (2) an argument supporting this appeal; (3) an alternative proposal. The second part can be further divided into three parts: (a) a general argument; (b) a personal argument relating to Tamar; (c) a personal argument relating to Amnon. A renewed appeal to Amnon to refrain from doing the deed is inserted between the general argument and the two personal ones. The phrase 'now therefore' ($w^e\ ʿatt\hat{a}$), which often serves as a structural element marking the transition between different sections of a speech and occurring particularly before a proposition or conclusion, appears before the third part, the alternative proposal.

Tamar's entreaty to Amnon to forbear from harming her is clearly stamped with emotion. The first phrase, 'Do not, my brother, do not force me', which is somewhat abrupt (because the first 'do not' is not followed by any verb which it negates), displays Tamar's emotional confusion and deep anxiety. She beseeches Amnon vehemently, with all the eloquence she can muster. The utterance 'do not' recurs three times: 'Do not, 'do not force me', 'do not do this', (and is reinforced by an additional negation, 'it is not done'). This reiteration of negatives expresses Tamar's desperate resistance as she cries from the depths of her heart: do not! do not! The negation is emphasized both by the repetition and by the fact that the first negative is at the beginning of the sentence. The absence of any word negated by this first 'do not' accords it an autonomous status, that of pure, unadulterated and absolute negation.

Tamar's term of address, 'my brother', should be regarded as her response to the term Amnon uses in addressing her, 'my sister'. It too is directed at the emotional affinity which devolves from their family relationship, as if to say: since you are my brother, do not ignore my supplication and do not injure me. It is not fitting for a brother to force his sister. A stranger would not do such a thing, how much less so a brother!

Tamar does not use the neutral verb 'lie' which Amnon employed but rather 'force', which has connotations of a far more negative and base nature. The implications of her choice of this term seem to be that Amnon will have to use force to achieve his end and that Tamar intends to resist him. Tamar's reply to Amnon's request, 'Come, lie with me, my sister' is not in the first person (I will not lie with you), but is an imperative, directed at him, 'Do not force me . . . do not do this wanton folly'. This means that the matter depends on him not on her. Tamar realizes that her refusal is not in itself sufficient to prevent the deed (for in addition to making a verbal request Amnon has also seized hold of her), and therefore does everything she can by pleas, arguments and an alternative proposal, to dissuade him from fulfilling his intentions.

After the appeal, which is imbued with emotion, Tamar proffers an argument based on rational considerations, starting with the word 'for'. The first argument is general and relates to accepted moral standards: 'for such a thing is not done in Israel'. Between the first and the second arguments Tamar bursts out in renewed entreaty: 'Do not do this wanton folly'.

Tamar uses generally accepted idioms as a means of persuasion (see above, p. 234). Both the first argument and her renewed entreaty are based on fixed collocations. The term, 'such a thing is not done' can be understood in two ways: a. such a thing is not customarily done, as in Gen. 29.26; 'It is not done in our country. . . '; b. such a thing ought not to be done, as in Gen. 20.9: 'You have done to me things that ought not to be done'. These two meanings are clearly interconnected; such a thing is not customarily done because it should not be done. In the present instance it seems that the first meaning is the main one while the second is subordinate, but both operate together as an argument aimed at persuading Amnon to desist from implementing his design.

Whenever the expression, 'to do a wanton folly in Israel' (*'āśâ nᵉbālâ bᵉyiśrā'ēl*) occurs in the Bible (Gen. 34.7; Deut. 22.21; Judg. 20.6, 10; Jer. 29.23) except for one instance (Josh. 7.15), the reference is to a sexual crime, and in all instances (including Josh. 7.15) the culprit pays with his life (in Deuteronomy the punishment of death is determined by law, while in Jeremiah it is asserted in a prophecy). The use of this phrase, which defines the deed Amnon intends to do as an appalling crime with the gravest consequences, is again designed to deter him. Tamar transfers the phrase 'in Israel' from this expression to 'for such a thing is not done' (whereby what she says comes to resemble the statement in Judg. 19.23: 'Do not do this wanton folly'. In both instances the expression is used in an attempt to avert a horrible crime, and it is one of several phrases in our narrative which are similar to those used in that of the concubine at Gibeah).

The following two arguments which Tamar raises allude to the personal aspect and the consequences of the deed rather than its nature, first in connection with Tamar and then with Amnon. The personal aspect of the arguments is clearly expressed by the emphasis on the pronouns: 'As for me, where could I carry my shame? And as for you, you would be as one of the wanton fools in Israel'. The phrase 'in Israel', which occurs twice in Tamar's speech (and is an integral part of the fixed collocation referred to above, as is clearly shown by its use in Gen. 34.7, since at the time of the rape of Dinah Israel did not yet exist), reflects the view that Amnon's deed would run counter to the accepted values of the whole nation, with all consequences of that.

There is a substantial connection between the 'shame' mentioned in the first personal argument, and 'wanton fool', cited in the second. A wanton fool causes shame, and consequently these two expressions occur together in various parts of the Bible: 'Let me not be put to shame by a wanton fool' (Ps. 39.8); 'Remember that the wanton fools put you to shame all the day' (Ps. 74.22); 'the shame to which I was put by Nabal' (1 Sam. 25.39; the name Nabal means 'wanton fool').

The argument pertaining to Tamar herself is intended to arouse Amnon's compassion. Tamar appeals to his sense of charity by describing how pitiful her situation will be after she has been raped. She uses two stylistic devices, the first being the formulation of her claim as a rhetorical question, and the second her representation of the abstract concept 'shame' as something of substance which can be led (only people, and sometimes the sea or rivers, are mentioned in the Bible as the objects of the verb 'to lead'). This achieves a vivid and impressive picture of the bitter fate which awaits Tamar.

The argument referring to Amnon is intended to point out to him the damage he will cause himself if he rapes her: he will be considered as one of the wanton fools, with all that this implies. By using the phrase 'wanton fool' Tamar repeats the term she has just used: 'Do not do this wanton folly'. Not only does the repetition provide emphasis and reinforcement, but by transferring the censure from the deed (wanton folly) to the doer (wanton fool) the condemnation of Amnon is made more powerful. At the same time, Tamar takes care not to aggravate Amnon unduly, and consequently does not say: 'You will be a wanton fool', selecting a milder expression: 'You would be as one of the wanton fools' (just as Job does—even more than Tamar—when countering his wife's rebuke;

he does not call her a wanton fool or compare her to one of them, but merely likens her words to those of the foolish women: 'You speak as one of the foolish women would speak': Job 2.10).

After pleading and putting forward arguments against the rape Tamar makes a positive proposal at the end of her speech, indicating that there is a solution to the problem which torments Amnon which involves neither damage or shame. It has been pointed out above that her suggestion, 'Now therefore, I pray you, speak to the king; for he will not withhold me from you', indicates that Amnon would have been permitted to marry Tamar. This view is substantiated by the fact that amongst the arguments Tamar raises to dissuade Amnon from raping her she does not mention the family relationship between them. If sexual intercourse had been forbidden on grounds of incest she would certainly have referred to it.

It should be noted that Tamar not only makes the suggestion but adds that the course of action she has proposed will succeed. If Amnon accepts her proposition he will undoubtedly win Tamar, for if he speaks to the king, 'he will not withhold me from you'. Thus, this procedure is worth Amnon's while, for it involves no harm and is assured of success.

> But he would not listen to her voice, and he overpowered her, and forced her, and lay with her (v. 14).

Tamar's efforts are unavailing. Amnon does not accept her suggestion because he is not interested in marrying her, it appears, but only in satisfying his desire. Now it transpires that the love mentioned at the beginning of the narrative is not elevated, spiritual emotion but mere carnal lust. The reader's attitude to Amnon is now indisputably negative.

Amnon's rejection of Tamar's plea is not transmitted by Amnon himself but by the narrator, despite the fact that till now the dialogue between Amnon and Tamar has been conveyed in direct speech. This reflects Amnon's disdainful attitude to Tamar, who is no more than a sexual object for him, for he disregards her lengthy speech, not bothering to reply or even refer to it. Though it is not unusual in biblical narratives for someone's response to an appeal to be brought to our notice through his deeds rather than his words, in the present case the narrator not only reports Amnon's actions but states explicitly that he would not listen to Tamar. This intelligence is redundant in terms of the information conveyed, as we are able to deduce this from the actual implementation of the rape. The narrator's remark throws Amnon's silence into relief, however, thus making it plain that Tamar's speech is of no importance whatsoever as far as Amnon is concerned.

At this point, when the deed itself occurs, narrated time is greatly accelerated. Whereas the narrator lingers on the details of what takes place before and after the rape, he gives absolutely no particulars about the act itself. Everything happens quickly. Three short clauses which are dominated by verbs create a rapid pace and emphasize the activity: 'And he overpowered her, and forced her, and lay with her'.

The phrases 'and he overpowered her', 'and he lay with her' refer back to what Amnon said and did according to v. 11, before Tamar's speech: 'and he took hold of her' (in Hebrew 'took hold' and 'overpowered' are from the same root), and 'lie with me'. Verse 14b is a direct continuation of v. 11 as if Tamar's long speech had not occurred. This also hints at Amnon's total disregard of her arguments. The fact that 'and he took hold of her' (*wayyaḥazeq bāh* becomes 'and he overpowered her' (*wayyeḥezaq mimmennā*) shows that Tamar not only argued verbally but also resisted bodily. *Wayyiškab 'tāh* (and lay with her) according to the Massoretic vocalization reading *'otāh* (her) as the object instead of *'ittāh* (with her) defines the intercourse as forbidden (cf. Gen. 34.2; Lev. 15.24; Num. 5.13, 19; Ezek. 23.8). The verb 'and he forced her', clearly defines the nature of the act. By using this verb the narrator reiterates Tamar's phrase, 'do not force me', thereby expressing his identification with her denunciatory stance.

> Then Amnon hated her with very great hatred; for greater was the hatred with which he hated her than the love with which he had loved her. And Amnon said to her, 'Get up, go' (v. 15).

After the actual rape there is an unexpected turn in the course of the plot. Amnon's love suddenly turns to hatred and as a result after the climax of the conflict—the act of ravishment—the expected decline in the plot line does not occur, another sharp conflict developing between the two protagonists instead. Beforehand, Amnon wanted to win Tamar, now he wishes to rid himself of her, and in both instances Tamar resists fiercely.

Verse 15, which informs us of the switch in Amnon's emotions, contrasts with the preceding verse or, to be more precise, with the

266   *Narrative Art in the Bible*

latter part of the preceding verse, as regards both form and content. Where before we found love, even if only carnal love, here we find hatred; where before there was the outside observation of action, here there is the inside view of emotion; where before there were three extremely short clauses, here there is one very long and complex sentence. The narrator does not require the reader to conclude from what Amnon says or does that there has been a change in his feelings towards Tamar, supplying precise information as to what has happened in Amnon's heart. This information concerns not only the reversal from love to hatred but also the intensity of the new feeling. Stylistic means are used to express the vehemence of the hatred in comparison to the love. The root 'hate' recurs four times in this verse as opposed to the two occasions on which the root 'love' is cited. The adjective 'great', qualifying the hatred, appears twice, despite the fact that in general there are very few adjectives in this narrative. Moreover, on the first occasion the adjective 'great' is intensified by 'very', and on the second by being placed at the beginning of the clause, after the conjunctive 'for'. Ten words (in Hebrew) are devoted to the subject of hatred and only three to that of love. In this way the intensity of Amnon's hatred is accentuated, and it is driven home to the reader that it is infinitely stronger than his love. This occurs after it has previously been made very clear how great was his love at the beginning ('And Amnon was so tormented that he made himself ill', 'Why are you so haggard, O son of the king, every morning?' etc.).

After this vigorous account of the hatred there is no longer any doubt in the reader's mind how to interpret Amnon's words to Tamar, 'Get up, go'. After having used her to satisfy his sexual appetite Amnon casts Tamar out like a vessel for which he has no further use. The reader's negative attitude to Amnon becomes even more intense, and his behaviour inspires loathing and disgust.

> But she said to him, 'No, because this greater wrong than the other which you did to me, to send me away'. But he would not listen to her (v. 16).

There is clearly a corruption in this verse, and it is therefore difficult to ascertain its precise meaning and examine its stylistic aspects. (The correct version may have been preserved in the Lucian recension of the Septuagint: 'No, my brother, for this wrong is greater than the other which you did to me, to send me away'). The general gist is clear, however. The importance of Tamar's declaration here within the framework of the narrative lies in the fact that it reflects the author's attitude to Amnon's action. The author does not judge Amnon directly, but his position can be inferred from what Tamar says. From this we learn that the banishment of Tamar after the rape is regarded as being worse and more reprehensible than the rape itself.

The question arises, however, how can the expulsion of Tamar be more nefarious than the actual rape? It would seem that the contrary is the case and that rape is the worse crime. The answer to this question seems to be contained in the conception underlying the law given in Deut. 22.28-29: 'If a man meets a virgin who is not betrothed, and seizes her and lies with her, and they are found, then the man who lay with her shall give to the father of the young woman fifty shekels of silver, and she shall be his wife, because he has violated her; he may not put her away all his days' (cf. Exod. 22.15). A similar directive is found in ancient Assyrian law: 'The ravisher shall give the (extra) third in silver to her father as the value of a virgin (and) her ravisher shall marry her (and) not cast her off'.[8] Laws of this kind were intended not only to punish the rapist but also to assure the position of the victim, guaranteeing her means of existence and social status. There is no need to suppose that Tamar is referring specifically to the formal infringement of the law. She may be alluding to the psychological and social suffering that will be her lot as a result of the rape because Amnon is sending her away. This suffering is mentioned distinctly at the end of v. 20: 'So Tamar dwelt, a desolate woman, in her brother Absalom's house'. Tamar is obliged to dwell as a desolate woman in her brother's house as she cannot marry. After the rape Amnon behaves in a disgraceful manner, disregarding Tamar's situation and future, indicating his moral baseness even more than by the rape itself (in this respect the present narrative contrasts with that of the rape of Dinah, where love grows after the act of violation; Shechem asks for Dinah in marriage and is even prepared to give everything and do anything in order to win her 'because he had delight in Jacob's daughter').

Tamar's aim is to change the fateful decision. This time she does not array her arguments at length because she has already seen how

8. J.B. Pritchard, *Ancient Near Eastern Texts*, The Middle Assyrian Laws, Tablet A, paragraph 55.

Amnon treats her requests. Amnon's reply to Tamar's appeal is not given this time either, but once again his silence is thrown into relief by the fact that the narrator does not only report Amnon's behaviour or, to be more precise, Amnon's instructions to his servant, from which it can be inferred that he does not accede, but states: 'But he would not listen to her'. There is a slight difference, however, between what the narrator says the first time, 'But he would not listen to her voice', and what we read here, 'But he would not listen to her'. This can be taken as intimating that whereas on the first occasion Amnon heard what Tamar said but did not accept it, this time he did not even listen to her.[9]

> He called the boy, his servant, and said, 'Pray, send this one away
> from me outside, and bolt the door after her' (v. 17).

The narrator introduces Amnon's order not only with the phrase 'and he said', as customary, but adds 'he called'. The phrase 'he called' is used here because the servant was some distance away, Amnon having sent everyone out. Amnon had to call him first, before he could give him the order. The double designation 'boy' and 'servant' serves to heighten Tamar's humiliation: the daughter of a king is to be expelled by someone who is only a boy and a mere servant.

Amnon uses the plural *šilḥû* (send away) even though he is addressing only one servant, possibly because he expects that Tamar will resist wildly again, making it impossible for one boy to deal with her. Since the action of locking the door afterwards can be implemented by the young servant on his own the verb *ûnᵉ'ol* (and bolt) is in the singular.

The order Amnon gives reflects his deep contempt and lack of consideration for Tamar, which is further emphasized by the polite form with which he addresses his servant, 'Pray'. The scorn with which the term 'this one' (*'et zo't*) is invested is clearly apparent. Amnon treats Tamar as something loathsome, as someone without identity, whereas previously he expressed his feelings of attachment by calling her 'my sister' (the possessive pronoun in the phrase 'my sister' also reflects affinity).

Moreover, after saying 'send this one away from me', Amnon unnecessarily adds the term 'outside', meaning, cast her out into the

9. Malbim (Rabbi Meir Leibush ben Yehiel Mikhal).

street. Amnon also instructs his servant to lock the door after her, as if she is a bothersome, stubborn and repulsive creature against whom every measure must be taken to ensure that she does not re-enter the house. The deliberate degradation of Tamar which accompanies her expulsion draws the reader's opinion of Amnon down to even lower depths. This man has deceived his father, raped his sister, cast her out of his presence and on top of it all humiliated her too. This kind of behaviour cannot fail to arouse intense revulsion, which increases as the narrative progresses.

> Now she was wearing a long robe with sleeves; for thus were the virgin daughters of the king clad. So his servant put her outside, and bolted the door after her. And Tamar put ashes on her head, and the long robe which she wore she rent; and she laid her hand on her head, and went away, crying aloud as she went (vv. 18-19).

The narrator reports that the order has been implemented, and we are shocked to read that Tamar is put outside and the door locked after her (the form of the verb, $w^e n\bar{a}\,\dot{}al$ (bolted) instead of *wayyin\,\dot{}al* is difficult; this verb is found in the same form in Judg. 3.23, after the killing of Eglon). Before this, however, we are informed that Tamar was wearing a long robe with sleeves which the narrator explains by: 'thus were the virgin daughters of the king clad'. It would seem that the explanation, which stops the flow of reported events, serves to provide the reader with the background information needed in order to understand what is happening. Is it really necessary to supply the reader with this item of knowledge, however? Can v. 19 not be understood without it, even if the reader lives in another age? There is, after all, no difficulty in grasping the meaning of 'And Tamar put ashes on her head, and rent the long robe which she wore', even if we do not know that this was the way the virgin daughters of the king were dressed. Moreover, from the passage stating that she rent the long robe which she wore anyone will understand that she was wearing a long robe. Why, then, is the fact noted at the beginning of v. 18 ('Now she was wearing a long robe with sleeves')?

Another question is why the details concerning the long robe are conveyed in the first half of v. 18, before the information that the servant put Tamar outside and locked the door after her? In their present position these details separate Amnon's order to send Tamar away from its implementation, while their correct place would seem to be adjacent to the information about Tamar tearing her robe, namely, between vv. 18 and 19.

It would appear, therefore, that the explanation about the long robe which appears in the first half of v. 18 serves less to communicate essential information than to hint at an additional meaning. As the narrator explains, the long robe was worn by the virgin daughters of the king, whereas Tamar was no longer a virgin and had at the same time been humiliated by Amnon and his servant as if she were nothing but a common prostitute. In order to stress the depths of her humiliation through contrast—the daughter of the king, wearing a long robe (the symbol of her status), is thrown out by a boy servant—the details about Tamar's apparel are situated at this particular point, between Amnon's command and its implementation by the servant.

Another possible interpretation is that Tamar was only wearing a long robe with sleeves, whereas the virgin daughters of the king also used to wear coats (*me'îlîm*), because the servant did not wait for her to put on her coat. According to this interpretation also Tamar's humiliation is emphasized.

From Tamar's point of view, tearing her robe, like putting ashes on her head, is merely a conventional way of expressing grief. The narrator, however, gives this tearing of her robe the additional significance of a symbolic expression of the deterioration in Tamar's status. This is reflected not only by v. 18 but also by v. 19. For if the narrator had wanted to indicate grief and pain alone it would have been enough to state that Tamar tore her clothes, without specifying the kind of garment. It is customary in the Bible to use the phrase, 'he tore his clothes', without adding further details. Similarly, we would expect to find a different word order here, first the subject with the predicate and then the object: 'And Tamar put ashes on her head, and rent the long robe which she wore, and she laid her hand on her head'. The position of the object at the beginning of the clause 'and the long robe which she wore she rent', stresses the long robe and thus hints at the additional, symbolic significance.

Placing one's hand on one's head was an accepted expression of grief and sorrow in ancient times, as is proved by Jer. 2.37: 'From it too you will come away with your hands upon your head'. The conventional nature of the gesture made its expressive meaning immediately clear to the audience.

The last clause in v. 19 consists in Hebrew solely of verbs: *wattēlek hālôk weˈzāˈāqâ* ('and went away, crying aloud as she went'). This hints at activity which expresses deep emotional shock. Crying aloud serves not only to express pain but also to request help (as in 1 Sam. 7.8: 'Do not cease to cry to the Lord our God for us, that he may save us from the hand of the Philistines'). The verb 'cry' (*zāˈaq*) also has a legal connotation, being sometimes used with regard to lodging a complaint with the authorities against an injustice (as, for example, in 2 Sam. 19.28: 'What further right have I, then, to cry to the king?' or in 2 Kgs 8.3: 'She went forth to cry to the king for her house and her land'). In the present case the expression of pain is the main point, but there are also the subsidiary meanings of appealing for aid and complaining against an injustice.

> And her brother Absalom said to her, 'Has Amnon your brother been with you? Now hold your peace, my sister; he is your brother; do not take this matter to heart'. So Tamar dwelt, a desolate woman, in her brother Absalom's house (v. 20).

Tamar does not hide her disgrace but gives prominent public expression to her despair. Absalom's words, 'Now hold your peace, my sister', are intended to put a stop to this display. Naturally, the assertion 'he is your brother', does not mean that the deed is less serious because the rapist is the victim's brother (on the contrary, the family relationship makes it graver still), but that because of the blood relation the matter should be kept secret and not be made a public affair.

We are not told how Tamar and Absalom met, and can only assume that Tamar made her way to her brother's house in order to find succour and protection there. At the encounter Absalom is the one to start speaking, but instead of asking Tamar the reason for her appearance and cries he asks her specifically whether her brother Amnon has been with her. Tamar's reply is not given, for it is clear from the way the question is phrased that Absalom realizes what has happened (the answer is included within the question, in effect). He immediately states the name of the person and the nature of the act that have caused Tamar to mourn and cry out, thereby indicating quite clearly that what David has failed to notice has not escaped Absalom.

Out of delicacy, Absalom uses the euphemism 'been with you', in speaking to his sister (the specific significance of 'been with you' can be learned from Gen. 39.10: 'he would not listen to her, to lie with

her and be with her') and the general term, 'this matter'. The phrases
Absalom uses are aimed at softening and blurring what has
happened. His counsel 'do not take this matter to heart', also
constitutes an attempt to minimize the gravity of the deed. It should
not be assumed that Absalom says these things only in order to calm
his sister, for if this were his sole intention it is unlikely that the
author would quote him. His advice has an additional purpose, one
which is important within the framework of the plot, and that is why
it is cited by the author. The nature of this purpose must now be
clarified.

Absalom's reaction to what Amnon has done to Tamar seems
surprising. He does not express anger at the injury inflicted on his
sister or evince any desire to take action on her behalf, but attempts
to suppress the entire affair. He tells his sister to hold her peace and
not to take the matter to heart, as if 'this matter' is but a trifle which
can easily be ignored as far as he is concerned. His statements do not
conform in the least with the baseness of the deed or the severity of
its consequences.

Further on in the narrative it transpires that the harm done to
Tamar is certainly no trifle for Absalom, and that he himself
definitely does take it to heart, to the extent that he does not forget it
until he has managed to take his revenge on Amnon. At that point it
becomes clear to us that Absalom's mild reaction here is intended
solely to camouflage and conceal his true intentions. In this way the
vengeance he wreaks two years later comes as a complete surprise
both to those surrounding him (this is necessary for the success of his
scheme) and to the reader.

In v. 20 the word 'brother' occurs four times, and 'sister' once.
These words also appeared frequently beforehand during the course
of the narrative, but not with the same intensity. The first time the
word 'brother' occurs in this verse it refers to Absalom, the second
time to Amnon, the third also to Amnon and the fourth to Absalom
again. The word 'sister', referring to Tamar, appears between the
second and the third times:

her brother	your brother	my sister	your brother	her brother
(Absalom)	(Amnon)	(Tamar)	(Amnon)	(Absalom)

Tamar is at the centre, constituting the focal point; Amnon is at
either side of her while Absalom is at both sides of Amnon and starts
and ends the sequence. This construction reflects the basic situation

in the narrative. The same construction is evident in the possessive pronouns accompanying the nouns 'brother' and 'sister': third person, second person, first person, second person, third person. These possessive pronouns indicate the propinquity between Tamar and Amnon ('your brother' twice) and the even greater closeness between Tamar and Absalom ('her brother' twice and 'my sister' once).

> When king David heard of all these things, he was very angry. But Absalom spoke to Amnon neither good nor bad; for Absalom hated Amnon, because he had forced his sister Tamar (vv. 21-22).

It should be noted that in the Hebrew version of this verse the customary word order (predicate, subject, object) of biblical narrative is altered, being replaced by a sentence in which the predicate is preceded by the subject. This sentence structure may be designed to stress the subject (king David) by placing it at the beginning. It may also indicate, however, that this passage is not a direct continuation of what has been related to date, owing to the tense (past simple) of the verb *šāma'* (heard). The action of the narrative ended in effect with v. 20, and vv. 21 and 22 report the reactions of Tamar's brother and father some time later (Absalom's immediate response is given in v. 20). In v. 22, too, the verbs *dibber* (spoke), *śānē'* (hated) and *'innâ* (forced) are in the past simple, but this is inevitable because *dibber* follows a negative (*lo'*), *śānē'* is not narrative past but an explanation ('for') and *'innâ* has the meaning of past perfect.

What is stated in v. 21 focuses our attention on what is omitted, for what is left unsaid is more important than what is included. When David hears of all these things, namely, that he has been deceived, that his daughter Tamar has been forced by Amnon and that she has also been thrown out in disgrace 'he was very angry'. But despite the fact that he was very angry we are not told that he took any action. The narrator does not report that David punished Amnon or even rebuked him, and this silence implies that David did not do anything. (The Septuagint includes a verse stating explicitly that David refrained from action, explaining why this was so and even clarifying the explanation: 'And he did not displease the spirit of his son Amnon, for he loved him, being his first-born'. This bears a certain resemblance to what is written of another of David's sons, Adonijah, in 1 Kgs 1.6: 'And his father had never displeased him...') David's failure to act is particularly prominent in view of the fact that he has been an indirect accomplice to the tragedy since it was he who told Tamar to go to Amnon's house.

We are informed that Absalom did not speak to Amnon. Does this mean that he too, like his father, did not reprimand Amnon, that is, did not speak to him about his violation of Tamar[10] or that he did not speak to him at all? The first possibility does not seem likely, for if it were so the phrase 'about the matter that he had forced his sister Tamar' would have to follow 'But Absalom spoke to Amnon neither good nor bad'. The words 'neither good nor bad' also make it difficult to interpret the passage this way, because it is inconceivable that Absalom should say anything good about what Amnon has done. 'Neither good nor bad' (cf. Gen. 31.24, 29; Isa. 41.23; Jer. 10.5; Zeph. 1.12) means that Absalom did not speak to Amnon at all. The narrator's explanation 'for Absalom hated Amnon' is also more appropriate to Absalom's total silence than to merely not discussing the rape. It is highly improbable that Absalom's hatred would only prevent him from talking with Amnon about the abuse of Tamar, while it is far more likely that his animosity would keep him from conversing with Amnon altogether.

Were it not for the narrator's explanation 'for Absalom hated Amnon because he had forced his sister Tamar', we might have understood the reason for Absalom's silence as being something else, particularly since he has said to Tamar, 'Now hold your peace, my sister; he is your brother; do not take this matter to heart'. If we were to interpret Absalom's silence in the same way as Tamar's—as acquiescence and suppression of the deed—the murder of Amnon would have to be seen in a different light. In effect, David and his courtiers did not understand the motive for the murder, and only Jonadab the son of Shimeah grasped it: 'for by the command of Absalom this has been determined from the day he forced his sister Tamar' (v. 32). From what both the narrator and Jonadab say it transpires that the motive for the murder was not Absalom's desire to get rid of his older brother as a rival for the succession, but Absalom's hatred for Amnon 'because he had forced his sister Tamar'. Thus it was family affairs, not political objective which according to the narrator, led to Amnon's murder.

The clause 'because he had forced his sister Tamar' explains

10. The phrase '*al dᵉbar 'ašer 'innâ*, translated here 'because he had forced', can also be interpreted 'about the matter that he had forced'.

Absalom's hatred, but is this explanation really necessary? Would we not have grasped the cause of Absalom's hatred of Amnon even without this elucidation? Similarly, did the narrator have to note at the end of the verse that Tamar was Absalom's sister? All this is well known and understood. The object of this is, however, to indicate what is going on in Absalom's mind and occupying his thoughts: his sister has been forced! The vague, general phrase, 'this matter' of v. 20 becomes here 'because (of the matter that) he had forced', defining the deed in clear terms and emphasizing its gravity. And whereas Tamar is defined as Absalom's sister, Amnon is not called his brother (in contrast to v. 26, for example, where Absalom is interested in hinting at the affinity between himself and Amnon), and the absence of this term is highly significant. By using the verb 'forced', defining Tamar as Absalom's sister and omitting to refer to Amnon as Absalom's brother, the narrator reflects Absalom's thoughts and emotions. In other words, through what the narrator includes and leaves unsaid Absalom's standpoint is revealed.

After the dramatic events the narrative ends tranquilly: Tamar sits, a desolate woman, in her brother Absalom's house, David is very angry but takes no action, and neither does Absalom. This serenity exists only on the surface, however. Underneath, in Absalom's mind, there is unrest and agitation, as the narrator insinuates, and these will burst out and be expressed in action at a later stage. Thus, the end of v. 22, 'for Absalom hated Amnon, because he had forced his sister Tamar', serves as a preparation for and transition to what is to happen later on. The reader will realize this only after the event, however, thinking at this stage that Absalom's hatred is manifested in his refusal to speak to Amnon, and that there is no need for it to be expressed in any other way. Consequently, Absalom's act of vengeance two years later comes as a complete surprise (in contrast to the events in the narrative of Dinah, where the vengeance does not surprise the reader because the narrator has given warning by saying that the sons of Jacob answered Shechem and Hamor *deceitfully* [Gen. 34.13]).

An overall view of the entire narrative of Amnon and Tamar discloses the following characteristic features:

The *narrator* is omniscient, but does not tell everything. The narrator hears the secret consultation between Amnon and Jonadab and is witness to the rape, at which nobody was present except Amnon and Tamar themselves. The unlimited knowledge is expressed particularly in the large number of inside views: 'and Amnon, David's son, loved her' (v. 1), 'And Amnon was so tormented. . .' (v. 2), 'and it seemed impossible to Amnon. . .' (v. 2), 'But he would not. . .' (vv. 14, 16), 'Then Amnon hated her with very great hatred; for greater was the hatred with which he hated her than the love with which he had loved her' (v. 15), 'he was very angry' (v. 21), 'for Absalom hated Amnon' (v. 22). Such a high concentration of direct information conveyed by the narrator concerning the internal states of the characters is unusual in biblical narratives, and leaves its imprint on this one. The intelligence about the emotions and desires of the personages helps us interpret their behaviour correctly. For example, without the knowledge that after the rape Amnon's hatred for Tamar was very great, we would doubtless find it difficult to understand the reason for his expulsion of her from his house. In other biblical narratives, however, it is also sometimes hard to interpret characters' behaviour, yet direct information about the motives, aspirations and desires which lead to their actions is rare. Moreover, not only is there a considerable amount of information of this kind in our narrative, but a comparison is also given of two emotions, the intensity of Amnon's love for Tamar and the vehemence of his hatred for her, which is not necessary for understanding his behaviour.

Consequently, it can be said that this narrative attributes importance to the characters' inner lives over and beyond what is customary in biblical narratives, and that emotions are accorded a place in their own right alongside external behaviour and not just beneath it. The accentuation and direct expression of emotions gives this narrative a special character. Many other biblical narratives display interest in the characters' inner lives, but it is in respect of the way these are expressed, that is in a matter pertaining to the art of narration, that the narrative of Amnon and Tamar is unique.

The narrator refrains from revealing what Amnon's real intentions are regarding Tamar, and these are exposed to us only when he is already putting them into effect. Similarly, the narrator does not divulge Absalom's plans concerning Amnon after the rape, and we learn of them only when Absalom gives explicit orders about implementing the murder, two years later. In both cases the narrator gives us only a very faint hint of the existence of these intentions by noting, in the first instance: 'and it seemed impossible to Amnon to do anything to her', and in the second: 'for Absalom hated Amnon,

because he had forced his sister Tamar'. The concealment of the aims
of both Amnon and Absalom introduces an element of tension into
the narrative, and also accords with the fact that both brothers keep
their plans completely secret.

On one occasion the narrator interrupts the narration of events by
adding the explanation, 'for thus were the virgin daughters of the
king clad'. Apart from this there is no intervention in the course of
events and the narrator's existence is not conspicuous. The horrifying
facts are related in a restrained, matter-of-fact way. Almost the entire
narrative is composed of scenes, the dialogues between the characters
occupying a prominent place (approximately 40%). This method of
narration involves a close view (or, rather, a close hearing) as well as
a vivid representation of events, engendering considerable involvement
on the reader's part. Thus, the dramatic design accords with and
reinforces the dramatic content of the narrative, which is distinguished
by the violent conflict between the protagonists.

The narrator does not take a stand or pass judgment directly,
though the attitude can be inferred from the selection of the verb
'force', which has negative connotations. The narrator's view is also
expressed indirectly through Tamar's phrases: 'do not do this wanton
folly', 'you would be as one of the wanton fools in Israel'.

The *characters* are presented in the exposition where the ties of
kinship between them are specified. A personality trait is also
mentioned, namely it is said of Jonadab that he was very wise. We are
told of Amnon's feelings (his love for Tamar) not only by the narrator
but also by himself ('I love Tamar, my brother Absalom's sister').
Amnon's appearance likewise provides evidence of his inner state
('Why are you so haggard, O son of the king, every morning?'). There
is, furthermore, direct information about Tamar's external appearance
(beautiful) and about the fact that she is a virgin. All these details
fulfil a very important function in the plot of the narrative.

The protagonists are characterized not only by direct means, but
also, and in fact primarily, by what they say and do. David is further
distinguished by his inaction (with regard to Amnon). Amnon is also
thrown into relief by the minor character, Jonadab (Amnon is
incapable of thinking up a scheme of his own for achieving his ends).
In addition, he is characterized by what Tamar says: 'You would be
as one of the wanton fools in Israel'.

The dynamic, indirect characterization causes Amnon's personality
to emerge gradually. At first the reader is not aware of Amnon's true

nature, and it is only during the course of the narrative, step by step, that it becomes apparent, in all its depravity. Each of Amnon's actions is worse than the previous one: first he deceives his father, then he rapes his sister brutally, and finally, after satisfying his appetite, he casts her out of his house in a particularly degrading way.

The *plot* of the narrative is made up of scenes which are arranged as a chain, each of its constituent links containing two characters. The exposition (vv. 1-3) is followed by the first link, in which Jonadab and Amnon appear (vv. 4-5), Amnon and David appear in the second link (v. 6), David and Tamar in the third (v. 7), Tamar and Amnon in the fourth (vv. 8-16), Amnon and the servant in the fifth (v. 17), the servant and Tamar in the sixth (v. 18) and Tamar and Absalom in the seventh (vv. 19-20). The seventh link is followed by what amounts to a conclusion, communicated by the narrator (vv. 21-22). All the links are connected to one another by the fact that the second character in each of them is the first in the succeeding one.

```
                        (4) Tamar  - Amnon
          (3) David  - Tamar    (5) Amnon - servant
    (2) Amnon - David                (6) servant - Tamar
(1) Jonadab -Amnon                        (7) Tamar  - Absalom
```

It should be noted that Amnon appears in the first two links and Tamar in the last two. Tamar also appears in the third from the beginning and Amnon in the third from the end. Amnon and Tamar meet in the central link, which is far longer than any of the others (nine verses) and constitutes the climax of the narrative. Thus, Amnon appears in links 1-2, Tamar in 3-4, Amnon in 4-5 and Tamar once again in 6-7. The symmetrical structure is also evident in the fact that Jonadab, who is close to and supports Amnon, appears in the first link, whereas Absalom, who is close to and supports Tamar, appears in the last one. The symmetrical parallelism between the links derives not only from the characters appearing in them but also from the content expressed within them. Amnon's feelings are dealt with in the first link, and Tamar's in the last. The second and third links concern the bringing of Tamar to Amnon's house, and the fifth and sixth her expulsion from it. The names of David, Absalom, Tamar and Amnon are mentioned in the exposition, and the same names are cited once again in the conclusion.

From the foregoing it is clear that the narrative of Amnon and

Tamar is a carefully constructed unit which is complete in itself. This unit, however, is the first part of a more extensive composition, which continues with the murder of Amnon by Absalom and concludes with Absalom's return from Geshur. An item of information noting that two or three years passed is inserted between each of the three parts.

The plot develops from an initial situation which contains the nucleus of the conflict. Amnon loves his sister Tamar to such an extent that he makes himself ill, but he cannot do anything to her. There is great tension between his love and his inability to do anything to her, and this needs to be released. The next stage in the plot is the planning of the action which will allay this tension. The planning stage is followed by the implementation, step by step: first Amnon's sham illness, then David's visit to him, Amnon's request that his father send Tamar to bake cakes in his sight, Tamar's appearance at Amnon's house, her preparation of the food and submission of it to Amnon, who is lying on his bed. Thus the plot gradually ascends to the rape itself. At the very last moments before the implementation of the rape the narrator shows us how Tamar attempts to prevent it, but to no avail.

There is no immediate descent in the plot line after the zenith of the rape, this being followed by another violent clash when Amnon wishes to send Tamar away and she tries to prevent this, once again unsuccessfully. After this the plot line descends, as Tamar cries out because of what has befallen her and her brother Absalom tries to calm her. The narrative reaches a (temporary) plateau of serenity when Tamar sits, a desolate woman, in her brother's house, David does nothing and Absalom does nothing either as yet, apart from not speaking to Amnon. Thus, the narrative ascends gradually to the climax, which is the rape, thence to another climax, the expulsion, and then subsides progressively until it finally reaches a point of general inaction (but since this does not constitute a solution events will flare up again two years later).

Tension in the narrative is achieved by the fact that at the beginning a plan for bringing Tamar to Amnon's house is presented, and it is not clear whether the stratagem will succeed. Similarly, it is unclear why, once Tamar is in his house and has prepared him food, Amnon refuses to eat and sends everyone away. All these steps are incomprehensible to the reader because Amnon's real intentions have not been disclosed and remain a mystery until he asks Tamar to lie with him. Tamar refuses, and the question arises as to whether she will manage to prevent the deed or Amnon will succeed in achieving his ends.

An ironic aspect of the story is found in the fact that by wanting to help his son David harms his daughter. Unknowingly he sends her to be forced, humiliated and disgraced, thereby bringing disaster on himself too. This irony intensifies the significance of the rape of Tamar for David (see below).

Time flows fairly evenly in the narrative. Most of the events are portrayed through scenic representation, in which dialogue occupies the central place, as has been noted above. Verses containing summary account are rare and refer only to limited periods of time. Most of the action takes place within a few hours, and from beginning to end does not extend over more than a few days (there are no denotations of time, so that it is impossible to determine the precise length of time). Thus, there are no great differences between narrated time and narration time, and in much of the narrative these two time-systems are virtually overlapping.

The narrative does not include simultaneous events or flashbacks. Time proceeds in one direction, without any deviation from the usual chronological order. It can, therefore, be said that in this narrative time fulfils no particular function. It is, nevertheless, clear that through the treatment of time (the varying relations between narration time and narrated time) the author makes it apparent to us that what preceded and followed the rape are more important in his opinion than the rape itself. The author dwells on all the preparations for the rape and the reactions to it, while reporting the actual deed in telegraphic terms; this leads us to infer that the emphasis in this narrative is on the human and psychological aspects of events rather than on factual facets. This finding accords with the large number of items relating to the inner states of the characters.

Space plays quite an important role in the narrative of Amnon and Tamar. Although space and the objects filling it are not described in concrete terms, in accordance with the norm in biblical narrative, several items mentioned, such as Amnon's house, Absalom's house, the (inner) chamber in Amnon's house, the door and the bed, serve to construct its space while at the same time fulfilling a role within the framework of the plot.

The entire story of Amnon and Tamar takes place within Jerusalem (in the narratives which follow and continue it the spatial horizon extends to Baal-hazor and Geshur, but Jerusalem remains the focal point). Within the limited space of this narrative there is movement from one place to another, constituting a vital element in the development of the plot. A central feature of the narrative is the fact that Tamar goes from her house to Amnon's, and from the room in Amnon's house where she prepares the food into the chamber where Amnon is lying. This is followed by movement in the opposite direction, which is also of crucial significance for the development of the plot, Tamar's expulsion from Amnon's house and the fact that she goes to Absalom's. The plot concludes when Tamar's movement ends, as she sits desolate in her brother's house.

The subject of the movement from one house to another brings to mind something which was recounted two chapters previously, in the narrative of Bathsheba and Uriah. At the beginning of that narrative Bathsheba goes from her house to the king's, at David's bidding, just as in this one Tamar goes from her house to Amnon's at David's direction; in both cases the result is unlawful intercourse. Later in that narrative David instructs Uriah to go down to his house, but Uriah does not wish to leave the king's house just as Tamar does not wish to leave Amnon's.

An additional connection between the narrative of Amnon and Tamar and that of Bathsheba and Uriah is established by means of the root *škb* (lie). This root occurs six times in our narrative, having two different meanings, cohabit and recline. While it could be claimed that the various repetitions of the word 'lie' are necessitated by the subject-matter, in the narrative of Dinah, which also deals with rape, it occurs only twice, and with the meaning of cohabit alone. The same root is reiterated frequently in the narrative of Bathsheba and Uriah too, six times in chapter 11 (relating the decisive events) and another four in chapter 12 (dealing with the consequences), and here it also has the two meanings referred to previously, the literal and the metonymic.

The root *brh* (sustain) also occurs frequently in our narrative, being repeated six times. This root is extremely rare in the Bible, appearing with that meaning in only two other places,[11] one of which is the previous chapter (12.17). This can be regarded as indicating a connection between the narrative of Amnon and Tamar and the

11. In 1 Sam. 17.8 and Ezek. 34.20 it occurs with a completely different meaning.

preceding one, or more precisely between the tragedy of the rape of Tamar and that of the death of the child, which both constitute serious blows for David within his family. The connection between these two narratives is also insinuated by the opening phrase 'Now after this', which is in all probability no mere formal overture but a hint at the substantial association between the two narratives.

These features serve to invest the narrative of Amnon and Tamar with significance extending beyond the limits of the narrative itself and fitting its wider context. In the light of these connections and the thematic parallel between this narrative and that of Bathsheba and Uriah (which both deal with unlawful intercourse) Amnon's abuse of Tamar is to be interpreted as David's retribution for his behaviour towards Bathsheba.

BIBLIOGRAPHY

Adar, Z., *The Biblical Narrative*, Jerusalem: World Zionist Organization, 1959.

Alonso Schökel, L., 'Erzählkunst im Buche der Richter', *Biblica* 42 (1961).

Alter, R., *The Art of Biblical Narrative*, New York: Basic Books, 1981.

Alter, R. & F. Kermode (eds.) *The Literary Guide to the Bible*, Cambridge Mass.: Belknap, Harvard University Press, 1987.

Arpali, B., 'Caution: A Biblical Story! Comments on the Story of David and Bathsheba and on the Problems of the Biblical Narrative', *Hasifrut* 2 (1970) (Hebrew).

Auerbach, E., *Mimesis*, Princeton: Princeton University Press, 1953: Ch. 1, Odysseus' Scar.

Bar-Efrat, S. 'Some Observations on the Analysis of Structure in Biblical Narrative', *Vetus Testamentum* 30 (1980).

Berlin, A., *Poetics and Interpretation of Biblical Narrative*, Sheffield: Almond, 1983.

Bertman, S., 'Symmetrical Design in the Book of Ruth', *Journal of Biblical Literature* 84 (1965).

Blenkinsopp, J., 'Structure and Style in Judges 13-16', *Journal of Biblical Literature* 82 (1963).

Buber, M. & F. Rosenzweig, *Die Schrift und ihre Verdeutschung*, Berlin: Schocken, 1936: M. Buber, 'Die Sprache der Botschaft'; *idem*, 'Leitwortstil in der Erzählung des Pentateuchs'; *idem*, 'Das Leitwort und der Formtypus der Rede'; F. Rosenzweig, 'Das Formgeheimnis der biblischen Erzählungen'.

Buss, M.J. (ed.), *Encounter with the Text: Form and History in the Hebrew Bible*, Philadelphia: Fortress—Missoula: Scholars, 1979.

Clines, D.J.A., D.M. Gunn, & A.J. Hauser (eds.), *Art and Meaning: Rhetoric in Biblical Literature*, Sheffield: JSOT, 1982.

Cohn, G.H. *Das Buch Jona im Lichte der biblischen Erzählungskunst*, Assen: van Gorcum, 1969.

Conroy, C., *Absalom Absalom! Narrative and Language in 2 Sam. 13-20*, Rome: Pontifical Biblical Institute, 1978.

Culley, R.C., *Studies in the Structure of Hebrew Narrative*, Philadelphia: Fortress—Missoula: Scholars, 1976.

Culley, R.C. (ed.), *Classical Hebrew Narrative* = *Semeia* 3 (1975).

—*Perspectives on Old Testament Narrative* = *Semeia* 15 (1979).

Dommershausen, W., *Die Estherrolle: Stil und Ziel einer alttestamentlichen Schrift*, Stuttgart: Katholisches Bibelwerk, 1968.

Eslinger, L.M. *Kingship of God in Crisis: A Close Reading of 1 Samuel 1-12*, Sheffield: Almond, 1985.

Exum, J.C., 'Aspects of Symmetry and Balance in the Samson Saga', *Journal for the Study of the Old Testament* 19 (1981).

Fisch, H., 'Ruth and the Structure of Covenant History', *Vetus Testamentum* 32 (1982).

Fokkelman, J.P., *Narrative Art in Genesis*, Assen: van Gorcum, 1975.

—*Narrative Art and Poetry in the Books of Samuel*, vol. 1: *King David*, Assen: van Gorcum, 1981.

—*Narrative Art and Poetry in the Books of Samuel*, vol. 2: *The Crossing Fates*, Assen: van Gorcum, 1986.

Fränkel, L., 'His Compassion is on all His Creatures: On the Meaning of the Book of Jonah', *Mayanot* 9 (1968) (Hebrew).

Galbiati, E., *La Struttura Letteraria dell'Esodo: Contributo allo Studio dei Criteri Stilistici dell'A.T. e della Composizione del Pentateuco*, Roma: Edisioni Paoline, 1956.

Goitein, S.D., *Iyunim Bamikra*, Tel-Aviv: Yavneh, 1957: 'Narrative Art in the Bible' (Hebrew).

Greenberg, M., 'The Redaction of the Plague Narrative in Exodus', *Near Eastern Studies in Honor of William Foxwell Albright*, ed. H. Goedicke, Baltimore: Johns Hopkins Press, 1971.

Gros Louis, K.R.R. *et al.* (eds.), *Literary Interpretations of Biblical Narratives*, Nashville: Abingdon, 1974.

—*Literary Interpretations of Biblical Narratives*, vol. 2, Nashville: Abingdon, 1982.

Gunn, D.M., *The Story of King David: Genre and Interpretation*, Sheffield: 1978. *The Fate of King Saul: An Interpretation of a Biblical Story*, Sheffield: JSOT, 1980.

Jackson, J.J. & M. Kessler (eds.), *Rhetorical Criticism: Essays in Honor of James Muilenburg*, Pittsburgh: Pickwick, 1974.

Kessler, M., 'Narrative Technique in 1 Sam. 16, 1-13'. *Catholic Biblical Quarterly* 32 (1970).

Krinetzki, L., 'Ein Beitrag zur Stilanalyse der Goliathpericope (1 Sam. 17, 1—18, 5)', *Biblica* 54 (1973).

Licht, J., *Storytelling in the Bible*, Jerusalem: Magnes, 1978.

Long, B.O. (ed.), *Images of Man and God: Old Testament Short Stories in Literary Focus*, Sheffield: Almond, 1981.

Magonet, J., *Form and Meaning: Studies in Literary Technique in the Book of Jonah*, Sheffield: Almond, 1983.

Martin, W.J., '"Dischronologized" Narrative in the Old Testament', *Supplements to Vetus Testamentum* 17 (1968).

Miscall, P.D., 'The Jacob and Joseph Stories as Analogies', *Journal for the Study of the Old Testament* 6 (1978).

—*The Working of Old Testament Narrative*, Philadelphia: Fortress—Chico: Scholars, 1983.

Muilenburg, J., 'A Study in Hebrew Rhetoric: Repetition and Style', *Supplements to Vetus Testamentum* 1 (1953).

Perdue, L.G., '"Is There Anyone Left of the House of Saul . . .?" Ambiguity and the Characterization of David in the Succession Narrative', *Journal for the Study of the Old Testament* 30 (1984).

Polzin, R., *Moses and the Deuteronomist: A Literary Study of the Deuteronomic History*, New York: Seabury, 1980.

Ridout, G.P., 'Prose Compositional Techniques in the Succession Narrative (2 Samuel 7, 9-20; 1 Kings 1-2)' (Ph.D. Diss.), Ann Arbor: University Microfilms, 1971

Savran, G.W., 'Stylistic Aspects and Literary Functions of Quoted Direct Speech in Biblical Narrative' (Ph.D. Diss.), Ann Arbor: University Microfilms, 1982.

Schulz, A., *Erzählungskunst in den Samuel-Büchern*, Münster: Aschendorff, 1923.

Seeligmann, I.L., 'Hebräische Erzählung und biblische Geschichtsschreibung', *Theologische Zeitschrift* 18 (1962).

Simon, U., 'An Ironic Approach to a Bible Story: On the Interpretation of the Story of David and Bathsheba', *Hasifrut* 2 (1970) (Hebrew).

—'Samuel's Call to Prophecy: Form Criticism with Close Reading', *Prooftexts* 1 (1981).

—'The Story of Samuel's Birth: Structure, Genre and Meaning', *Tyunei Mikra Ufarshanut* 2, ed. U. Simon; Ramat-Gan, 1986 (Hebrew).

Sternberg, M., *The Poetics of Biblical Narrative: Ideological Literature and the Drama of Reading*, Bloomington: Indiana University Press, 1985.

Talmon, S., *Darkei Hasippur Bamikra*, ed. G. Gil; Jerusalem: Hebrew University, 1965.

—'The Presentation of Synchroneity and Simultaneity in Biblical Narrative', *Scripta Hierosolymitana* 27 (1978).

Walsh, J.T., 'Genesis 2, 4b—3, 24: A Synchronic Approach', *Journal of Biblical Literature* 96 (1977).

Webb, B.G., *The Book of Judges: An Integrated Reading*, Sheffield: JSOT, 1987.

Weiss, M., 'The Craft of Biblical Narrative', *Molad* 169-70 (1962) (Hebrew).

—'Einiges über die Bauformen des Erzählens in der Bibel', *Vetus Testamentum* 13 (1963).

—'Weiteres über die Bauformen des Erzählens in der Bibel', *Biblica* 46 (1965).

—*The Story of Job's Beginning: Job 1-2, A Literary Analysis*, Jerusalem: Magnes 1983.

Witzenrath, H., *Das Buch Rut: Eine literaturwissenschaftliche Untersuchung*, München: Kösel, 1975.

—*Das Buch Jona: Eine literaturwissenschaftliche Untersuchung*, St. Ottilien: EOS, 1978.

INDEX

INDEX OF BIBLICAL REFERENCES

INDEX OF SUBJECTS